P9-CMW-607

The HeART of Nursing

Second Edition

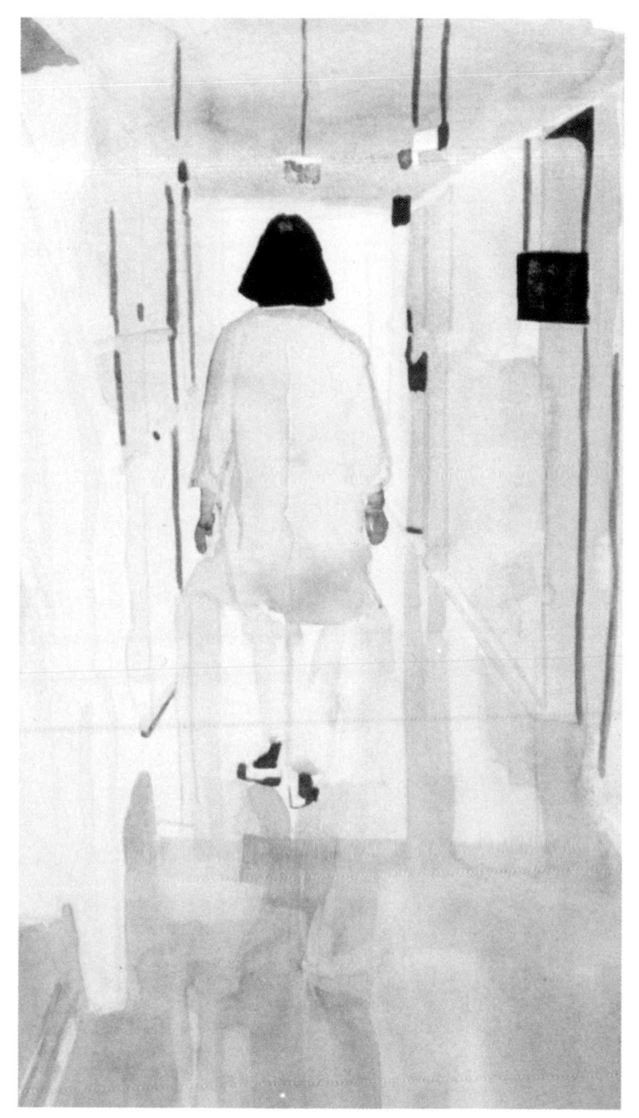

Nurse
by Catherine Fraser

The HeART of Nursing

Second Edition

Expressions of Creative Art in Nursing

Edited by M. Cecilia Wendler with a Foreword by Jean Watson

Sigma Theta Tau International

Editor-in-Chief: Jeff Burnham
Acquisitions Editor: Fay L. Bower, RN, DNSc, FAAN
Editor: Carla Hall
Proofreader: Linda Canter

Second edition cover design by Gary Adair
First edition design by Perna Design

Printed in the United States of America
Printing and Binding by: V.G. Reed & Sons

Sigma Theta Tau International
550 West North Street
Indianapolis, IN 46202 USA

Visit our Web site at **www.nursingknowledge.org/STTI/books** for more information on our books and other knowledge solutions.

ISBN: 1-930538-16-2

Library of Congress Cataloging-in-Publication Data

The heART of nursing : expressions of creative art in nursing / edited by M. Cecilia Wendler, with a foreword by Jean Watson.— 2nd ed.
p. ; cm.
Includes bibliographical references.
ISBN-13: 978-1-930538-16-0
ISBN-10: 1-930538-16-2
1. Nursing in art. 2. Nurses as artists.
[DNLM: 1. Medicine in Literature. 2. Nurses. 3. Art. 4.
Creativeness. 5. Nursing. WZ 350 H436 2005] I. Wendler, M. Cecilia.
II. Sigma Theta Tau International.
NX652.N87H43 2005
704.088'61073—dc22

2005028374

05 06 07 / 9 8 7 6 5 4 3 2 1

Dedication

This book is dedicated to nurse-artists from around the world who are committed to artistic practice. It is also dedicated in recognition of the importance of aesthetics in nursing. As an example of the exquisite intimacy that emerges between nurse and patient, it is a testament to the resilience of the professional nursing spirit. May it serve as an inspiration to other nurse-artists finding their humanistic voice in a highly technological age. ♥

About the Cover Artist and Art

Catherine Fraser, RN, BScN, is a public health nurse who believes that art-making and creativity is healing and has great value in practice, in client self-expression, and for health workers' self care. The title of the cover art is "Freedom to Be," which is #10 of 29 images from "The Gesture Series." (The back-cover images are the remaining 28 images. They can be viewed in larger size with titles on Catherine's Web site at www.members.shaw.ca/catherinefraserart.)

Artist's Statement: The series started with a contact from a friend through dance. The idea evolved to share in a creative process to learn about myself and another person—how we moved and how we used energy. My friend shared his practice of movement and yoga. I was inspired by the movements, a sacred experience honoring each other's creative experience. The resulting 29 drawings became The Gesture Series. I drew continuous contour drawings using thin and thick lines with pencil, pen, and charcoal. Later, during a period of recuperation from surgery, I reduced the images and used curvilinear shapes randomly woven to create the feeling of movement using watercolor pencils of red, yellow, and blue. I applied colors in a quiet, meditative way, layering color and waiting for form to appear. In this series I wanted to capture the figure, the heart of expression, the feeling or illusion of continuous movement and emphasize the idea of the soul gesture of a movement, qualities of color, and the spiritual aspects of color and light. The color was layered emphasizing form and shape. With each image there came words to describe the experience and these words became the titles of each respective piece.

by Veneta Masson

A baby's born. Its first faint cry is drowned
In mother's tears both for what is and for
What should have been—a perfect child. Around
Them nurses set about their healing chores.

A breast is gone and in its place a gash
Across the very heart of womanhood
Still bleeds in tiny kills. Unabashed
A nurse keeps vigil, willing loss to good.

A beam collapsed and left him less a man.
He rattles bedrails, pelts the air with curses.
A nurse confronts him eye to eye and hand
To trembling hand.

I want to ask these nurses

Do you face the dark because you trust in light?
Or is it that you've come to terms with night?

Contents

CHAPTER 1—THE NATURE OF NURSING *continued*

CHAPTER 2—ART IN RESEARCH

CHAPTER 3—BOOKENDS: BIRTH AND DEATH

CHAPTER 4—THE EXTRAORDINARY ORDINARY

CHAPTER 5—DELICATE ARTISTRY: NURSING OF CHILDREN

CHAPTER 6—IN THE PROCESS OF BECOMING A NURSE-ARTIST

CHAPTER 7—REFLECTIONS: NURSES' INTERIORITY UNFOLDING

CHAPTER 8—THE OTHER IS ME

CHAPTER 8—THE OTHER IS ME *continued*

CHAPTER 9—PREPARING OTHERS TO NURSE: TEACHING

CHAPTER 10—HOPE: LOOKING FORWARD

AFTERWORD

The Change

by Durae Pfeffer

The change
the conscious decision
then the unexpected transformation
not unlike the
nature of seasons
of evolution ... gradual, brilliant, real
magnificent in the transformation

The change
the inescapable struggle
the tumultuous storms
intense and seemingly destructive
yet somehow
purifying and enhancing
revealing the colorful awareness in the tranquility

The change
the pain
of laborious birth
fighting towards a self creation
of enlightenment
inhaling the first breath of knowledge
to recognize the truth in personal being

The change
the courage
the growth despite the fear
the nerve to attempt to blossom
like the flower of academia
rooted in the soil of knowledge
and flourished by the sunlight of understanding

The change
the challenge
eloping expertise
to embrace a novice
to erase self doubt and continue the climb
carrying the entity of personal experience
as the flag to plant at the summit

The change
the self reflection
unrecognizable, but yet familiar
the mirrored awareness of comprehension
in the serene pond of personal knowing
the appreciation
the praxis

The change
is my change
my challenge, my belief
my transformational journey and
my success
of life
of nurse
of spirit

Foreword

This unique text is not a text at all but rather a poignant adventure into the art and beauty of nursing and humanity itself. It explicates, reflects and reveals the complexity, diversity, intimacy and depth of the heART of nursing, the majesty and beauty of human caring processes and relationships.

This national project, initiated from a Sigma Theta Tau International conference, elicited artistry from nurses who did not know they were artists—from nurse-artists and artist-nurses—but who found their expressive form and voice to create new ways to communicate the art of nursing. The result is an intellectual, emotional and aesthetic dance of texts and visual sensations that integrate and synthesize spirit into matter made whole. It is offered as one loving gift honoring the humanity of nursing and nurses, as well as the deeply human dimensions of caring and healing practices.

The creative scholarship it embodies moves the intellectual focus of nursing art from a modern mindset that asks expected questions such as "What is nursing?" or "What is art in nursing?" toward postmodern ambiguities and another frame of reference in which the reader, silently, alone or in groups, asks different questions and finds his or her own meaning and answers.

The postmodern question in this work becomes open-ended inquiry that asks "When is nursing art?"

These creative revelations span a variety of art forms, shapes, colors, sensations, moods, moments, emotive expressions that are as diverse and artistic as the humans we are. Whether viewed through the lens of the theoretical, the postmodern discourse, the historic, or from the collected art forms themselves, the stories, words, visuals, texture and poetry are the human spirit made whole. Once you enter this work, it is almost impossible to put it down. It is evocative, emotional, intellectual, exciting, sad, joyous, creative, intimate, private and public. It is a dance with our humanity and all the vicissitudes of nursing and nurses' engagement with caring and human experiences.

As Kandinsky reminds us: The spiritual resides in art and art bestows significance to the soul. So too does this work reside in that special place where spirit and art converge in the heart, mind and soul of the human condition. Ultimately, we are forced to conclude that art is not separate from science, from practice, from life, from living and dying. Thus, just as art mirrors the infinity of the human soul, this work is about healing the spirit and soul of nursing and our shared humanity.

Finally, the special combination of having the diversity of nursing heART made visual in one collection makes this truly a one-of-a-kind classic, a collectors' item, a work that points the way toward a new revelation about the compassionate, humanitarian nature of nursing at its finest depth and beauty. ♥

Jean Watson, PhD, RN, HNC, FAAN
Distinguished Professor of Nursing
Murchinson-Scoville Chair in Caring Science
University of Colorado Health Sciences Center
School of Nursing
Denver, Colorado

REFERENCE:

Kandinsky, W. (1977). *Concerning the spiritual in art.* New York: Dover.

Introduction to the Second Edition

M. Cecilia Wendler

When *The HeART of Nursing: Expressions of Creative Art in Nursing* was originally published in 2002, it was received with enthusiasm and embraced as a landmark collection of modern nurse-artistry. Since that time, the book has been used as a textbook for undergraduate and graduate students; given as gifts; even purchased for placement in countless nursing report rooms where nurses from all shifts and all specialties might escape into aesthetics amid a busy shift. Nurses have used the book to help explain nursing to people in their lives with no connection to health care and to laugh and cry over the universalities revealed in these pages. It has even inspired a new wave of nurse-artists, some of whom have provided the wonderful new material for this second edition.

This second edition features expanded and new chapters, including a focus on caring for children. Christina Impoco Nieves, a highly regarded nurse artist, tells us about her inspiring and transformational journey into artwork as an expression of herself. Throughout the book, new visual art helps illuminate aspects of nursing—and of nurses—that are often hidden from view. Overall, the book has nearly doubled in size, reflecting the talent of dozens of men and women in nursing.

As editor, I have joyfully collaborated with the nearly 100 contributors to bring this important work into your hands. I am deeply grateful for the humanistic caring these expressions of creative art represent. I am humbled at the sheer talent of my colleagues, and I am convinced that this book will continue to facilitate dialogue about nurse artistry in all its varied forms. Join us in that engagement. Share a poem with your loved ones. Read one of the essays to a classroom of high school students. Find yourself in one of the pictures. However you do it, take time from your busy life to exercise your own artistic expressions that convey your passion for nursing. We invite—and await—your unique creative engagement. Begin! ♥

Introduction

The "HeART" of Nursing: Origins

M. Cecilia Wendler

Contributions provided by Mary Elaine Kiener

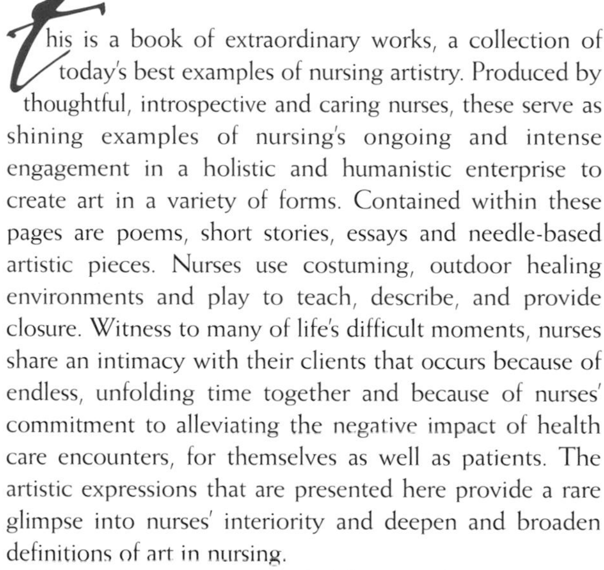

This is a book of extraordinary works, a collection of today's best examples of nursing artistry. Produced by thoughtful, introspective and caring nurses, these serve as shining examples of nursing's ongoing and intense engagement in a holistic and humanistic enterprise to create art in a variety of forms. Contained within these pages are poems, short stories, essays and needle-based artistic pieces. Nurses use costuming, outdoor healing environments and play to teach, describe, and provide closure. Witness to many of life's difficult moments, nurses share an intimacy with their clients that occurs because of endless, unfolding time together and because of nurses' commitment to alleviating the negative impact of health care encounters, for themselves as well as patients. The artistic expressions that are presented here provide a rare glimpse into nurses' interiority and deepen and broaden definitions of art in nursing.

This book portrays a broad definition of art in nursing, informed by Chinn (1994) who asserted, "The art of nursing is the art/act of the experience in the moment" (p. 24). This art/act can be within the present flow of time, as in the unfolding artistic ballet of an experienced nurse rendering professional care. There is also recognition that art may unfold through quiet and thoughtful reflection of a critical, or everyday, event in a nurse's life (Johns & Freshwater, 1999). Art may evolve during an engagement in diversionary activities as nurses play, relax, or connect with friends and family. Art in nursing may also emerge in the understated elegance of a parsimonious research design. The book is designed to illuminate the question "when is nursing art?" in such a way that students, clinicians, educators and scholars can identify the influence of art within nursing and celebrate the expressive and creative artistic acts of nurses.

Origins: Sigma Theta Tau International and "The HeART of Nursing"

The idea to showcase nursing's artistry arose during a brainstorming session of the planning committee participants for the 1999 Biennial Convention of Sigma Theta Tau International (STTI). During the discussion, Dr. Mary Elaine Kiener challenged nurses to reach toward a new view of scholarship, one which required "a dedicated spirit, which necessitates the heart of an explorer, coupled with the soul of a poet" (M.E. Kiener, personal communication, October 2000). The goal was to nurture the ontology or 'being' of nursing through the courageous expression of art in its many forms.

Dr. Nancy Brown-Schott, a member of the committee, asked Dr. Kiener to spearhead this effort. With the assistance of Sue Wheeler and Dr. Brown-Schott, Dr. Kiener drafted the following call for abstracts highlighting artistic nursing:

As nurses, we often interact with individuals who are facing difficult periods in their lives. Very often, it is the richness of our interactions with those who are undergoing life-threatening challenges that also offer nurses their most memorable experiences.

No matter which model of nursing guides our practice, the nature of our work involves an exploration of the meanings and values surrounding health, illness, death and dying. While physical factors often influence an individual's ability to perform 'those activities contributing to health or its recovery (or to a peaceful death)' (ANA Social Policy Statement, 1995), an often stronger influence derives from how each person actually interprets and incorporates their health challenges within the individual tapestry of their life experience.

Many nurses find that their own involvement in one or more of the creative and expressive arts... enables them to more deeply explore the inner nuances of these experiences. With their own understanding enriched, they are then able to more effectively work with other patients.

As a first step in celebrating the heART of nursing, we invite STTI members to share examples of their own expressive and creative artwork. Selected submissions will be showcased throughout the 1999 Biennial Convention in San Diego.

The response was overwhelming—despite a short turn-around time, 65 submissions were received; 36 of which are featured in this book. In many cases, the story behind the work—and the poster displays themselves—added additional artistic dimension to the original pieces and were artworks unto themselves. Convention-goers enthusiastically received the displays and people would often weep when reading and/or experiencing the poster presentations.

A similar call for artwork in subsequent years brought additional submissions from the 2001 and 2003 Creative and Expressive Arts in Nursing presentations, which are also included in this edition.

Much more importantly, though, the "HeART of Nursing" displays allowed the silent, often marginalized artistic expressions of nursing to shine in the spotlight for the profession. This book allows that message to be carried further, to future generations of nurses, so they might also see the richness of a life in nursing nurtured by the humanities. This book provides an avenue for educators to teach students about the nature of art, its role in a highly technological world and the importance of developing an aesthetic sense for nurses. The essay that follows—"When is Nursing Art?"—asks the critical questions that help to frame our examination of these issues. We suggest that you read and reflect upon (Johns & Freshwater, 1999) Dr. Gramling's thesis question and, then, engage in an aesthetic exchange with each of the art forms presented. See what you might learn about nurses, nursing, clients, or yourself in the process. Then, create a space for your own aesthetic expression. See what kinds of experiences—healing, caring, presence, understanding—arise as a result. Enjoy! ♥

REFERENCES:

American Nurses Association. *Social policy statement.* Washington, DC: Author, 1995

Chinn, P. , & Watson, J. (Eds.). *Art and aesthetics in nursing.* NY: National, 1994

League for Nursing Press. Johns, C., & Freshwater, D. *Reflective nursing practice.* London: Blackwell Science, 1999

When is Nursing Art?

by Kathryn Louise Gramling

After the death of a nine-month-old infant, a Minnesota emergency department nurse, tears streaming, presented the draped and lifeless baby's body onto the lap and into the waiting arms of his mother. Her gesture was interpreted as one of exquisite compassion and respect. A record of this "work of art" lives in the full story and in the hearts and minds of those who experienced it. There is no canvas for critics to dispute. No framed and pedestaled beauty in an endowed hall. For many, the image evoked is too deep to penetrate, too private to view, and too soaked in horror to embrace. Nurses live and create such stories daily. The impact of the nurse's actions on the grieving mother's health and healing remains undisclosed and untapped in an economic, technological, and scientific system of "care." Occasionally, people are so affected by their care experiences that they make unsolicited powerful testimony similar to that shared in the *Boston Globe* by Kenneth Schwartz (1995). More often, the art of nursing remains invisible, ineffable, cloaked in mystery and myth.

For over a century, nurses have referred to their practice as an art. Hailed as nearly the "finest of Fine Arts" by Nightingale in 1856 and illustrated as the "oldest of arts" by Donahue (1985, p. 2), nursing has sustained and cherished a claim to art. However, a classic treatise noted that the discipline had only given a "tacit admission" (Carper, 1978, p.16) of the art of nursing through vague associations with manual and technical skills. A recent examination of nursing art in the literature revealed "immensely diverse" characterizations that were confusing and unclear and had little common ground for debate (Johnson, 1994).

Although the delineation of nursing art remains a challenge to the discipline, the "idea" that nursing is an art is communicated as a given, a truth, and an essential fact. Nurses may "know" what nursing art is but may lack the words to effectively describe it or the words that may help form questions to advance an understanding of it. Indeed, art is considered difficult to represent using words (Carper, 1978; Jacobs-Kramer & Chinn, 1988). Additionally, there appears relatively little opportunity or discursive space for such a heady discussion in "real world" nursing.

Language may serve as a force that shapes or, conversely, obscures an appreciation of nursing's art. Therefore, nursing's art discourse deserves our attention and a reflective, self-conscious appraisal. This discussion examines the questions and vocabulary used to characterize nursing as an art in the literature over time. The question "What is art?" is critiqued and a new question proposed, as a way to open the dialogue and reframe the conversation. "When is nursing art?" is offered as a way to illuminate how nursing serves as an aesthetic force in the dynamic human health experience.

Significance

Knowledge of both nursing science and nursing art is needed for excellence in practice. Since the 1960s, the discipline of nursing has made strong strides in building a science base. Yet, the art of nursing has had a restricted meaning (Carper, 1978; Boykin, Parker & Schoenhofer, 1993), a devalued place in disciplinary discourse (Carper; Johnson, 1994; Rhodes, 1990), and has changed in nature as roles and operational definitions have evolved (Donahue, 1985). Unexplored dimensions of art limit the possibilities of uncovering the healing power of nurses' work in health care. Without language or discussion, nurses have no tools to name or claim nurse-sensitive outcomes of artful care. There is no legitimacy without language, no power without words, no answers without penetrating questions and debate.

Educators struggle to prepare compassionate, competent practitioners for the twenty-first century without clear tools for describing or enhancing artfulness in practice. The teaching and learning of the art of nursing is a less formalized, illegitimate aspect of the educational process. Left to chance and without a developing knowledge base, the educator and the student remain impoverished.

However, the artistry of nursing—the creative construction of the science—when exposed and developed discipline-wide, may provide the nurse with a legitimate avenue for further professional fulfillment and joy. Essentially, the everyday life of nurses—and of patients—could be enriched through a fuller aesthetic development. Certainly nursing artistry evolves in spite of a lack of formal facilitation and system validation. But for those who feature nursing as "caring in the human health experience" (Newman, Sime, Corcoran-Perry, 1991, p. 3), it is essential that the discipline actively explore the art of nursing and aesthetic ways of knowing. Careful attention to questions and the use of language may direct us to or away from the aesthetic being of the nurse and the caring relationships in which the nurse participates.

♥

WHAT IS ART?

History of the Question

Philosophers of art have long been frustrated by attempts to answer the question "What is art?" (Goodman, 1978). In general, art and knowledge about art is a human construction (Collingwood, 1938; Dewey, 1934; Goodman, 1978; Howard, 1982). Asking "What is art?" has traditionally directed us to a definition, a theory, boundaries, and universal criteria (Parsons & Blocker, 1993). Closely aligned and sometimes implicit is "Is this good art?" (Goodman, 1978, p. 66). Asking "What is art?" calls forth answers from a distinguished and formidable legacy. Notable thinkers and philosophers of art have developed strong arguments about what a claim to art entails and what it does not.

One of the earliest views of art was that it is an imitation or copy of reality. This was Plato's (c. 427-347 B.C.) view, which was described in the *Republic*. Plato believed that the highest attainment for man was to come to know "Absolute Truth." Such an ideal, he was convinced, could only be attained through reason (Ritcher, 1967). Since Plato understood art to primarily appeal to a person's emotions and passions, he did not believe that art would strengthen reason or wisdom (Ritcher). As guardian of the ideal Greek city-state, Plato communicated his suspicions about the value of art through dialogues in which aesthetic problems were addressed in the 'voice' of Socrates.

Aristotle studied at Plato's Academy but he differed from his master's teachings by defending some of the arts that Plato condemned. Aristotle's (384-322 B.C.) *Poetics*, considered one of the most significant treatises in the history of aesthetics (Ritcher, 1967), viewed art as catharsis. People created art because they desired emotional expression. From this perspective, the function/value of art was to purge emotions (Ritcher). Aristotle theorized that art could bring a clearer understanding of the universals in experience and therefore was constructive (Ritcher). It is beyond the scope of this discussion to attempt to trace specific conceptions of art through the ages. However, in asking "What is art?" today, we must acknowledge that our answers will, to some degree, be influenced by thousands of years of powerful voices that reach as far back as these Greek scholars.

Interpretations

When we ask "What is art?" we are asking whether "it" conforms to "our" idea of art (Parsons & Blocker, 1993). Yet, ideas are learned. Interpretations of art can change. As

Howard (1996) reminds us, ideas about art are not all subjective, in "the mind;" because culture also shapes thinking. Goodman (1978) believes that a work may function as art at some times and not at others. He gives an example of a Rembrandt painting that stops functioning as a work of art when used to patch a broken window. Such fluidity begs the question "What is art?" Asking a "what is art?" question disavows the influence of intention in what constitutes art and through omission neglects change, perspective, function, and culture. Today, artworks are being "discovered" in Anasazi ruins. The reinterpretation of those works are colored by our present understandings of past events. The useful objects created by Native Americans now represent something beautiful and symbolic. In a similar way, Nightingale's ministrations have been revisioned from today's position.

Disconnection from Experience

Dewey (1934) reminds us how often the question "What is art?" conjures up images of "precious objects" separated from the experience of real life and divorced from the circumstance of its creation. "Fine art" has been glorified and alienated, says Dewey, from community life of which it used to be a significant part. When art is isolated from reality, segregated in museums, or performed for the elite only, art becomes "an affair for odd moments" (Dewey, p. 53). Conceived as such, art does not have any relationship to the day-to-day reality, is thought a luxury, a decoration, or entertainment (Dewey; Howard, 1992) and is considered "far from the core of our interests and our urgent concerns" (Kupfer, 1983, p. 1). However, art is not by nature on the margins of life; it has been actively disengaged from experience by our minds, theories and philosophies and in our culture (Dewey; Howard, 1992; Kupfer). Nursing art cannot be fully conceptualized apart from the experience of it or of someone's experience of it (Benner & Wrubel, 1989; Bournaki & Germain, 1993; White, 1995) and the circumstances of its execution (Jacobs-Kramer & Chinn, 1988; Silva, Sorrell & Sorrell, 1995; Stewart, 1929).

Dismissive of Thought

Answers to the question "What is art?" by the 19th and 20th Century romantics focused on the power of art to express the emotions and the inner world of the artist. Sometimes this part of the truth is presented as a whole truth (Howard, 1996). If expression is considered to be the only property of making art or if art is equated with emotional expression alone, artists are depicted as thoughtless or out of control (Howard, 1992). An artist can then be thought of as "a sensitive collector of emotional vibrations" (Howard, 1992, p. 32). Although art is much more than a "spewing forth" (Kupfer, 1983, p. 83) or a "discharge of emotion" (Dewey, 1934, p. 61), the expressive nature of art can tend to supercede the intellectual effort and purpose embedded within (Dewey). A comprehensive view of art would be portrayed by a balance of thinking, doing, making and feeling (Dewey; Howard, 1992). Dewey warns that too much emotion impedes purposeful expression whereas too little produces a sterile, lifeless product.

Contrary to Plato's description of the poet (in ION): "a light and winged and holy thing, and there is no invention in him until he has been inspired and is out of his senses and the mind is no longer with him" (cited by Ritcher, 1967, p. 27), creating art requires thinking. In particular, Chinn (1994) asserts that nursing art "is expressive of a deep understanding of common human experience" (p. 37). Thus, nursing as art employs "an embodied grasp of situations and intimate experience with the deepest, most significant life events that have traditionally and cross-culturally been associated with women's experiences—birth, death, sorrow, joy, pain, and life transitions " (p. 37).

WHAT IS NURSING ART?

Changing Characterizations

From a domestic art, a helping art (Wiedenbach, 1964), a technical performance (including hospital housekeeping), a practical art learned in "nursing arts' labs," to a "science creatively lived" (Parse, 1992, p. 147), nursing art has changed. The artist, the context, the tools, the techniques, the preparation of practitioners, the health situations, the delivery systems and the collective experience upon which nursing are based is ever changing. Human knowledge and ways of knowing have expanded. The very universe has grown. Our amplified worldviews and dynamic nursing paradigms are begging for space from linear, static notions and language about art.

Some of the adjectives employed in the past twenty years reflect an effort to break the traditional static barriers by creating discipline-distinct language. Nursing art has been called an enabling, an empowering or a transforming art (Peplau, 1988), a creative art (Skillman-Hull, 1994), an existential art (Patterson & Zderad, 1988), a performing art (Parse, 1992) and a transpersonal art (Watson, 1985). Nursing art is believed to have meaning and mystery (Cody, 1994), healing energy (Quinn, 1992), soul (Watson, 1995), generativity (Mayeroff, 1971), harmony (Jacobs-Kramer & Chinn, 1988), and beauty (Boykin, Parker & Schoenhofer, 1993). Through an illustrated history, Donahue (1985) portrays the "active, dynamic and developing" (p. 467) aspect of nursing art as a form of "qualitative inquiry" (p. 467). However, it is difficult to carve out a reflection of the complexity and density of the human, interactive art of nursing using a vocabulary and ideas originally utilized in the expression and appreciation of art as an autonomous, static, permanent object. Consider the questions that have been asked: "What is nursing art?" "What is the nature of nursing art?" These questions imply there *is* one right answer; *a* set of fixed criteria for what nursing art is and what "it" is not, and that *the* answer remains the same over time and circumstance. The century-old query "What is nursing art?" may not, in fact, permit access to the complexity, intricacy and human experience of the art of nursing. The answers may be larger than this particular question allows.

"What" assumes an answer in absolutes; "what" implies that there is a concrete product, a measurable finite object like a painting or a piece of music. "What" assumes that there is an essential, immutable character to any art that one can point to and all can "see" and experience identically. Newman, Sime and Corcoran-Perry (1991) described this perspective as emulating from a particulate-deterministic paradigm—one where phenomena are reduced, isolated and measured apart from experiences. These scholars advocate a shift to a fuller explication of nursing with questions that honor/respect change, wholeness, and complexity. "What is nursing art?" is a question that continues to systematically obscure the interconnected, relational, rich circumstances from which and with which nurses create art.

When the profession began to develop its knowledge base, it did so within an empirical science focus and moved away from the "seemingly unscholarly domain of art" (Rhodes, 1990, p. 2). The "truth" of nursing was defined within the parameters of the "received view" perspective of science (Watson, 1981a). More than twenty years ago, Watson lamented, "[W]hile nursing is on its Odyssic quest to develop the science of nursing practice the universal humanistic art of nursing lies unattended" (1981b, p. 244). Further "some of the rich, nonquantifiable, qualitative, subjective, emotional *wholes* of nursing became submerged... because they weren't scientific, researchable or testable" (Watson, 1981a, p. 414). However, there is renewed enthusiasm for articulating the art of nursing (Appleton, 1991,1994; Bournaki & Germain, 1993; Boykin, Parker & Schoenhofer, 1993; Burke, 1992 ; Chinn, Maeve & Bostick, 1997; Chinn

& Watson, 1994; Hess, 1995; Johnson, 1991, 1994, 1996; Kolcaba, 1995; LeVasseur, 1999; Parse, 1992; Patterson & Zderad, 1988; Rhodes, 1990; Rose & Parker, 1994; Silva, Sorrell & Sorrell, 1995; Watson, 1996; White, 1995). Recent characterizations of nursing art have been more expressive of the dynamic nature than the practical mid-century representation of the techniques and procedures of nursing care. For example, nursing art is described as "the capacity of a human being to receive another human being's expression of feelings and to experience those feelings for oneself" (Watson & Chinn, 1994, p. xvi). Chinn and colleagues (1997) have depicted nursing art as a "synchronous arrangement of narrative and movement into a form that transforms experiences into a realm that would not otherwise be possible" (p. 90). Such an ability to shape patients' reality was reported to be rooted in solid nursing knowledge, personal knowledge, and technical skill (Chinn, Maeve & Bostick, 1997). Other accounts of the character of nursing art have emphasized the forms that art takes (Parse, 1992), the properties art displays (Peplau, 1988), the aesthetic response (Appleton, 1991), the artist (Skillman-Hull, 1994), the theoretical stance of the nurse artist (Boykin, Parker & Schoenhofer, 1993; Parse, 1992; Watson, 1985), the product of the artistry (Kolcaba, 1995) and the sociopolitical context out of which the art arose (White, 1995).

Nonetheless, the literature also retains shades of deterministic ideology, competitive-comparative values, universal criteria rooted in power and tradition, and lack of attention to the context from which nursing arises. Is the changing nature of nursing art problematic? Is the diversity of views about art in nursing a barrier to understanding? Shall we never "entirely capture the true art and caring spirit of nursing" as Donahue suggests (1985, p. 468)? Does the discipline expect to create one narrative, one image? Are we looking for "it" as in the search for one permanent truth, frozen in time, framed and isolated from the lived, human experience of art? Or does the language and traditions upon which art theories stand fail to serve our expanding paradigms and ontology?

Often, Nightingale's (1856) famous words are evoked in today's art discourse:

"[F]or what is having to do with dead canvas or cold marble, compared to having to do with the living body—the temple of God's spirit? It is one of the Fine Arts: I had almost said, one of the finest of the Fine Arts" (as cited in Donahue, 1985, p. 469). Powerful and challenging as these words may be, do they help contemporary nurses focus on the uniqueness of our practice or do they put nurses in a comparative, competitive place, steeped in universal essentialist empirical boundaries? Or does the discipline not wish to stand on the power of fine art distinctions that have systematically excluded experience (Dewey, 1934; Everett, 1991), women's experiences (Chinn, 1994; Duncan, 1993) and nursing (Chinn, 1994)? Nursing scholars (LeVasseur, 1999; Rhodes, 1990) argue that many aesthetic theories are not compatible with nursings' notion of art.

Explorations of Nursing Art

Carper (1978) challenged the discipline to consider that nurses' knowledge extended beyond the empirical. Carper equated the art of nursing with "aesthetics" while identifying it as one valid way that nurses know; She presented art as "... the creation and/or appreciation of a singular, particular, subjective expression of imagined possibilities or realities" (Carper, 1978, p. 16). In art, wrote Carper, the nurse's thinking is converted to a fuller understanding of the significance of patient behavior in the moment. Artful nurses sensed, felt, perceived, observed and imagined meaning and significance in patient care, according to Carper. They became "subjectively acquainted" with the whole rather than with the isolated parts of patient situations. Carper's work brought attention, credibility, and validity to the study of nursing as art.

Although there are many views and diverse writings about nursing art, few scholars have chosen to systematically investigate this concept. In part, the methodologies for studying art are not readily available. Chinn (1994) addressed this issue by developing a process of "aesthetic experiential criticism" (p. 32) that was utilized in studying practicing nurses' characterizations of art (Chinn, Maeve & Bostick, 1997). Rhodes (1990), Johnson (1994), Burke (1992) and LeVasseur (1999) have undertaken philosophical analyses. Experiential studies have been conducted by Appleton (1991), Skillman-Hull (1994) and Gramling (1999). While this is not an exhaustive list of contributors to the developing body of knowledge, they represent diverse scholarly efforts to develop understanding of nursing's artistry and thus will be briefly summarized.

Philosophical

Believing that the difficulties in clarifying the definition of nursing art were related to a lack of understanding of the nature of art in general, Rhodes (1990) studied the philosophy of art as depicted in the metatheory of Sparshott (1982). She found that nursing's historical emphasis on intersubjectivity and interpersonal processes was under-represented in major theories of art. As an experiential caring entity, much of nursing appeared to Rhodes to lie outside the bounds of traditional past philosophical notion of art. Rhodes elaborated on the interpersonal core of nursing art stating that "creative interaction is the art of nursing" (p. 180). She urged the discipline not to discount the value of traditional thought but to proceed critically.

Burke (1992) undertook a philosophical study to inquire into how a nurse develops nursing artistry. She confirmed that this encompasses the imaginative and sensitive spirit of the nurse, which Burke described as the nurse's "perceptual palette" (p. 1). It is this palette that guides the artistry of nurses. Burke found a range of subjective and objective perspectives that may be reflected in artful caring and made a strong case for nurturing and deepening the caring being who employs the science of nursing.

Johnson (1994) surfaced areas of agreement from over a century of nursing literature. Through a comprehensive dialectic examination of 41 writings in nursing, Johnson uncovered some of the implicit understandings about nursing art in order to make substantive debate possible. Identifying the diversity of views as problematic, confusing and unclear, the derived characterizations were structured into "five senses" of what is meant by nursing art. The categories are described in terms of a nurse's *ability* to: 1) grasp meaning in encounters with patients, 2) connect meaningfully with the patient, 3) perform nursing functions skillfully, 4) rationally choose appropriate nursing action and 5) behave morally in practice (Johnson, 1994). Johnson's work provides a framework for discussing conceptualizations of nursing art. She is clear that art may be a vehicle for debate and she invites argument stating that scholars have not acknowledged each other's constructions. This type of examination removes a scholar's characterization from its history, context and knowledge perspective; as Johnson noted, it treats the literature as an ongoing dialogue when in fact there has been no discourse. Johnson succeeded in synthesizing diverse and fragmented literature and setting out concrete ideas and language for challenging future debate.

LeVasseur (1999) acknowledged the lack of agreement in the discipline but suggested one of the problems lies in the fact that "currently, the idea of nursing art is unformed theoretically" (p. 49). She examined broad aesthetic theories for goodness of fit with nursing art and found that most theories separate art and science, and craft from art in a way that makes these less relevant to nursing. LeVasseur described how Dewey's (1934) theory of aesthetics could be a strong ground for building a nursing aesthetic theory. This complementary feature was also noted by Carper (1978), Appleton (1991), Gramling (1999) and Rhodes (1990). "The art of nursing" writes LeVasseur (1999), "is not an indulgent nicety, but instead, an essential activity grounded by practice and manifest in helping patients create coherence and meaning in lives threatened by transitions of many kinds" (p. 62).

Experiential

In contrast, Appleton (1991, 1993, 1994) derived descriptions of artful nursing from the perspective of both patients and clients who have lived the experience. Appleton (1993) conducted a phenomenological inquiry to answer the question "What is the experience of the art of nursing for you?" (p. 893). Artful experiences were found to be those in which there was a "very special" process of being really engaged with a nurse over time; the giving and receiving between nurse and patient transcended "conventional human boundaries" (Appleton, 1991, p. 238). Important characteristics of nurse patient engagement were: 1) a way of being there in caring, 2) a way of being with in understanding, 3) a way of creating the fullness of being through caring, 4) a transcendent togetherness and 5) the context of caring (Appleton, 1991, p. iii). Summarily, these metathemes led to a unified statement about the art of nursing as a "transcendent togetherness in love—the true spirit of understanding creates a liberating way of helping" (Appleton, 1991, p. 237). Appleton (1991) concluded that the findings reflected a "new paradigm" (p. 277), which challenges biomedical approaches that fail to put the patient in the center of nursing. She essentially portrays nursing art as "The Gift of Self" (Appleton, 1994, p. 91). Reminiscent of Clayton's (1989) investigation of the intersubjective caring encounter, Appleton's work (1991) tapped into the world of the nurse and client to provide substance to theory development. Both works support the link between caring and nursing art. Appleton's abstractions do not make explicit the art act, but they provide new language to consider in the discourse. Appleton's stories – art unto itself – communicate deep insight in this way.

Skillman-Hull (1994) looked for the art of nursing in stories from persons who were both nurses and also artists. She hypothesized that nurses who were also traditional artists might be particularly able to articulate the dimension in both areas. This phenomenological study provided new understandings about nursing art depicted in the metaphor "she walks in beauty" (Skillman-Hull, 1994, p. 215), which was chosen to reflect the respect and comportment of nurse-artists as they create human caring art. Knowledge about nursing as art came from journals, stories and reflections on the personal experiences of human care relationships in nursing. Participants agreed that nursing as caring and art were one. Qualities of authentic being, truth, transcendence, oneness, and beauty were persistent themes communicated about nursing as caring art.

Skillman-Hull (1994) constructed personal stories about each nurse artist to give the reader deeper detail about how they lived and grew an artistic process inside and outside of nursing. While the metathemes are very global, the experiences depicted in the individual stories offer detail and personal insights.

Chinn (1994) published initial findings from an exploratory study of the "art/act" of nursing practiced by selected acute care nurses. Using and refining a methodology called "aesthetic experiential criticism" (p. 32), Chinn worked closely with the nurses to identify, share, and communicate what they experienced as their art. A group process was used to critique and explore vignettes and photographs that had been selected as representations of their art. Overall the purpose was to gain "compelling insights" (p. 34) through reflection, diverse perspectives and collective wisdom. The critique was not meant to construct a "correct view" but rather to expand consciousness about nursing's art.

An early finding revealed that the art of nursing was communicated through the body of the nurse. "Our bodies constitute the carrier of our art—they tell the story, convey the message, and portray the experience" (Chinn, 1994, p. 35). Body movement, touch and posturing were noted to be core elements of nursing art. For example, Chinn explains that particular body movements by the nurse may be invitations to patients while others indicate endings. Although these performances were spontaneous artistic movements, they were grounded in knowledge and experience. Chinn suggests that practice or rehearsals may be found to strengthen the art of nursing in the future.

Chinn and colleagues (1997) extended this work and reported success in coming to some clarification of the term "nursing art." Sixteen nurse-artists became critics reflecting on their own and other nurses' experiences of nursing art through stories, poems, observations and photographs. The group came to see nursing art as an intentional shaping of the experience of the patient through the mediums of movement and narrative. A definition of nursing art was advanced. The art of nursing is "the nurse's synchronous arrangement of narrative and movement into a form that transforms experiences into a realm that would not otherwise be possible" (Chinn et al., 1997, p. 91).

This movement of nursing art was conceptualized as a "rhythmic flow" (Chinn, Maeve & Bostick, 1997, p. 91), which usually involved some type of healing touch. In fact, Bostick found that the flow "touches the human realm of unrevealed emotions and sensations, bringing participants and observers to dimensions not otherwise accessible to awareness" (Chinn, Maeve & Bostick, 1997, p. 91). Rhythmic flow is said to produce inner pleasure and harmony with the possibility of decentering external stimuli.

Another significant form of nursing art revealed in this investigation was the narrative. "Stories are told to patients, in clinical time, that situate the patient's current dilemma within a plot structure meant to reflect future possibilities and realities" (Chinn, Maeve & Bostick, 1997, p. 93). Therefore patients were able to reformulate their experiences with new knowledge. This work appears to be a promising contribution to accessing the process and product of nursing as art.

Gramling (1999) interviewed critically ill patients to discern when they considered their nursing care to be art. Patients told stories of very deep, intimate, healing engagements with nurses. While patients may not "know" nursing's art as nurses do, the perspectives they offer may help illuminate our art anew and facilitate an understanding of the notion of "appreciation" of nursing as art. Themes that emerged from patients' stories of nursing art were "perpetual presence," "knowing the other," "intimacy in agony," "deep detail" and "honoring the body" (p. 174). Both the themes and the stories help reveal the artful presence of nurses during and within the most agonizing of times.

Shaping

An examination of nursing art may come from different perspectives and take different directions. All are important in knowledge development. Eventually, we want to get to this rich "perceptual palette" (Burke, 1992, p. 1), the "transcendent togetherness" (Appleton, 1993, p. 264), the comportment of a human care artist (Skillman-Hull, 1994), the "existential moments of caring" (Krysl & Watson, 1988, p. 13) and the "integrated experience" (Chinn, Maeve & Bostick, 1997, p. 86) of artful practice. It is enlightening to listen critically to the diverse and changing nature of depictions of nursing art. In so doing, nurses may find that we cannot answer the question "What is nursing art?" From the point of view of Howard (1996), a philosopher of art and education, as soon as the question is answered it will become insufficient. The problem is partly the question, but it is also contained in the strength of centuries of carefully crafted responses to the question that has nothing and everything to do with nursing art.

"Our so-called modern assumptions and worldview about humanity have tainted our openness to what it means to be human, what it means to engage the human spirit through our nursing arts" (Watson, 1996, p. 33).

Summarily, "What is nursing art?" is a question that may keep the profession struggling in a particular-deterministic paradigm (Newman, Sime, & Corcoran-Perry, 1991). The question itself continues the objective and definitive functions of nursing, perpetuates the dichotomy of utility versus beauty, in a context-poor construction. This question gives deference to more objectively explicit professions, keeps nursing in the shadows of tradition and power, reinforces non-relational worldviews, and sustains competitive and comparative discourse, resulting in confusion and marginalization.

♥

WHEN IS NURSING ART?

Instead of being restricted to the "what" of artwork, we might expand the question to: "When is nursing art?" Goodman (1978) and Howard (1996) promoted new dialogue in art proper by posing a *When is art?* query. Howard (1982) suggests "avoiding some of the ontological hazards of a frontal assault" [on art through a] "reconceptualization of the problem in terms of transient function rather than fixed ontology" (p. 15). By asking this question in nursing, we may open up the characterization of art, by providing context, meaning, strength and visibility (Gramling, 1997b). As a new query, "When is nursing art?" may evoke more storytelling, as it is less authoritative, and more open to ideas and answers. "When is nursing art?" suggests that there may be a variety of ideas and answers that should and could be entertained.

Stories have demonstrated they are a powerful passage to understanding in nursing (Benner, 1984; Boykin, Parker & Schoenhofer, 1993; Chinn, Maeve & Bostick, 1997); they provide fresh images, insights and experiential language upon which to build further dialogue about nursing as an art. For instance, asking a patient to "Tell me a story about when your nursing was artful" (Gramling, 1999, p. 124) was utilized as one "easy concrete way to start the storytelling off, to create an inviting space that may be filled" (Reason & Hawkins, 1988, p. 90).

"When is nursing art?" is a powerful query. The question itself possesses the strength to modify or change paradigms and may elicit responses that create a collective bridge to understanding. The question is highly open-ended; it does not call for prescribed defined answers but requests expanding, diverging concepts. "When is nursing art?" is open to life, thought and multiple theoretical perspectives. "When is nursing art?" may be an inquiry consistent with the disciplinary shift in perspective referred to as "the unitary transformative paradigm" (Newman, Sime & Corcoran-Perry, 1991, p. 5), a view with access to human experience. "When is nursing art?" is a promising probe for removing nursing's artistic shroud.

Diversity

The diverse and multiple characterizations of nursing art reflect the complexity of a human practice discipline. These diverse depictions act as many windows to full understanding. We may hear many stories with a "when" question. For instance, nursing evolved as a service to the sick, in homes as domestic art, on battlefields, in the streets and in hospitals (Donahue, 1985). To dehistoricize the "art of nursing" is to misrepresent its significance and its usefulness. To some degree, the character of nursing art has been related to health/illness, however, health has been culturally defined. When germ theory was discovered, nurses gave penicillin. When homelessness and alienation were viewed as responsible for ill health, providing connections for housing became a shared nursing responsibility. When technology threatened to dominate, caring theory arose to combat mechanical isolation. When there was no one to care for crack/cocaine babies, nurses ensured that the void was filled.

The art of nursing has evolved within a global social context of ever-changing views of life, health, and human existence. The art of nursing is a response to human need.

Visibility

The nursing profession has not always taken a position in all this history, but the nursing literature chronicles a struggle to do so. Some urgency is registered in the present as the economy and technology threaten nursing's integrity and viability. As opaque as language is, the ability to describe the contributions of nursing to health care will in part determine the future of the nurse and nursing's art. Poetry (Krsyl & Watson, 1988) as well as metaphor (Appleton, 1991; Burke, 1992; Hess, 1995; Skillman-Hull, 1994), story (Benner, 1984; Boykin & Schoenhofer, 1991; Vezeau, 1994) and art forms such as painting (Breunig, 1994), photography and drawing (Malkiewicz & Stember, 1994), dance (Boyle, 1994), and music (Gramling, 1997a; Updike, 1994) have enhanced understanding of art where proscribed discursive presentation falls short. However, there is a need to tell others, to talk about our art in the traditional sense in order to be funded, to be heard, to be visible and to matter. Art can be described retrospectively and comprehensively when the whole of the experience is contemplated (Jacob-Kramer & Chinn, 1988, p. 36). A "when" question will circumvent the problems of the "what" question while still keeping us *in dialogue*.

Context

Professional self-understandings have evolved, and they will continue to do so. When nurses were considered physician handmaidens, they created art within prescribed patriarchal roles mindfully, but not independently. As scientism was embraced, empirical research and rational thinking were cultivated into professional practice. Now thanks to Carper's (1978) pioneering work in nursing, there is interest in more than scientific knowing (White, 1995) within the profession.

Aesthetic, intuitive, ethical, personal, and sociopolitical knowing are being given attention in the nursing literature. All ways of knowing are said to enfold "to bring about a harmonious and pleasing whole—an artful nursing act" (Jacobs-Kramer & Chinn, 1988, p. 137). Munhall and Oiler-Boyd (1993) urge the discipline to understand the value of qualitative methods in arriving at full knowledge of nursing practice. "The isolation of parts suitable for scientific analysis in the empirical model discourages those who would envision the acceptance of other ways of knowing, particularly ways of grasping wholes and complex meanings in nursing situations" (p. xvii). The question "When is nursing art?" is congruent with the paradigmatic, methodological and ontological shifts called for by nurse leaders such as Newman, Rogers, Watson and Parse.

Connection of Art and Utility

Additionally, "When is nursing art?" can help nurses remember that what functions as art at certain times may not be particularly artful at another or for another. For example, using Johnson's (1994) typology, when nursing a woman in childbirth, the nurse must have the ability to perform procedures; grasp the meaning of the situation (has this woman had four stillbirths?); interact/connect with the woman, husband, partner, others; deploy knowledge (the monitor reading indicates the baby does not have enough oxygen) and act morally (not discuss this nursing case with others). All these abilities merge artfully, as a whole, in the service of caring.

Thoughtful Action

The whole represents a confluence of creativity, intelligence, sensitivity and judgment that the nurse uses in the deployment of nursing under certain circumstances (Stewart, 1929). For instance, when a woman's fear of stillbirth has the potential to interfere with labor and delivery, how does the nurse use knowledge and skill to safely assist her with comfort and peace? "When is nursing art?" Bournaki and Germain (1993) contend that the practice of family nursing is art when there is "an understanding of the uniqueness of individuals in their clinical complexity, the significance of context, the value and use of creativity, interpretive ability and the integration of all types of knowing" (p. 86). Hold that idea alongside the categorization of nursing art as an immediate perceptual capacity unaffected by the intellect (Johnson, 1994).

Utility and thought are important in a professional practice, but they need not overshadow the aesthetic face of nursing. Asking "When is nursing art?" may help us validate that beauty/art, thought and utility coexist in spite of the profession's history to categorize them otherwise.

Theory

Cody (1994) postulates that the performance art of nursing takes on the distinctive characteristics of the nursing theory embraced by the nurse-artist. For example, Cody envisions the artistry of a Newman-driven practice would find expression in facilitating expanded levels of consciousness. A Watsonian artist would bring about transpersonal caring moments. But as Smith (1995) points out, it is imperative that the nurse express the science of nursing from nursing's disciplinary perspective, not from that of some other science; this is at the core of advanced practice.

Within caring theory, the overall context is the moment to moment human encounter (Watson, 1985). Watson posited nursing is art *when* the nurse who detects a person's feelings can express those feelings in a way that helps the person reach a fuller experience and release. Expressions take the form of acts, movements, sounds, silence, forms or color... "the process allows for combinations of expressions of human feelings in different moments and contexts, and with different outcomes, that can never be fully explained or predicted" (p. 70). "It is all art," says Watson (p. 68). Sometimes there is a product that can be seen or felt; sometimes there is not. The product may be a new way of seeing, a new way of approaching one's life and challenges, or a new perspective. Sometimes it is a more authentic way of living or of dying.

Nurse scholars (Doona, Haggarty & Chase, 1997; Gilje, 1992; Liehr, 1989; Pettigrew, 1990) continue to investigate the nurse's presence as a core feature of excellence in practice. Indeed, to develop the symbolic systems—the behavior, the words, the gestures, the voice, the skill, the touch, and the wisdom and to deploy each with intelligence and sensitivity remains our challenge. "When is nursing art?" is a question that will move the intellectual energy in the direction of how nursing acts as art in the lives of human beings generally and on particular occasions.

♥

CONCLUSION

Nursing has long claimed to be an art. Yet a distinct portrait of nursing art has not developed. "What is art?" has been a question that has directed the discourse regarding nursing art in the past century. The question may not serve nursing well. "What is nursing art?" may instead hinder interpretation within nursing by comparing nursing art to criteria of fine art; remaining invisible due to an inability to capture its inherent complexity. Instead of clarity, there is confusion and disunity because of a lack of fruitful discourse and a persistent intolerance to differing views. The result is a loss of understanding and insight into nursing art. An alternative question "When is nursing art?" is proposed here as a way to reframe the discourse, redirect intellectual energy, respect diversity, and assault the traditional shadows of language and thinking that have obscured an understanding of nursing as art/artistry. As has been called for in these postmodern times, nursing must continue in a process of "endless self revising and self reflecting" (Watson, 1995, p. 630) to participate in the construction of its own unique possibilities. To do so, we must expand the conversation and acknowledge expressions of our art and that of other nurses. ♥

REFERENCES:

Appleton, C. (1994). The gift of self: A paradigm for originating nursing as art. In P. Chinn & J. Watson (Eds.), *Art and aesthetics in nursing* (pp. 91-113). New York: National League for Nursing.

Appleton, C. (1993). The art of nursing: The experience of patients and nurses. *Journal of Advanced Nursing, 18*, 892-899.

Appleton, C. (1991). *The gift of self: The meaning of the art of nursing*. Doctoral dissertation, University of Colorado, Denver.

Benner, P. & Wrubel. J. (1989). *The primacy of caring: Stress and coping in health and illness.* New York: Addison Wesley.

Benner, P. (1984). *From novice to expert; Excellence and power in clinical practice.* Menlo Park,CA: Addison-Wesley.

Boyle, D.E. (1994). The use of dance/movement therapy in psychosocial nursing. In P. Chinn & J. Watson (Eds.), *Art and aesthetics in nursing* (pp. 301-316). New York: National League for Nursing.

Bournaki, M. & Germain, C. (1993). Esthetic knowledge in family centered nursing care of children. *Advances in Nursing Science, 16*, 81-89.

Boykin, A., Parker, M., & Schoenhofer, S. (1993). Aesthetic knowing grounded in an explicit conception of nursing. *Nursing Science Quarterly, Winter*, 158-161.

Boykin, A. & Schoenhofer, S. (1991). Story as link between nursing practice, ontology and epistemology. *Image: Journal of Nursing Scholarship, 23*, 245-248.

Breunig, K. (1994). The art of painting meets the art of nursing. In P. Chinn & J. Watson (Eds.), *Art and aesthetics in nursing* (pp. 191-201). New York: National League for Nursing.

Burke, C. (1992). *Pentimento praxis: Weaving aesthetic experience to evolve the caring beings in nursing*. Doctoral dissertation. University of Colorado, Denver.

Carper, B. (1978). Fundamental patterns of knowing in nursing. *Advances in Nursing Science, 1*, 13-23.

Chinn, P. (1994). Developing a method for aesthetic knowing in nursing. In P. Chinn & J. Watson (Eds.), *Art and aesthetics in nursing* (pp. 19-40). New York: National League for Nursing.

Chinn, P., Maeve, M.K. & Bostick, C. (1997). Aesthetic inquiry and the art of nursing. *Scholarly Inquiry for Nursing Practice: An International Journal, 11*(2), 83-94.

Chinn, P., & Watson, J. (Eds.). (1994). *Art and aesthetics in nursing*. New York, NY: National League for Nursing.

Clayton, G. (1989). Research testing Watson's theory: The phenomenon of caring in an elderly population. In J.P. Riele-Siska & C. Roy (Eds.), *Conceptual models of nursing practice* (pp. 245-252). Norwalk, CT: Appleton-Century-Croft.

Cody, W. (1994). Meaning and mystery in nursing science and art. *Nursing Science Quarterly, 7*, 18-51.

Collingwood, R.G. (1938). *The principles of art.* Oxford, MA: Oxford University.

Dewey, J. (1934). *Art as experience.* New York, NY: Perigee.

Donahue, M.P. (1985). *Nursing: The finest art, an illustrated history.* St. Louis, MO: Mosby.

Doona, M.E., Haggarty, L., & Chase, S. (1997). Nursing presence: An existential exploration of the concept. *Scholarly Inquiry for Nursing Practice, 7*, 183-193.

Duncan, C. (1993). *The aesthetics of power: Essays in critical art history.* Cambridge, MA: Cambridge University.

Everett, S. (Ed.). (1991). *Art theory and criticism: An anthology of formalist avant-garde, contextualist and post modern thought.* Jefferson, NC: McFarland.

Gilje, F. (1992). Being there: An analysis of the concept of presence. In D. Gaut (Ed.), *The presence of caring in nursing* (pp. 53-67). New York, NY: National League for Nursing.

Goodman, N. (1978). When is art? *Ways of worldmaking.* Indianapolis, IN: Hackett.

Gramling, K. (1999). *The art of nursing: Portraits from the critically-ill.* Doctoral dissertation. University of Colorado, Denver.

Gramling, K. (1997a). Photography and music give expression to caring from the heart. In S. Roach (Ed.), *Caring from the heart: A convergence of caring and spirituality*. Manwah, NJ: Paulist.

Gramling, K. (1997b). *When or what is art? That is the question.* Unpublished paper, University of Colorado, Denver.

Hess, J. (1995). The art of stained glass: Metaphor for the art of nursing. *Nursing Inquiry, 2*, 221-223.

Howard, V.A. (1996). Philosophy of art. *Lecture series* (Fall). Boston: Harvard University.

Howard, V.A. (1992). *Learning by all means: Lessons from the arts.* New York, NY: Peter Lang.

Howard. V.A. (1982). *Artistry: The work of artists.* Indianapolis, IN: Hackett.

Jacobs-Kramer, M.K. & Chinn, P. (1988). Perspectives on knowing: A model for nursing knowledge. *Scholarly Inquiry for Nursing Practice, 2*(2), 129-143.

Johnson, J. (1996). Dialectical analysis concerning the rational aspect of the art of nursing. *Image: Journal of Nursing Scholarship, 28*(2), 169-175.

Johnson, J. (1994). Dialectic examination of nursing art. *Advances in Nursing Science, 17*(1), 1-14.

Johnson, J. (1991). Nursing science: Basic, applied or practical? Implications for the art of nursing. *Advances in Nursing Science, 14*(1), 7-16.

Koithan, M. (1994). Incorporating multiple modes of awareness in the curriculum. In P. Chinn & J. Watson (Eds.), *Art and aesthetics in nursing* (pp. 145-161). New York: National League for Nursing.

Kolcaba, K. (1995). Comfort as process and product, merged in holistic nursing art. *Journal of Holistic Nursing, 2*, 117-131.

Krysl, M. & Watson, J. (1988). Existential moments of caring: Facets of nursing and social support. *Advances in Nursing Science, 10*, 12-17.

Kupfer, J. (1983). *Experience as art. Aesthetics in everyday life.* Albany, NY: State University of New York.

LeVasseur, J. (1999). Toward an understanding of art in nursing. *Advances in Nursing Science, 21*(4), 48-68.

Liehr, P. (1989). The core of true presence: A loving center. *Nursing Science Quarterly, 2*(1), 7-8.

Malkiewicz, J. & Stember, M. (1994). Children's drawing: A different window. In P. Chinn & J.Watson (Eds.), *Art and aesthetics in nursing* (pp. 263-289). New York: National League for Nursing.

Mayeroff, M. (1971). *On caring.* New York, NY: Harper & Row.

Munhall, P. & Oiler-Boyd, C. (1993). *Nursing research; A qualitative perspective.* New York, NY: National league for Nursing.

Newman, M., Sime, A., & Corcoran-Perry, S.A. (1991). The focus of the discipline of nursing. *Advances in Nursing Science, 14*, 1-6.

Nightingale, F. (1856). *Notes on nursing.* London: Harrison and Sons.

Parse, R. (1992). The performing art of nursing. *Nursing Science Quarterly, 5*(4), 147.

Parsons, M. & Blocker H.G. (1993). *Aesthetics and understanding: Disciplines in art education: Contexts of understanding.* Chicago, IL: University of Illinois.

Patterson, J. & Zderad, L. (1988). *Humanistic nursing.* New York, NY: John Wiley.

Pettigrew, J. (1990). Intensive care nursing: The ministry of presence. *Critical Care Nursing Clinics of North America, 2*(3), 502-508.

Peplau, H. (1988). The art and science of nursing: Similarities, differences and relations. *Nursing Science Quarterly, 1*(1), 8-15.

Quinn, J.F. (1992). Holding sacred space: The nurse as healing environment. *Holistic-Nursing Practice, 6*(4), 26-32.

Reason, P. & Hawkins, P. (1988). Storytelling as inquiry. In P. Reason (Ed.), *Human inquiry in action: Developments in new paradigm research* (pp. 79-101). London: Sage.

Ritcher, P. (Ed.). (1967). *Perspectives in aesthetics; Plato to Camus.* New York, NY: Odyssey Press.

Rhodes, J. (1990). *A philosophical study of the art of nursing explored within a metatheoretical framework of philosophy of art and aesthetics.* Doctoral dissertation. University of South Carolina, Charleston.

Rogers, M.E. (1980). The science of unitary human beings. In J.P. Riehl & C. Roy (Eds.), *Conceptual models for nursing practice* (2nd Ed.). New York, NY: Appleton-Century-Crofts.

Rose, P. & Parker, D. (1994). Nursing: An integration of art and science within the experience of the practitioner. *Journal of Advanced Nursing, 20,* 1004-1010.

Schwartz, K. (1995, July 16). *A patient's story.* Boston Globe, pp. 15-20, 23-26.

Silva, M., Sorrell, J., & Sorrell, C. (1995). From Carper's patterns of knowing to ways of being: An ontological shift in nursing. *Advances in Nursing Science, 18,* 1-13.

Skillman-Hull, L. (1994). *She walks in beauty: Nurse artists lived experience of the creative process and aesthetic human care.* Doctoral dissertation. University of Colorado, Denver.

Smith, M. (1995). The core of advanced practice. *Nursing Science Quarterly, 8,* 2-3.

Sparshott, F. (1982). *The theory of the arts.* New Jersey: Princeton University Press.

Stewart, I. (1929). The science and art of nursing. *Nursing Education Bulletin, 2,* 1.

Updike, P. (1994). Aesthetic, spiritual, healing dimensions in music. In P. Chinn & J. Watson (Eds.), *Art and aesthetics in nursing.* New York, NY: National League for Nursing.

Vezeau, T. (1994). Narrative inquiry in nursing. In P. Chinn & J. Watson (Eds.), *Art and aesthetics in nursing.* New York, NY: National League for Nursing.

Watson, J. (1996). Art, caring, spirituality and humanity. In E. Farnes (Ed.), *Exploring the spiritual dimensions of care.* Wiltshire, PA: Mark Allen.

Watson, J. (1995). Postmodernism and knowledge development in nursing. *Nursing Science Quarterly, 8*(2), 60-64.

Watson, J. (1985). *Nursing: Human science and human care.* Norwalk, CT: Appleton-Century-Crofts.

Watson, J. (1981a). Nursing's scientific quest. *Nursing Outlook, 29*(7), 413-416.

Watson, J. (1981b). The lost art of nursing. *Nursing Forum, 10,* 244-249.

Watson, J. & Chinn, P. (1994). Introduction: Art and aesthetics as passage between centuries. In P. Chinn & J. Watson (Eds.), *Art and aesthetics in nursing.* (pp. xiii-xviii). New York, NY: National League for Nursing.

White, J. (1995). Patterns of knowing: Review, critique and update. *Advances in Nursing Science, 17,* 73-86.

Wiedenbach, E. (1964). *Clinical nursing: A helping art.* New York, NY: Springer.

Creating Art: Messages from the Artists

by M. Cecilia Wendler

Awakening the artist within is a challenging and intense feeling for nurses, who intuitively, I think, draw from the humanities when caring for patients and their families, and in an effort to make sense of all the suffering they witness. The arts and humanities help to balance the mechanistic approach of some of our health care colleagues, restoring a sense of integrity to humans who are sometimes shattered by their illness or injury experiences. In editing this book, I have stumbled upon many gems of creative wisdom from the contributors, and I wish to share some of that with you, the reader. Perhaps it will facilitate your own budding efforts at nurse artistry, be it art-in-the-caring-moment with patients and families, or in the development of your own artistic voice or talent. Here are some ideas and suggestions I hope may nurture your own artistic journey.

Awakening the Artist Within

For Laurie Shiparski, a poet, (see Chapter 1) the challenges in health care are what sparked her interest in art in nursing. She says, "Many [nurses] are desperate to find passion, purpose and meaning in their work and lives; I, too, have been a seeker of such wisdom in my journey as a nurse, healer, teacher, and leader. The success experienced in my career was not enough, and I found answers in a most unlikely place. Nine years ago, I learned to meditate and tap my spiritual wisdom that ignited a spiritual journey. I began to journal and in writing found pearls of wisdom, that I felt compelled to capture in poetry. Soon I had many poems that reflected my learning from patients, from colleagues and from my own emerging voice." For Shiparski, these poems emerged from the inward journey that came to her while engaged in meditation and journaling.

Priscilla Kline's painting, "After Mother's Fall" was created when she, too, was contemplating. However, her contemplation was anticipation of her dear mother's death. She describes the painting as a reflection of holism and spirituality, "transition between life and non-life and the possibility of an afterlife... The realistic flowers represent known life, the bud is hope for new life; the mists of seas are the life force flowing in ways we may not fully understand." Kline notes, "The creative process is both a struggle and a healing in itself; it holistically enhances empathy with the life/death crisis. Subsequent sharing of this painting and poem... has directly fostered insight, interaction, mutuality and connectedness far more effectively than just the spoken word." Indeed, creating a space for healing is one of the most important functions of art in nursing; healing for patients, healing for families, healing for ourselves.

Be Prepared for Healing

This idea, of art as an opportunity to heal, is echoed by Josephine McCall (see Chapter 5) who states, "The heart of nursing has often experienced disappointment, loss, illness and pain. This heart should also be allowed, encouraged and provided the opportunity to participate in the journey of healing." For McCall, this arises from writing poetry, reflecting healing after recognition of sometimes crushing injustice and loss.

Presence is also an important idea emerging here. Described in the work of Lynch (Chapter 2), Wesorick (Chapter 7) and myself (Wendler, Chapters 4 and 7), presence as a theme of healing is expressed in poetry and essay. Wesorick says, "Nurses are present at birthing; birth; across the life spans; in schools, homes, churches, neighborhoods, work settings; and again at dying and at death." She asserts, "The beauty of beginnings and endings become familiar. Nurses are present during the most painful and the most loving intimate moments of life. With this work comes a wisdom about what matters most in life." Indeed. As Borawski (Chapter 4) also says, "Writing is a healing activity when used to express what we cannot otherwise say."

Taking care of others also means taking care of ourselves. For example, Carlisi and La Brosse (see Chapter 3) describe their use of horticultural therapy that "provides an opportunity to self-nurture through the nurturance of plants." They also noted, "This art form fostered trust and self-disclosure... facilitated holistic communication and provided a new and innovative experience of mutuality in caring." By participating with patients in horticultural therapy, nurses' sense of connection to the natural world—the earth—provides a diversion as well as a space for healing.

Taking care of one's self means just that: eating well, exercising, tending to one's needs and nurturing one's personal sense of spirituality. Most of my best artistic work is done as I walk every day. Or, when I am swimming: Each stroke of the arms through the satin warmth of water cocoons me from the world, for it is completely silent underwater, except for the controlled rhythm of my breathing. When I swim, I cannot be distracted by the national news, music, or the conversations of others nearby. Swimming leaves me completely encased within my own body and with my own thoughts. With the creative power of endorphins that are released with aerobic exercise, I can be present with my creative self in a very powerful way—away from the demands of my family, my critically ill patients, and my students. It is blessed and nurturing, and this daily time exercising provides a meditation space, a

International Perspectives
Fabric art by Terri Pauser Wolf

place to write "in my head." This interior dwelling within one's self creates a fertile ground for productive artistry. Later, energized, the words flow smoothly and fluidly from my fingers... like my body through the water. It is an apt simile. Take care of yourself. Engage in the journey within. Learn your own interior landscape, know and claim your own wisdom. Then, create from that deep well of wonderful nursing experience.

Look at Ordinary Things through New Eyes

One of my favorite chapters of this book is called "The Extraordinary Ordinary." It consists of works that bring to light items—events, people—that may be invisible but help create a spotlight of attention, followed, perhaps, by a new appreciation, a new understanding and a new respect. For example, Fitch's poem, "Automatic," (see Chapter 3) describes beautifully that panicked moment when a child's ventilator alarms cause the nurse to race to the bedside, checking out everything, only to discover...a child laughing! In this poem, Fitch makes extant something that is often hidden from view, a common moment or experience of terror, for a patient's well-being...followed by self-realization and hearty laughter—at self! This is also true for DeCrane, (also Chapter 3) who brings a new understanding and appreciation to a battered wheelchair. Masson has now written and published countless poems illuminating the ordinary, everyday experiences she encounters as a nurse, bringing her wisdom, awe and understanding of ordinary events, people, and situations to us through her work.

My advice? Follow the example of these artists and look again at the extraordinary ordinary. I work on a surgical ICU where we occasionally have patients undergoing nursing care while their hearts are actually visible, beating within their chests. An ordinary event perhaps, that is—incredible! Other times, we have patients who are with us for many weeks... their cluttered rooms are a mute testimony to their "unit seniority." These patients get one of the few rooms with a good view... and so do their primary nurses. We also have a tradition of Sunday shift "pot luck" meals. Those lucky nurses who float to our unit are treated to a homemade supper, a rare treat in any hospital environment.

What ordinary event is extraordinary to you? What defines your practice, your unit and the spirit of your practice environment? Capture these in photos, poems, essays or sculptures. Celebrate the ordinary with your focused attention and your developing awareness.

Let the Big Stuff Inspire You, Too

Our profound life experiences become part of our story, and nurses witness so many stories, so much unfolding of the human experience. Sometimes the Big Stuff is theoretical thinking, as for McNeely, (see Chapter 6) who crocheted a bookmark to show the intertwined relationship among the four areas of the discipline of nursing: "Clinical practice, theory, research and education." Jerzak (see Chapter 6) used the medium of painting to communicate her growing understanding of nurse leadership, and Wagner (see Chapter 5) was inspired by the Oklahoma City Bombing to express her feelings in poetry.

Passages from one form of life to another are also Big Stuff, and nurses are often the silent witnesses to these events. Nieves' beautiful painting "The Passage" (see Chapter 2) is a wonderful example. She says, "My work embraces themes of religion, spirituality and elements found within the natural world" and attributes to her "extensive background in healthcare, as well as [my] own personal quest to experience God as avenues of connectedness with the human condition as inspiration" for her art. Werner's (see Chapter 2) unlikely encounter with two butterflies... or was it one?... expresses a similar connection between the present and afterlife.

Bryner (see Chapter 1) celebrates nursing's presence at birth in her wonderful poem about a 1950s midwife. In contrast, Lynch (Chapter 2) celebrates a sensitive and caring nurse at a time of death-not-birth as a beautiful expression of an artistic nursing moment, personally experienced and remembered through poetry. Raingruber, (see Chapter 2) a prolific poet who teaches her lucky students how to write, says, "Poetry gives voice to intense feelings… assisting to express the depth of meaning" in practice. These important events, often hidden from non-nurses, enlarge our connection to other humans and to our own humanity and mortality. It also makes the nurse prematurely wise. Art can help us pass on this wisdom, facilitate illumination of these interior events, and provide an opportunity to learn and experience for those who know our world and for those who wish to know our world.

The Importance of Supportive Others

When you are ready to show your stories, experiences, poetry or painting to others, be sure to create a circle of safety for yourself. For some budding artists, having someone interested in their artistic work is all that is needed to support and encourage. One artist describes herself as a "closet writer" who never felt as if her work was "good enough." Indeed, it was terrific… and published here. Another submitted the first poem she ever wrote for this publication… and, with only a few tiny changes, was also exquisitely matched to this book. We, indeed, are our own worst critics.

For me, to stand at my poster at the 1999 and again at the 2001 Biennial Conventions and to watch people read my work… and weep… was all the encouragement I needed. Upon returning home from both conventions, I heard from several people, asking permission to use one or more of the essays in a newsletter… in a class… in a clinical conference. Their responses to my efforts encouraged me to gather these works together in this book. It is clear to me that nurses ache for these expressions of nursing art, the recognition that the everyday challenges and experiences we face are, in fact, fluid opportunities upon opportunities to express our love and support of patients and our own humanistic roots. This book celebrates all of this, and more.

Just Do It

With my apologies to Nike and their athletic shoes, it is important, in the end, to just create. Let the inspiration from your experience, your witness to patients' suffering and triumphs in the presence of adversity, be the energy behind your artistic work. Begin by journaling your stories. Choose a medium that appeals to you. Also explore others. Dance. Sing. Write. Remember. Play. Talk to children. Watch the stars. Listen to the rain. Spy the moon sparkling on a fresh blanket of snow. Spend some time completely alone, in a new and beautiful place. Think. Write. Care. Create. As Rossman (see Chapter 1) so wisely asserts, "true caring is the most supreme thing [nurses] have to offer." So know deeply that your work, ALL of your work—nursing's art as well as its science—is vitally important. ♥

The Nature of Nursing

Standing There

by Jeanne Bryner

Our history isn't an album of healers
Dressed in snowy uniforms, white oxfords,
And halo caps. We do not saunter hallways
And giggle pink words.

This narrative is not about Merlin
Or medicine men chanting blue power
Over steamy rocks, nor is it a fist
Against mahogany conference tables
Or the kitten's whimper
In a rainstorm.

Our logbooks record moments
Where pain was thunder, and we waited,
Worked in a world of raw light
So bright its camera blinded.

Our story is a sea of brave faces
With grit teeth and shussed wings
And stalled hearts below gazed eyes.

Our story is how we did not shrivel,
Though we were soaked, how we did not
Freeze in cold almost beyond bearing.
Our story is how we did not break
And run—no matter how close
the lightning gouged.

Reprinted with permission from The Kent State University Press.

Maples

by Jeanne Bryner

So much depends
upon

the needle
hitting

each blue vein
as though

it had tapped
a living tree.

Reprinted with permission from The Kent State University Press.

The Old Man

by Brenda Rushing French

I looked into the eyes of a real old man today
He had yellowing eyes with red streaks
He hadn't spoken an intelligent word in days
But I took time to look
And I saw a young man helplessly trapped in a wrinkled body
A man who silently was screaming for help on the inside
He stayed for a few days
no one ever came to visit him
and then he died.

The World's Smallest Church

by Rebecca J. S. Elsbernd

Time Between Times

by Barbara Kay Pesut

Sunlight ascending
Pushing back the garment of the night
Time suspended in a cloak of grey
The time between times.

I yearn to the east
Soul eyes locked face to face
Warmed by eternal beauty and light
Caught in His fiery embrace

But the time between times
Holds my heart still
Patiently waiting
Soul afire

Night at my back
Heart drenched by dawn's clammy dew
Longing...
Come quickly
The night grows colder before the dawn

Alarm Anatomy

by Bonnie Jean Raingruber

A red second hand
floats over the face
of twelve hours.

All is automated.
where is your care?
The peepers crawl,

penlights focused,
weasel-willed,
in their own skin

In stark white
anonymity, nurses
parade ahead

The snap of plastic
substitutes for touch. Skin
has been homogenized.

Straight-ahead faces
with the life ironed out
decree a hard love.

Lab tubes are tinkling
waiting to drink
down black blood.

A hydraulic bed
grunts itself up. Drip
rate regulates life.

Tick, tick, tick—heart
measures mechanical
and will not respond.

Schedule does not
make meaning.
Such structure jails us all.

Person has flown.
Apparatus anatomy
measures me cold.

Rush, rush, rush.
Who will we follow—
structure or function?

....alarmclocks
are going off.

Yellow Asphodel
by Candace Matthews

Welcome
by Mark H. Clarke

Though you fear this abyss,
where darkness appears endless
first entry feels like falling
and the chill takes your breath,
once you let go
you will arrive at a separate place
where everything, everything matters.

The grief space,
where healing begins,
seems close, intimate,
yet open to a soft wind
from purple hills beyond a broad plain,
scented lightly
with asphodel.

Reprinted with permission from Myrmex Press.

Nursing Genesis: Our Cross Road
by Mercy Mammah Popoola

We have come to a crossroad
and we must
Either go or come with you
we linger over the choices
And in the
darkness of our doubt you lifted the
LAMP of hope and we saw in your
Face the road that
we
should take

Nightwatch

by Marietta P. Stanton

Sweet Child
I'm so worried about you
Your vital signs are now stable
Your respirations are normal
Your damp curls have dried
But still...
Sweet child
I've read and reread your chart
I've checked and rechecked your labs
I've monitored your IVs
I've given you antibiotics
But still....
Sweet child
I'm so worried about you
You'll never know how I've watched you this night
You won't remember how often I've checked you as you rest
You haven't heard my prayer for you to pass this crisis
For you
Sweet child
Are my patient, my heart,
The reason I do what I do
I'm here to nurse and protect you.
Where else should I be this night?

Florence Nightingale: We are Contemporary Nightingales

by Rita Bergevin

Louisiana Hot Sauce Blues

by Sr. Connie Beil

I remember the first time I saw Robbie Rochambeau. He was wearing tight, black leather pants with a black silk shirt and hand-tooled leather boots and a matching black and gold leather belt. The gold rings on his fingers and in both of his ears sparkled in the light of his private room as he placed a large, very expensive Bose radio/tape recorder on his night stand. He had a Rolex watch and beautifully manicured nails. He asked if he could change into his pajamas because he said he was very tired from the trip to Washington and needed to rest. His black silk oriental pajamas with matching scuff slippers shimmered as he sat on the side of the bed. I had never met anyone quite like Robbie. The initial information needed for the nursing assessment was noted rather quickly, and I left him so that he could relax and visit with the few friends who came to help him get settled. His physician had called and asked for some private time to be scheduled so that he could further explain the thoughts he had on the proposed course of treatment. Robbie moved his long, wispy blond hair out of his eyes and sighed as we put his fourteen-page assessment form with his laboratory test results aside for later. 12 West, an AIDS Oncology Unit, was very busy that day, and the nursing staff was deciding whether taking Robbie would be too much for my present assignment. We decided I would share the initial assessment duties with Janice, another RN. The primary nurse role was very demanding and truly comprehensive but very satisfying. Robbie needed to rest. His paperwork and nursing assessment as well as initial nursing care plan needed to be entered into the computer, and with two nurses working on it we would finish most of it before the evening shift came on duty. We were busy, but we could wait until he had rested. This first day was to get him oriented to the National Institutes of Health and our nursing regimen. His bright blue eyes looked tired as

Whatever!
Fabric art by Terri Pauser Wolf

he tried to make jokes about having to leave his larger electronic equipment and audio system at home. His small shoulders slumped as he sat on the pale blue sheets of his opened bed. He seemed to melt into the clean linen of his bed as his eyes closed and his breathing became deeper as he drifted off to sleep. His friends left to get something to eat and give Robbie a chance to rest.

After Robbie awoke, Dr. Marco Pentangele, in his crisp white lab coat with his name embroidered on the breast pocket, shared the initial information on the protocols that were available for Robbie. Robbie's diagnosis was AIDS. Further tests would reconfirm this diagnosis and then he would be randomized into the section of the study that would hopefully bring positive results for Robbie.

Robbie had come to the NIH for treatment. He had verbalized being lucky that he had been accepted into the clinical trials. He was here and very glad to be part of the AZT clinical trials. Tomorrow he would continue the evaluation process and be randomized to his particular protocol. A huge fruit basket and a floral arrangement of cymbidium orchids were delivered. "We love you Robbie" signed the rock band Aerosmith. Robbie had directed the light/sound crew for several rock bands and their concerts throughout the world. He had truly lived in the fast pace lane. Robbie was bisexual and had been married and had several children. That first day he had several visitors, and as we got ready for the evening shift and report, we shared the fact that we were almost finished with his assessment and needed to pass that on so we could get started tomorrow. Visiting hours and the number of visitors were very relaxed, and patients usually did what they wanted with the watchful support of the primary nurse. It was important that Robbie get the rest he needed and felt comfortable and as unstressed as possible. As long as medications and tests we completed were within the protocol expectations most everything else was permitted including bringing food in. My shift was ending and Janice and I said good-bye as we introduced Robbie to the evening nurse who would be caring for him. We agreed that he would continue the assessment as soon as report was over.

In the days that followed, Robbie and I had many wonderful conversations. We talked a lot about traveling, philosophy, and the south and music. Robbie was involved in a multimedia production company and had traveled all over the world. He listened to hot southern jazz and blues. Robbie loved listening to the blues. Robbie shared his love for the south and southern cooking, especially food from New Orleans. I could almost smell cornbread and fresh greens and blackened catfish. We talked and tasted in our minds. We spoke of Bourbon Street and Robbie's love for blues and all types of music. He was a promoter and production manager who would have loved to play or sing but said he had no musical talent other than to set up other people to perform successfully. Robbie shared his frustration about his family and need to embrace a different lifestyle. He loved his two sons but wasn't able to spend more time with them because of his production company. He stared out the window as he talked about missing their growing up years and needing to find himself. He was open and shared easily. His connections had brought him all over the world,and he was in demand as an individual who made it happen and was paid very well for his results. All the money in the world could not help him now. He was here at the NIH to get in on the ground floor of a cure. There was hope. The nursing team had discussed the need to focus on the therapeutic relationship with Robbie and to take care in not getting too dangerously close. The focus was on the therapeutic relationship and supporting the patient in his process. I felt happy I had been able to care for him but appreciated the support and nursing wisdom of my fellow, more experienced nurses.

It took about a week to get Robbie settled. I was one of his primary nurses and enjoyed working with him and caring for him for three weeks before I had some time off. A two-week vacation took me away to a family vacation in Pennsylvania, and I had temporarily signed off on my primary care of several patients. Janice would take the lead until I returned. My vacation gave me a much-needed break to be with family and friends. I loved my work and was looking forward to getting back, even if it was on the night shift. The evening shift hadn't been very busy, and I was looking forward to spending time with my patients. I loved caring for my patients and enjoyed nursing. The night was the time when many patients were in need of some extra support from their nurses. They missed their homes and families and needed extra support. Many times they could not sleep. I could talk with my patients, listen to them and even pray with them if the situation was appropriate. We were beginning to do some gentle massage as well as energy work and relaxation techniques with some of the patients who were receptive. It was a very exciting time. When Robbie's name came up for report, Janice, who was now on evenings, stopped and paused. She focused on her notes and provided the update. Medications and tests continued per his protocol. Robbie's lab values were showing the continued need for hospitalization as he said that he felt ill, he had a low-grade temperature and was unable to sleep. He needed to be under close observation according to the protocol with round-the-clock intravenous antibiotics. Many AIDS patients had been able to come in for medication and then go home and return for additional medications and hospitalization as needed according to their protocols. Robbie had been selected for the AZT clinical trials but was not responding as hoped.

Once you were on a protocol at NIH, you were able to continue in most cases no matter what happened. They wanted to know what was going on to the last day, especially with AIDS. Janice continued, "Robbie was rude to me today and refused to eat and speak with me." I was shocked. He just nodded his head yes and no.

How could this happen? No one on the day shift could put any light on this situation. They had tried to connect with some friends and family to see if they were able to find out what, if anything, had happened. No answers were shared because there weren't any. I was sure that my relationship with him as I returned from my vacation would be different. I could fix this.

I made my rounds after the evening shift nurses left and saved Robbie for last as I wanted to have extra time to spend with him. I quietly walked in and greeted him. He had earphones on listening to jazz. I gently touched his arm as I sought to check his IV lines and medications. He turned and looked at me and blinked and nodded. Not even a smile, no conversation and very little eye contact. What room was I in? This was not the Robbie that I had left two weeks ago.

I quietly continued to greet him smiling. Robbie's eyes looked past me and then closed. I asked if he would like to talk for a while. Robbie stared out the window and didn't turn his head. I felt myself talking just to me. I touched his arm and stated my proposed schedule for nursing assistance throughout the night. He turned and looked me squarely in the face and said, "I don't need anything from you." This struck like a knife. I started his triple antibiotics made a note on my schedule and left the room.

Robbie was at the NIH five weeks now. My mind went back to my first interactions with Robbie when he verbalized hope as IV lines were started and medication was administered. As the treatment progressed, Robbie had asked questions and was very active in wanting to know his lab values. Occasionally, some of his production company would come to visit, and once several evening shift nurses saw Aerosmith come in after they had called Robbie, who asked them to bring some special Louisiana pork ribs. Robbie longed for southern food and made every attempt to have the foods he craved. I was amazed that he was so thin. Since he was not on any special diet and was very thin, his physicians encouraged him to eat whatever and whenever he wanted. One particular evening after being off for a weekend, I received my regular report before beginning the night shift. Several of his medications had been changed. I made several notes and then got ready to make my initial rounds as I began my shift. It was eleven thirty and as I entered Robbie's room, I was surprised because Robbie's lights were off and he appeared to be sleeping but was listening to his Bourbon Street Blues. He greeted me as I entered the room and asked that I not turn on the lights. I used a flashlight to check the IV fluids and his IV sites. I counted the bottles of fluid and there was an extra one. I looked at the tubing and felt a sudden panic as I tried to figure out what was going on. A small thin bottle in a light green plastic case had tubing that appeared to be connected and was flowing into his main IV line. I needed to turn on the light to read the label on the bottle. The bottle, unlike any other I had ever seen, was upside down, and as I unhooked it from the IV pole I realized that this bottle was not a medication it was Louisiana Hot Sauce. A joke! One of his Aerosmith buddies from Louisiana had brought hot sauce in a plastic sleeve and then taped it to the IV line. Robbie said he missed his spicy hot food, and his friends wanted to see that he got it. I was initially taken back but then joined in the laughter of the joke. Robbie and I laughed and chatted about southern food with the most important ingredient of hot sauce. We laughed and smiled the entire shift. He stayed awake the entire night listening to music. When day shift came on duty, he decided he wanted to sleep. I felt a smile come across my face as I remembered this incident and then continued my work.

My mind flashed back to my busy schedule and refocused on the tasks of the night. Robbie was getting several antibiotics, and I would be in his room quite often. Robbie offered no conversation or positive communication that shift. I felt sad and upset and had to continue my shift and do my job. Robbie demonstrated no attempt to communicate in a positive manner. The uneventful shift ended with me making the same statement as Janice had made. I had patients refuse to speak with me, but this was a new experience for me.

In the days to come, the entire staff worked on this with our psychiatric liaison. Robbie withdrew. He refused to wash, eat, let us change the linen and only spoke when he absolutely had to. Supervisors on several levels were involved in helping the nurses to provide the care we needed to do for him. He never returned to the Robbie I had known during the first days of his admission. Opportunistic infections associated with AIDS exacerbated, and he was transferred to the ICU. Several of the staff went to visit him in the ICU before he died. His life ended so abruptly leaving no opportunity for the nurses to provide some kind of closure and support for him as well as us. As nurses, we think that we can do most everything and help everyone. Sometimes that is not possible. Sometimes no matter how experienced we are and no matter how much we know, we just have to "let it be." How could I prepare myself for this situation? What could I have said or done differently? Probably nothing. I still reach out to establish that caring therapeutic relationship with patients and their families and realize that the patient may, for whatever reason, choose not to respond. The nurses on 12 West talked about Robbie in several of our staff meetings and support group sessions. I still think of him and his silk pajamas when I hear hot southern jazz or the blues or taste Louisiana Hot Sauce. ♥

Thank You For Letting Me Care

by Carol Rossman

Thank you for letting me care for your little one,
Many the days I sat by your bed
The dim lights of the room a sharp contrast
To the bright monitor lights 'bove your head.

I was busy with meds. And machinery
The labs, vent, changes and treatments.
The virus that raged in your body
Was a challenge of wits and commitments.

I instinctively knew what action to take
From my constant watching and learning,
Your every move, your every breath…
To beat this illness, my yearning.

What image is pressed on my memory
From the months I cared for only you
Is the constant watching and waiting,
The slight, subtle changes, my cue.

I knew you so well that it scared me,
Every bump on your smooth baby skin,
Your cherub cheeks, the golden curls,
The heart and lungs, which just wouldn't mend.

I remember the lighthearted banter
As your mom and I discussed the world,
But beneath lie the ever-present knowing
We shared a great bond in "our girl."

I willed you to respond to our efforts,
Many the days I just kept you alive.
Another alarm, another ventilation,
Another eight hours survived.

Your special nurses came to your funeral.
We cried over memories we shared.
I am grateful to you little angel,
So grateful that you let us care.

For it's as we cared that we grew,
When we were giving, and loving, and sharing.
We found the essence to nursing—
To make a difference by caring.

Shades of Gray

by Mary Lou Denatale

In my work interviewing caregivers, I have found it important to listen to their stories and respond with words or some display of silent support. It was not surprising that these individuals provided me lessons about respect, humility, and patience, but I truly was not prepared for the impact these family caregivers would have on my life.

Nurses and other authors frequently write about caregivers, trying to understand the moments in time their stories offer us. The moment in time I include here in the photograph shows Corky and his mother Dolores. It was taken on a scheduled home visit with them. At this visit, I experienced a feeling of calmness and peace that I had not experienced with other families at other home visits. Through their genuine respect for each other, Corky and Dolores showed me that life is not just black and white. It is what one individual does with the shades of gray that matters most.

Corky and Dolores, thank you for this home visit and the opportunity to listen to your story.

Photograph by Mary Lou Denatale.

Photograph by Mary Lou Denatale.

Sweetie Baby

by Karen Roberts

Hello, Mrs. Jacobs.
–Hello, Sweetheart. How you doin'?
I glance at the chart again, frowning slightly.
I think I have seen her before, I just can't remember…
–What's new with you, darling?
Oh, you know, working hard—cold and flu season.
–Oh, baby, I know it. I hope you're keeping well, honey.
Her tenderness warms me. She likes me.

I'm new here. Here's the pitch:
"Would you like to see the Nurse Practitioner?
She's very good. Yes, she can write prescriptions.
Oh, yes, the doctor trusts her. And she can see you today."

Mrs. Jacobs and I get down to business.
She answers my questions
–Yes, honey; oh no, sweetie; uh-uh, baby;
–that's right, darling.
I am faintly pink at the flood of endearments,
this embarrassment of riches.
I tell her my diagnosis—bronchitis,
and recommend an antibiotic and an inhaler.
I ask her if she has any questions.
She looks at me pleasantly; fondly.
I wait.
–Honey, I don't even know you. Who are you, now?

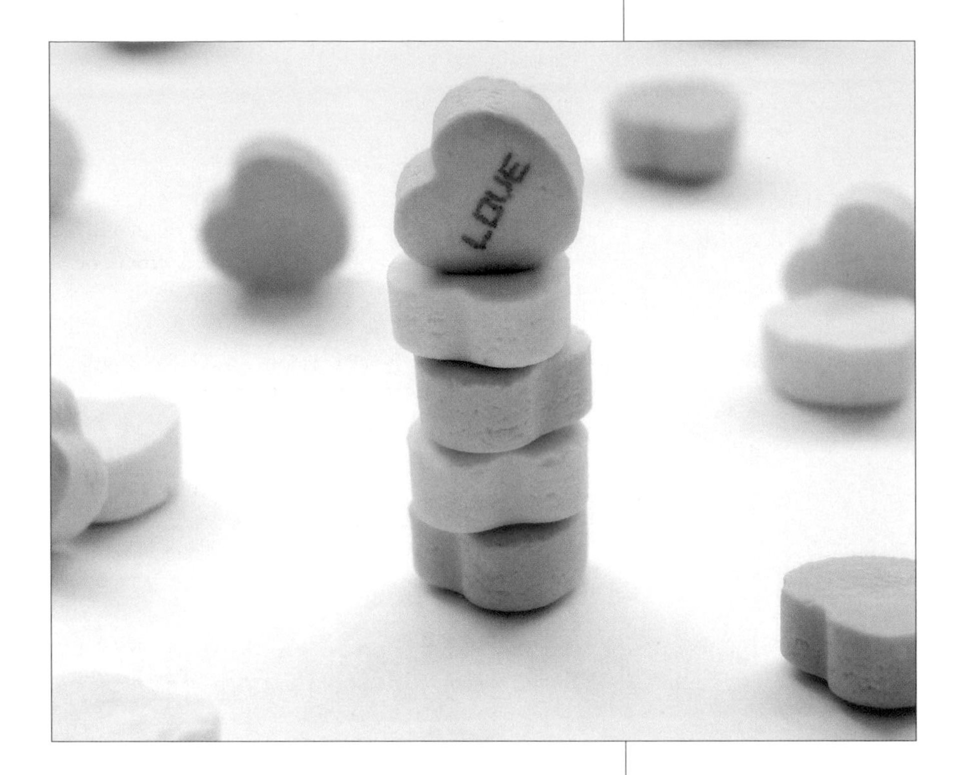

Passion

by A. Lynne Wagner

Reflective Listening: A Model

Caring requires a multifaceted knowing of another person's needs and the ability to respond to those needs. Although much is known about physiological and social changes of aging, the lived experience of aging in our society is an isolating process that is feared and little understood, with wide gaps between the perceived realities of the younger caregivers and the old in need of care. Personal stories teach about one's reality. Shared storytelling often softens the boundaries between different realities, allowing each to know the other more wholly within the context of mutual humanness. Understanding the intricacies of growing older through storytelling provides insight into gerontological caring for this ever increasing population. Inviting the aging population to voice their stories, however, demands that health care providers reflectively listen with their hearts and heads. A nurse's poetic response to a story validates a deeper understanding.

The Story:

E. O. is an 85-year-old widow of 10 years who had been married for 50 years. She has four daughters, 12 grandchildren, and five great grandchildren, none of whom visit her very often. She has been in a nursing home for three years since she first suffered a stroke with right-sided weakness and incontinence. She has diabetes, failing eyesight, and peripheral vascular disease with ulcerated legs. She is lonely but speaks more of her loss of independence and the burden of pain in her legs. She is a retired school teacher and loved to sew, garden, and do crafts until she lost the physical abilities to do so. Her days seem endless to her.

The Poetic Reflection:
Mrs. O'Malley: Pain

You sit, lap covered with frayed blanket,
framed by two wheels;
one leg firmly against metal plate,
the other shortened by disease
not knowing where it belongs;
face twisting at bright light
that streams through your window
filtered by cobwebs on the glass
and cloudy cataract vision.
You sit enjoying a moment of warmth
that brings late afternoon memories.
But then the pain,
that pain whose source is deeper
than ulcers on your leg,
merges past and future with present space.
Your swear word breaks the sacred
mood of brief escape;
reality beckons you to pay attention,
nudging you back to prison
that you describe as shrunken world
of chair with wheels that goes no where.

Mrs. O'Malley
by Maria Witt

"The room box celebrates the progression and evolution of nursing practice."

The Nurse Practitioner's Clinic

by Carol A. Williams

"The Nurse Practitioner's Clinic" is a 1-inch scale room box that reflects the autonomy of the advanced practice nurse. This particular nurse practitioner's practice is pediatric orthopedics. Skeleton wallpaper, an X-ray box, crutches, IV pole, eye chart, and water bottle are featured in the room. Nursing textbooks and a medical dictionary are available for the difficult diagnosis. Copies of The Cat in the Hat and Highlights for Children are available for the little patient's reading pleasure. Outside scenes include a poster that promotes hand washing and immunizations. Proudly displayed over the desk are the nurse practitioner's credentials.

It is the artist's wish that children looking into the room box will be mesmerized by the little world and respond by asking questions about nursing and the care they receive from the nursing community. As for adults, the artist wishes to evoke reminiscence and hope for their future. All ages may imagine health care given in the warm, friendly atmosphere the room box portrays.

The artist hopes that nurses gazing into the box will remember special moments or patients that evoke positive feelings about practicing in the wonderful profession of nursing. The room box celebrates the progression and evolution of nursing practice.

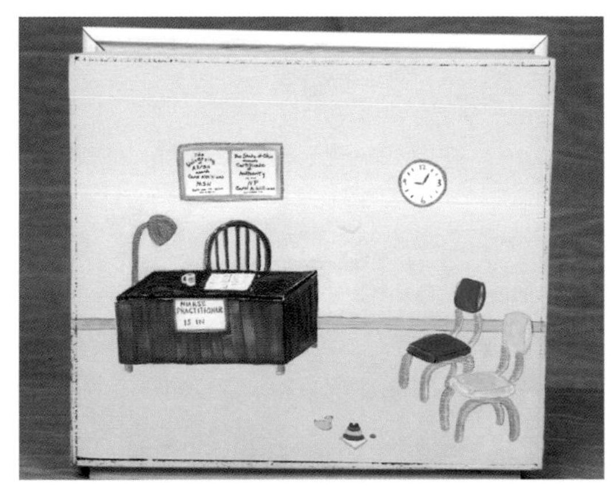

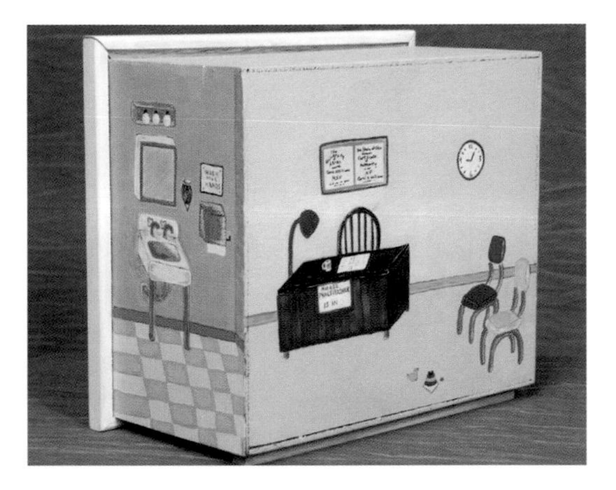

The Voice of Courage

by Laurie Shiparski

From the deepest depths it comes,
a voice.
At times it bubbles up
slowly, meekly
calling to be heard
begging attention.
At times it rushes out forcefully
a screaming outcry,
compelling action.
A powerful voice in
meekness or might.
Could it be the voice of the soul…
Offering direction,
Purpose, possibilities,
Self,
Offering freedom?

Listen to the voice.

Icarus I Fly

by Bonnie Raingruber

Folds of flesh fly.
Winged-Icarus-free
toward the sun I soar,
skin layers burnt
brown by excitement.
Tapioca freckles
dance energy blisters up,
gloving my hand.
I hear who I am, calibrated
radar loud as a homing signal buried in my brain,
taking wings, soaring up and out,
exploding life around me
until reality blooms forth bright.
I am an ER nurse.

Passion

I want to write about passion,
how it is always there
deep in the well of my soul.

How it is the vital substance
for a life worth living.
Without it I am incomplete,
left to lurk in the shadow of my soul.
Trapped outside of the real me
unable to give what the world
is calling to be.

In my thirst for purpose,
direction, and vitality
I sip from the well.
Finding the opening,
I draw the bucket up
from this everlasting source
and taste the thrilling life force.

Real passion comes in my
moments of surrender.
It is power and possibility,
love and creativity.

I want to write about passion
and how it is always there
deep in the well of my soul.

We all have passion…

What is your passion?

Compassion.

Poetry excerpted from:
Alive with Passion Poetry/music CD

Passion

by Laurie Shiparski, RN, MS

This painting is by artist Madonna Walters, the piece is titled "Fire On the Lake" and is a multi-medium, watercolor. I purchased this painting from a gallery a number of years ago because it represented for me that fire or passion that sits within each of us. When it came time to design a cover for my poetry/music CD called "Alive With Passion," the painting seemed perfect. To my surprise, when I contacted the artist I learned she was an RN in a trauma nurse coordinator role with a local hospital. The synchronicity of the universe continues to amaze me.

Fire on the Lake
by Madonna Walters

Throwaways

by Ethel C. Ragland

The humanities offer us a unique way of understanding the human experience. Through literary works, we can see the other as ourselves and actualize the concepts of empathy and transpersonal caring. Written from the client perspective, this poem challenges us to see the humanity of the diverse clients we serve in the community. The refrain urges an unconditional acceptance of all clients regardless of their life circumstances.

In my work as a community health nurse educator, I am constantly struck by the differential valuing of lives in our society. Through this poem, I hope to challenge us as nurses to confront and reject the "throwaway" mentality of rank, the ordering of human beings by their perceived worth. It is only through seeing the humanity of all our clients that we can live the ethic of caring.

Photograph copyright 1982 by Gabrielle Beasley

Throwaways

you've seen me but you don't

crackhouse, outhouse, no house

you've seen me but you don't

mother too soon, daughter too little, sister too late

you've seen me but you don't

dream for more, expect no more, hope no more

you've seen me but you don't

waste of time, waste of money, waste of you

you've seen me.

Prairie Man*

by Karen Roberts

straight from the field,
he comes to sit on my table
dusty jeans rolled up
revealing the gash
that won't heal despite
six days of penicillin
that the vet gave him for
the dog two years ago.
he will take my samples
and use them just until
the redness goes
putting aside the rest for a day
when he's not feeling
so damn good.

*Reprinted with permission from the *American Journal of Nursing*.

Shamanic Healing Journey

by Valerie S. Eschiti

This work consists of a handcrafted ritual rattle and medicine bag. As nurses, we are often wounded healers who need to attend first to our own inner woundedness before venturing to care for patients. The sound of the rattle provides a sonic meditation for the nurse to journey within to discover the sources of her wounds and the methods by which to heal them. The rattle is made of a turtle shell, which carries the energy of Mother Earth. The medicine bag is decorated with beads and sacred items. It is made of deerskin. Deer is known for gentleness. The gentle nurse supplies the environment conducive for healing to occur. The green stone on the bag is moss agate, a stone with healing properties. The shells represent the feminine, caring energies present in the healing encounter, whether the nurse is woman or man. The dove feathers stand for peace which is a grace of the sacred healing process. The rattle and medicine bag are symbolic of the instruments of healing that we as nurses are as spiritual beings. Many cultures throughout the world utilize shamanism as a vehicle to access inner resources. I have had the blessing of experiencing the depth of shamanic healing within the Native American cultures. Such richness of tribal cultures that are so embedded in respect of Mother Earth has facilitated my self healing, as well as supplied the energy for me to serve as an instrument to facilitate self healing for my patients.

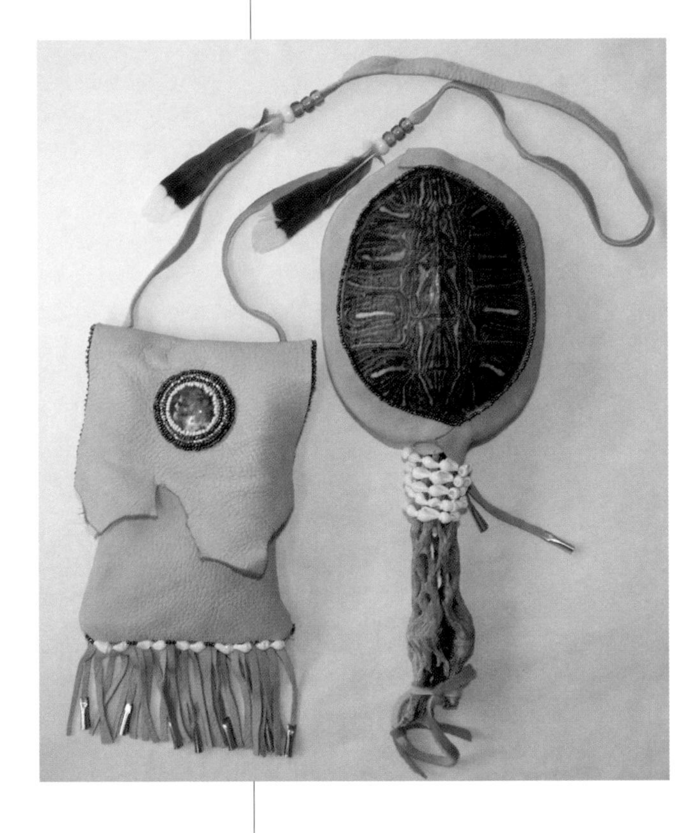

Music: A Universal Healing Modality

by Sarah Hall Gueldner, in collaboration with Janis Bible and Cheryl Bible Miller

Janis Bible is a remarkable woman of modest means in her 80s who has played the piano all her life and continues to play, even though she (and her piano) now live in an assisted-living facility. I visited her in her new quarters and asked her to play. What happened next was one of the most remarkable displays of individual and group energy that I have ever seen. It was as if fairy dust had been sprinkled throughout the room to create a very magical moment. Janis sat down and folded back the cover to the keyboard, as she has done for eight decades. Then she looked up, her eyes bright and smiling, and began to play the songs that were popular in her youth, one after another, from memory. She never missed a note and embellished her rendition with flowing chords and scale runs for a full, rich melodic sound. Other residents began to come into the room, some with walkers and canes, but all were smiling. Two residents "boogied" in, keeping time with their shoulders and snapping their fingers. And as we left, a resident who looked to also be in her late 80s was leaning against the piano on her elbow, crooning the words expressively like a vintage torch singer. The room, empty and quiet less than half an hour before, became vibrant with smiles and fun and movement. As I watched Janis, smiling and feeling happy and useful, I was reminded that humans have a multitude of talents and abilities, and that loss of ability in one area must not be casually generalized to signify the loss of others. We must find ways for people to continue to express themselves as fully as possible. It would have been a tragedy if Janis Bible had been separated from her piano. Her incredible gift of music is too precious to lose.

Janis Bible at her piano

Art at the bedside: Reflections of a Lifetime

by Sandra M. Walsh

The challenge to describe my work as a nurse-artist presented itself in my 66th year. It has been a long time coming.

When others view one of my paintings, they often ask, "How long did it take you to paint that?" I tell them, "66 years?" Some appear amused, some appear confused, and some think I did not understand the question. During a lifetime of trying to find myself, my role as a nurse-artist has evolved.

Without personal and professional tragedies, I would not have come to this place. Reed (2003) would call my journey "self-transcendence." Perhaps so ... I will let the readers decide.

I have saved a small wooden art box given to me as a child that contained a set of beginner paints. I remember carefully writing my name on the top of the box. My signature on paintings today is similar.

My decision to become a nurse was pragmatic and passionate: I wanted to support myself and, like most nurses, I wanted to help others. I left my art behind.

Yet my life has led me to become a hybrid—a "strange blend" of nursing art. I am a nurse, scientist, teacher, *and* an artist.

During doctoral study, the seeds of my growth as a nurse-artist and researcher began while I worked in a psychiatric facility with suicidal adolescents. I noted their despair about life's possibilities and for encouragement drew portraits portraying them in future professions. While I drew, we talked. Many began to express a renewed interest in their futures. Dr. Sally Hardin, my mentor and dissertation chair, listened to my stories and said, "Design and test an intervention." And I did (Walsh & Hardin, 1994; Walsh, 1993). Since then I have shared my workbooks with professionals, patients, and students and receive requests from around the world to help others implement my "Future Images" Intervention.

A final turning point was a personal one. As I sat at the bedside watching my father die of cancer, I felt helpless and hopeless. In other times of despair I had turned to art for comfort, so I began to draw. My father, watching, asked, "Why not draw me?" Startled at first, I agreed. Dad proudly insisted that these portraits of his last days be displayed on the walls of his room.

Later, I came to appreciate that these activities strengthened our relationship at the end of his life. I began to ask if art-making could help others. A future "Art at the Bedside" program began at the bedside of a dying man.

Following my father's death, I relocated to Miami, joined the Watercolor Society, and continued to paint. I also found a friend and another nurse-artist, Dr. Sharlene Weiss, who shared my passion for nursing and art. With Ms. Sue Radcliffe, coordinator of volunteers at Sylvester Comprehensive Cancer Center, we established an "Art at the Bedside" program (Walsh & Weiss, 2003).

For us, dissemination of research outcomes continues (Walsh, Martin, & Schmidt, 2004). We have received local, regional, and national recognition

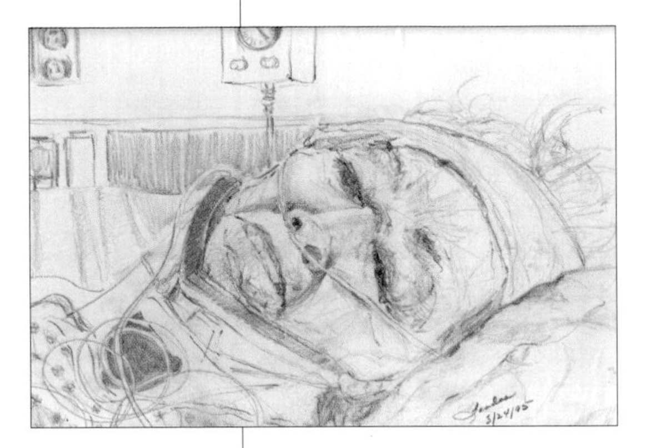

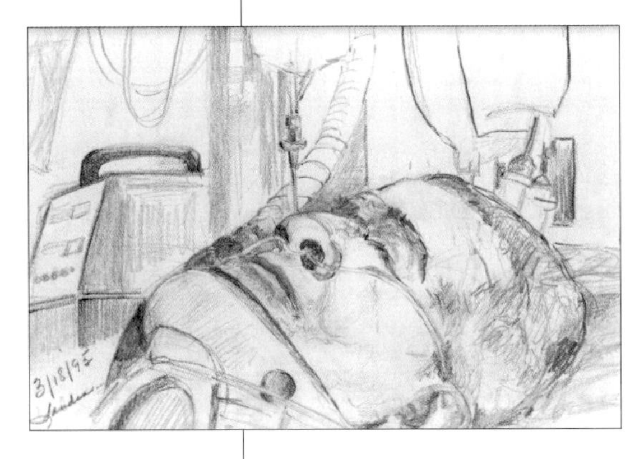

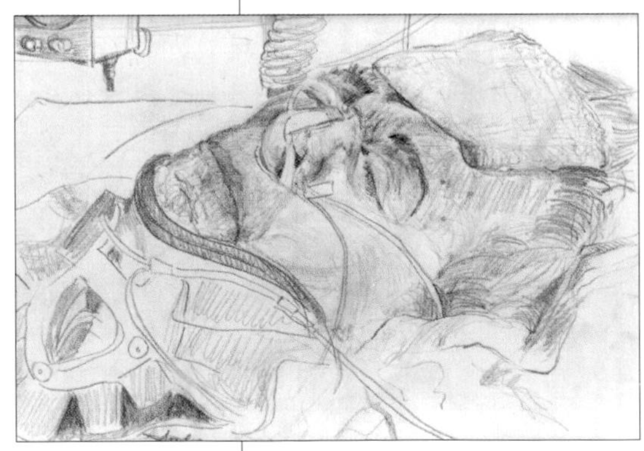

Charcoal drawings by Sandra Walsh

Tapestry by Sandra Walsh

for our efforts, including a Blair Sadler International Award for Arts in Health Care in 2004. Yet, as so often occurs in arts programs, the idea flounders from lack of funds or lack of enthusiasm from others who see art as an interesting but trivial approach to care. A colleague once said, "I know you are doing some type of research about art, but it seems to have little importance to nursing."

While we have obtained significant results from our investigations (Walsh, Chang, Schmidt, & Yoepp, in press; Walsh, Purnell, & Milone, in press; Walsh et al., 2004), I feel the real significance is not in the findings but in the ways of knowing (Carper, 1978). My aesthetic way of knowing occurs while helping and watching others create. My ability to offer brief respite from despair has led me to encourage nurses to consider how similar work could be implemented in their practices.

Last spring, two of my family members became seriously ill during the time I was adjusting to a joint appointment as a professor and research clinician. Again, I expressed my frustrations and passions through art. The painting I created won first prize in the Miami Watercolor Society spring show. Since this and several other awards have come with cash prizes, I began an "Arts and Healthcare Fund" at Barry University School of Nursing. I find myself less shy about selling and promoting my work when I donate proceeds to this fund.

I teach a graduate nursing theory class to nurse clinicians who balance work, family, and school, along with the associated stressors of multifaceted lives. After discussing the applicability of King's (King, 1971) goal attainment theory and my work, they "transacted" with me to create one life goal in a "Future Image" portrait. They also pondered linkages between this unique goal setting experience and aesthetic ways of knowing (Carper, 1978).

Recently a young father brought his four-year-old daughter and 18-month-old son to our Saturday morning art class—part of our "Art at the Bedside" program. His wife lay seriously ill at a nearby hospital. For two hours a father/daughter team created a crown of flowers, a yarn necklace for "my Mommy," and a portrait of the girl as a future veterinarian. A graduate research assistant provided entertainment and baby-sitting for the younger child. When the family departed, I asked the father if the children would share their art with his wife. He said, "No, she is unconscious. The children do not visit anymore. She was diagnosed with cancer a year ago, the day before our daughter's fourth birthday."

Neither words nor pictures can adequately describe this journey. I have witnessed the joys of art-making—the making of positive memories in the midst of despair.

Carper (1978) wrote of aesthetic ways of knowing. I have come to know nursing aesthetically in a different way through my art. I think I have found myself.

REFERENCES:
Carper, B. A. (1978). Fundamental patterns of knowing in nursing. *Advances in Nursing Science*, 1(1), 13-23.
King, I. (1971). *Toward a theory of nursing: General concepts of human behavior*. New York: John Wiley & Sons.
Reed, P. G. (2003). *The theory of self-transcendence*. In M. J. Smith, & P. R. Liehr (Eds.), *Middle range theory for nursing* (pp. 145-165). New York: Springer Publishing Company.
Walsh, S. M. (1993). Future images: An art intervention with suicidal adolescents. *Applied Nursing Research*, 6(3), 111-118.
Walsh, S. M., Chang, C., Schmidt, L., & Yoepp, J. (in press). Teaching research and lowering stress: A creative arts intervention in the classroom. *Journal of Nursing Education*.
Walsh, S. M., & Hardin, S. B. (1994). An art future image intervention to enhance identity and self-efficacy in adolescents. *Child and Adolescent Psychiatric Nursing*, 7(3), 24-34.
Walsh, S. M., Martin, S. C., & Schmidt, L. A. (2004). Testing the efficacy of a creative-arts intervention with family caregivers of patients with cancer. *The Journal of Nursing Scholarship*, 36(3), 214-219.
Walsh, S. M., & Weiss, S. (2003). Art at the bedside for family caregivers of patients with cancer. *Oncology Nursing Forum*, 30(6), http://www.ons.org/publications/journals/ONF/2003exclusives.shtml

Dancing Daisies
by Sandra Walsh

Art in Research

Understanding the Family Experience of Neutropenia: Hope

by Mary Bliesmer, Sandra Eggenberger, Norma Krumwiede, and Sonja Meiers

Understanding the Family Experience of Neutropenia: Hope was co-created by family nurse researchers and a professional artist based on an empirical research study. The Family Nursing Research Team at Minnesota State University was searching for a way to capture a family illness experience and evoke the emotion of nurses to help them feel the family experience more deeply and embrace family caring in their nursing practice. The family researchers believed that through visual art the empathic perception of a family's illness experience would encourage a nurse to immediately embrace the art of caring for families. The 30 X 40 acrylic painting revealed insight, understanding, and meaning of the family experience of cancer greater than the scientific findings of the original grounded theory study. Blending empirics and art generated an understanding of human experiences that reached beyond the objectivity of numbers and language.

The empirical family research study used in the creation of this painting was a grounded theory study designed to discover how rural families understood and managed the neutropenic experience caused by cancer chemotherapy. Twenty-one family members of rural, adult patients being treated at a Midwestern regional cancer center were interviewed as family groups within their homes. Families included spouses, children, grandchildren, siblings, in-laws, and parents of the person with chemotherapy-induced neutropenia. Data text was derived from audio taped interviews that had been conducted by research team members using a semi-structured, interactive approach. Dyad and team analysis revealed family processes and family variables in the context of a family illness experience of cancer. The researchers then contracted for the services of a professional artist to create a visual interpretation from findings of the initial empirical study. Dialogue between the nurse researchers and the artist was an exchange of ideas regarding the data themes and meaningful data text. The outcome was a unity of understanding. This understanding and the artist's immersion in two months of studio work resulted in the creation of the painting depicting the family data.

Metaphors Brought to Life

- A family is together on one long couch.
- The powerful bond of a family emerges as they experience cancer and neutropenia.
- Family members spoke of feeling with and for the members with cancer and their family. Yet, there is a sense of separateness and aloneness in the experience, as they sit on their sections of the couch.
- The subjective nature of an illness experience emerges as one views the family as a whole while also viewing its separate members.

- ❖ The storm outside represents the turbulent times surrounding neutropenia and the shattered glass in the window represents treatment disruption.
- ❖ Chemotherapy represents the hope for curing cancer while the neutropenia is a forced interruption in the chemotherapy that triggers an increased sense of family vulnerability.
- ❖ A threat of mortality and uncertainty looms outside the family.
- ❖ Family vulnerability emerges as they recognize the threat of being harmed by the neutropenia or losing their loved one.
- ❖ Unknown outcome of cancer, the unexpected event of neutropenia, and ambiguous information contribute to family uncertainty.
- ❖ Slivers of light continue to stream in on the family, in spite of the storm.
- ❖ The storm of turbulence, vulnerability and uncertainty does not wipe out the glow of the family's hope. Families develop strategies, roles, and processes that maintain family integrity through the neutropenic experience.
- ❖ The family, within reach of their loved one and one another, maintains a connection that works to protect them from the turbulence of the cancer and neutropenia. Families work together to develop a protecting environment for their family and the member with neutropenia and maintain their hope for a cure and calm from the storm.

"Blending creative art and nursing research can move the nursing discipline toward new avenues of knowing."

- A grandfather clock in the background depicts the time standing still while waiting for the neutropenia to resolve and chemotherapy to resume. Family waiting is a crucial time, often filled with anxiety, urgency, fear, confusion, and feelings of helplessness. The experience of waiting has a never-ending timeline attached to it. Family life and individual life is somewhat suspended while the chemotherapy induced neutropenia and cancer become a priority of family life.
- In the center of the painting, the family member with cancer is confined to a separate square on the couch, depicting that the ill member has a central position in a family, and dressed in white symbolizing innocence and neediness. The family often views the ill member with a certain reverence and wanting.
- Nonspecific faces represent unique family experiences and diverse family types. Individual interpretations are possible because of the nonspecific faces of the family members.
- The out-of-perspective depictions, such as the twisted legs and thin elongated arms represent the pain and yearning throughout the cancer experience. Illness often brings a sense of family torment with an aspect of gauntness and emptiness. Families describe the experience of struggling alongside the ill family member and other family members. Yet, there is a sense of working together as a family to support each other.

Understanding the Family Experience of Neutropenia: Hope depicts the depth of emotion that surfaces in families with cancer. The visual experience of viewing this painting has been powerful to viewers, including families, nurses, and nursing students. It has engaged the viewer and created a somewhat unsettling experience as the viewer makes a silent connection with the meaning of the painting. The subjective nature of art has surfaced as personal experiences influence interpretations of the painting. Viewers have also noted the profound emotional impact of the painting which the researchers believe emerges as a powerful force. At times, viewers have focused on the darker side of the experience and the painting, while others have directed their attention to the lighter and hopeful tones. Viewing the painting from different angles and distances provides viewers with various perspectives on the turbulence of the storm, the light of the rays of hope shining through the window and family members.

The intent of our approach of blending research and art was to help nurses feel a family illness experience, find a new avenue for nurse researchers to present family data, and encourage the nursing discipline to embrace family caring. *Understanding the Family Experience of Neutropenia: Hope* did it! This painting evokes emotion with acrylic paints on canvas in ways that words in our research findings could not. This visual art captured a family experience and evokes the emotion of the viewer so that they embrace the art of nursing and family caring to transform nursing practice. Blending creative art and nursing research can move the nursing discipline toward new avenues of knowing. The painting expresses a family illness experience and the need for family caring, which our Family Nursing Research Team believes is the HeART of nursing.

Wave of Colours
Fabric art by Norrie MacIlraith

Bookends:
Birth and Death

For Maude Callum: Nurse Midwife, Pineville, SC, 1951

by Jeanne Bryner

I speak of a woman, blue black midwife
Of April fog, flood, swamp, and July nights
When Maude Callum's hands layered newsprint
In circles as a weaver works her loom,
Slow, to catch blood straw, placenta, save sheets.
I sing kitchen lamplight, clean cloths, Lysol,
Cord ties, gloves, gown and mask; she readies
For this crowning, first mother, purple cries.
I sing of sweat and gush and tear, open thighs
And triangle moons, ringlets, charcoal hair.
I sing sixteen-hour days, Maude's tires bare.
Mud country roads, no man doctor for miles.
I sing transition, collapse of mountains,
Crimson alluvium, the son untangled.

Reprinted with permission from The Kent State University Press.

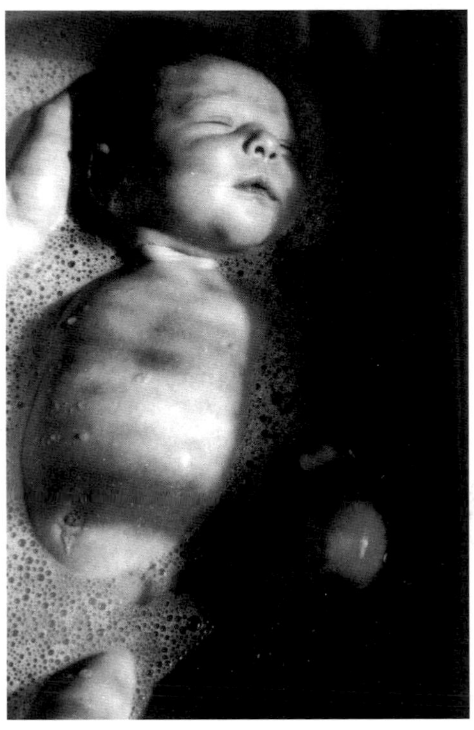

Photograph copyright Nicole O'Reilly, Melbourne, Australia. http://www.kids-fun-and-games.com/.

The Pause Between: Looking Back on Life

by Bonnie Jean Raingruber

Clouds reshape themselves
ever so subtly.
One hardly notices
darkness and daybreak
twinkling in descent.
You lie recumbent
arms folded pristine
over chest after
mahogany and marble
have lost all meaning.

The pause between breaths
sifts o'er your heart.
Silence sinks to toes.
Worry wanders away,
drifting to sleep.
Sleep eventuates
to death.
In the silence
a cat-eyed intuition
sees even

at night
hearing all,
filling your lungs
with nothing but peace.
It is in the quiet
before winter's glare
that enveloping love
holds you safe
in tears and in joy.

After Mother's Fall

by Priscilla M. Kline

Somewhere, inside this crumpled shell of aging cells ... mother still ...
Glimpsed in a singular twinkle in the eye as memory catches momentarily
... in the smile, the occasional burst of hooting laughter,
the sharing of a thought with hints of the once-rich vocabulary.
When asked in an attempt to stimulate connecting thoughts
with reference to a parakeet similar in color and named for one of long ago
provided by a well-meaning daughter, "I have no affinity for that bird."

The daily tedium of struggle, "Why won't God let me die?"
Unmeasured, unreal time spent with the daughters from far away after
the fall... a broken limb... confinement miles from home in strange, new,
sterile surroundings in hopes that bone will knit.

Daily visits with hours of few words, occasional flashes of meaning,
touched interlaced with shadows of fear.
Wheeled down the longest hall past similar sufferers, the trembling begins
... the whimpered, tremulous, "I'm scared."
"What are you scared of, Mother?" "I don't know... I'm just scared."
A pause... "I know...it's all right, *you're* all right."
More shivers... "I'm afraid I'll never go home again... will I?"
"That's the plan...what we're working toward. We don't know *when*."
No empty promises for one so proud, so long now humbled by infirmity.
Frail bones, loose connections between brain and body.

Home again, months passed, but nothing "fixed," little healing,
thoughts meander, time has little relevance.
"Where's Scilla? I want to see her once more before I die."
The intermittently yet oft repeated query, painful to the daughter present,
now, giving daily care, engenders feelings not unlike those perhaps felt
by the brother of the prodigal son.
Not intended to be hurtful, indeed, understandable,
Yet, nonetheless small, pointed arrows to the heart.

Long after the visit, unrelated in time or space but present in the fog-filled brain,
connections unexpectedly occur... I can die now... I've seen Scilla again."
Yet she lives another day.... and another.

Escape Velocity

by Scott Chisholm Lamont, RN

Sunlight streamed in the window
186,000 miles per second
Shimmering waves of photons
Washing over your body

Sounds flitted about the room
770 miles per hour
Sinuous rises and falls
Shivering tiny membranes

Heartbeats clocked on the monitor
60 – 40 – 30 beats per minute
Bright electrons darting
Furious bounces off glass

I have no idea
How quickly your soul left.

Only a sense
Of reluctance.

Photograph copyright Anna Moore.
http://www.littleparachutes.com/.

Cancer

by Bonnie Jean Raingruber

I am a fat frog Buddha,
sitting swollen and sick,
scratching my breasts
… looking for escape valve
exits from the pressure cooker
my body has become
clothed by cancer.

I open my closet door to find
nothing suitable, except death.
Ascites insulates pain and pallor enwraps
what was my life. Jack Daniels urine burns into
Bile, belching up out of awareness.
My absorption quotient cannot carry
a ration. I can only see myself.

…. death is making love to me.

The Well

by L. B. Sossoman

Gathered around the edge
afraid to get too close
Foreboding and cool it seems.

The echo calls to them.
Encouraged, they
Drop the pail into the abyss.

The coolness of water,
A drink from the knowledge of experience
Quenching their thirst.

Presence

by Sandra J. Lynch

I'm afraid.
alone.
"We've never done this before...
...it hurts."
"She's been through it,
with others."
"You are not alone."

This: the death of a dream
...a future...
Comes forth from my womb.

Her presence
...quiet
...supportive
...encouraging
...present.
The remnant
of what only days before
had been life, within me...
now is... lifeless, voiceless.
tears, my tears...

A gentle touch,
her hand
"Oh look!
Look at his perfect little fingers"
she utters

I look...
Yes.
They are perfect
He fits the palm of my hand
the warmth of my life still in him.
In my moment of grief
she sits beside me
her quiet presence

Strength.

Who is she
who sits beside me
in my moment of private horror...
and yet finds such quiet beauty
in my lifeless son?
"I'll be OK,
won't I?"

Yes.

Photograph by Gary Cowles

Rocky's Horror Dying Show

by Linda Norlander

My name is, or at least it was, Rocky and I am, or was, 42 years old. I think I'm dead, but I've never done this before, so I'll get back to you on that one. I've been married to Darryl for 24 years. We have no kids. He's worked for the county in the maintenance garage since right after high school. I'm the grade school playground supervisor.

I was born Cynthia but I always thought that was a pretty dumb girl kind of a name. My family called me Rocky because I collected stones and carried them around in my pockets. Up until my hormones kicked in, I wanted to be a boy. The only other Cynthia in my grade wore white anklets and shiny patent leather shoes. She used to waltz around school in dresses and say to me, "Cindy, girls shouldn't carry dirt and stuff around in their pockets." One day I got mad and stared her down. "My name is Rocky. If you call me Cindy one more time, I'm going to stomp on your pretty shoes and cut all your hair off." At least, that's the story my mother always told. I do not remember it well.

Anyway, I digress. Darryl's in big trouble right now. I want to tell you about Awful Marion and Doctor Scrub Suit and the Junior Scrub Suits and all the rest so you understand why he did what he did. It's the least I can do for the sweet old buffalo.

It all starts around Easter when I pick up one of those late winter colds, you know, the kind that hang on and hang on. Anyway, the cough gets so bad that Darryl threatens to move out if I do not see the doctor. I hate doctors. They always lecture me on smoking. I remember once telling the little exam room nurse when she opened her mouth to say something about my two-pack-a-day habit, "You're wasting your lecture, Kiddo. I'm not going to quit. I like to smoke. I like the way it feels coming in, and I like the way it feels going out."

So I cough and sputter my way into the doctor and ask him to please give me some cough syrup and skip the smoking lecture. By then, I have such a nagging backache that I figure I've broken a rib hacking so hard.

Damn if the chest X-ray doesn't show some "suspicious shadows." After three doctor appointments they finally send me down to the Cities for a biopsy.

I hate the Cities doctors. Back ten years ago, when Darryl and I weren't producing little Darryls, we went to some specialists down there. They poked and prodded and mumbled about how they could do this and they could try that and we'd have a twenty percent chance here and a fifty percent chance there. When it was all over, the specialists had all the money we'd saved up for Darryl's fishing shack up on the lake, and we had no little Darryls and no little Rockys.

But here we are again, back in some specialist's office. Once they've got the report, they stick Darryl and me into this dinky room about the size of a coffin. It's got one chair and the paper-covered exam table. I'm still coughing but now it hurts more because of the needle they stuck through my ribs. Darryl paces while I try to catch my breath. The only poster on the wall shows this toothless old bum with a cigarette hanging out of his mouth. It says something like, "Smoking is glamorous." Okay, I get the point. I decide right then and there that if the news is good, I'll quit.

The doctor walks in wearing a white lab coat. She has a ponytail that bounces like a cheerleader. After she introduces herself, she stands real near the door, like she wants to make sure she can escape. I'm thinking, this is bad news.

It is. The big C. Darryl looks stunned. I feel this crazy kind of relief. Now I do not have to quit smoking. Anyway, Doctor Rah Rah rattles off a bunch of stuff like, "We can try this and we can try that and you've got a twenty percent chance of this and a ten percent chance of that." I've heard it all before.

Then she stops and looks right past me to the damn poster on the wall. "Any questions?"

Darryl just stands with his mouth hanging open, wringing his hands. I'm about to ask the big one, "Is this going to kill me?" when someone knocks on the door. Doctor Rah Rah looks so relieved that I let her go. As she's backing out, she says, "I'll get the nurse in here to schedule you."

I give Darryl a little kick and say, "Let's get the hell out of here." I do not want to be around for the nurse to schedule anything. I want to go home.

Well, of course, Darryl won't let me go. I end up agreeing to chemotherapy. It's this battery acid stuff they pour through your veins. It's supposed to kill the big C cells. In the process it also kills everything else in sight. Makes you throw up, too. A month later I've left all my

hair in the shower drain, I've lost fifteen pounds, and I can barely get up in the morning.

It's now the beginning of May. I may not look like the green thumb goddess type, but I love my garden. Long about February when I'm ready to set fire to the living room, because I've been in it so long, the seed catalogues start coming. I spend as much time reading my seed catalogues as Selma next door spends praying for her dead husband Edgar's soul.

I tell Darryl I'm not going back down to that hospital for more of those pesticides they're pumping through my veins. Something tells me it's not doing much good anyway. I feel like hell. Some nights I spend an hour at bedtime just coughing up chunks of crud. I can hardly walk from the front door to the kitchen without taking a nap. Besides, I am bald as a newly hatched robin and I look about as bad.

Poor Darryl, he's this big burly guy who looks like a Hell's Angel. He's got a gap between his front teeth and a big scar running down his cheek. People look at him and figure he must have been in one hell of a bar fight. Darryl is about as mean as a ladybug. The scar came from a car accident when he was a kid. Went right through the windshield. My Hell's Angel, Darryl, wouldn't consider driving away in his pickup without buckling up.

Anyway, Darryl is beside himself. "You gotta go, Rocky. The doctor says it takes time."

But I've made up my mind. "It's my life. I'm going to plant the goddamn garden." It's hard to sound tough when you're wheezing and coughing.

Well, sometimes stubbornness can get me into big trouble. I figure that's the moment when we really start the roller coaster ride into hell.

Darryl fusses for a little while, then shrugs and heads off to work. That night he slams around the garage and pulls out the tiller. I can tell by the look on his face, he's an unhappy man.

I sit on our back deck smoking a cigarette and taking in the spring smells. I watch him and think about the last time we went motorcycling together. It must have been at least ten years ago, before we spent all our money trying to produce more Darryls and Rockys. When we were younger, Darryl and I used to bike a lot. One year we made it out to Sturgis for the rally. It was the first time I'd ever been out of the state.

God was that a great trip. I love the cycle roaring and the wind whipping through my hair. I remember watching the telephone poles whiz by and thinking that this must be heaven.

For at least a moment, as Darryl turns over the heavy black dirt, life is good. Then it hits me. I might not see another spring and another garden. Darryl will be all by himself. For a second I get so cold and so numb, I can't breathe. I start coughing like a son of a bitch and the tears come pouring. I have to go inside so Darryl won't see me like this.

Darryl doesn't say much about the skipped poison therapy. He lets me do my thing. My thing consists of making deals with myself. If I can get this row of lettuce in, my cough will be better. If I can just drive downtown to the hardware store and back, it's a sign I'm on the mend.

Meanwhile, Selma brings me over these god-awful concoctions to give me strength. She says the recipes are right out of *Prevention* magazine. I think she puts everything she can think of, including the Drano, in the blender, then adds Cool-whip.

Every day, I poke around in the garden for a while, nap for a couple of hours, then work up the energy to fix myself some toast and gag down some of Selma's Drano juice. I'm pretty happy not to be hooked up to some machine pouring poison in my veins. But I know I'm not getting any better. Somehow I can feel the Big C working it's way into other parts of my body. I hurt more. There's an ache, kind of like the time my back molar abscessed. Except it's in my gut. The pills I have cut the ache a little, but they make me so constipated I hardly ever take them.

Of course, I do not tell Darryl about the pain or the constipation. He's already to the point of pacing every night when he finds me half-dead on the sofa trying to watch television.

Selma tells me about reading in a magazine that some woman concentrated on her tumor so hard she made it go away.

"It just disappeared, Rocky. The doctors called it a miracle."

One sunny warm morning, I try the concentration thing. I sit on the deck with my eyes closed and try to see those damn cancer cells. I can't seem to see anything but that rotten molar the dentist pulled when I was eighteen. I end up in a coughing fit that brings up bright red blood.

Next thing I know, Darryl comes trotting out on the deck followed by his sister Marion. I call her Awful Marion because she acts like she's God's gift to the world. I sometimes think that someone left Awful Marion with Darryl's parents as a baby because they couldn't stand her. She doesn't even look like Darryl. He's got round rosy cheeks, like Santa Claus except for the scar. Hers are caved in, and she's got the biggest mouth and teeth of anyone I've ever seen. Honest, Awful Marion looks like a horse. To top it off, when she talks, she likes to run her tongue across her upper teeth. There's many a time I've wanted to give her a carrot, slap her on the rump, and send her on her way.

I've just coughed up a tissue full of blood that I'm trying to hide from Darryl. Awful Marion stands over me with her tongue lapping on those giant teeth. For the moment, I'm too sick to be rude.

She sits down next to me and pulls something out of her bag. Awful Marion always carries this gigantic straw bag. I can't imagine what she could possibly keep in it besides oats and sugar cubes.

"Now, Rocky, Darryl tells me you do not like your doctor."

I'm not in the mood for a lecture. I'm about to ask her how she'd like to leave her dyed hair in the bathtub, but Darryl looks at me with such puppy eyes that I shut up. Actually, I start coughing and hacking so hard I almost throw up.

Awful Marion waits with the patience of a nun on a holy mission. Then she spreads out this newspaper ad on my lap. At first I think she's trying to get me to fly down to Mexico for peach pits or whatever they're selling these days. But, no. It's a full-page ad from one of the City hospitals showing a nice looking doctor in a scrub suit. He's got his arms folded and he's smiling. The ad says, "The word 'terminal' is not spoken here."

Awful Marion smacks her finger on the ad and says, "That's where you need to go. They'll cure you."

I should have said, "Okay, I'll go tomorrow." I could have gone down there, told Doctor Scrub Suit, "no thanks," and been back on my deck by evening. Instead, I shake my head and say, "I'm fine." Never mind that most of my body aches like a truck ran over it and that I'm hiding a tissue full of blood.

Awful Marion clicks her tongue and shakes her head. "You should listen to me."

When hell freezes over, I think.

For the next couple of weeks, I keep up my bargaining game. Only the deals became simpler and simpler. If I can just get in a half a row of carrots, I know I'll get better. If I can get the seed pack open, I know I'll get better. Darryl grills me every night. How are you? What did you get done today?

I lie a little to him. I do not tell him I took twice as many pain pills as the doctor said I should, and it still didn't help. I tell him the garden is going well. He seems relieved. I do not tell him that inside, where the Big C is taking over, I'm pretty damn scared.

One day in late May, after the opening of fishing season, I tell Darryl I'm fine and that he should go with Bill and the boys up to the lake and fish for the day. Darryl says he will only if I'll let Marion check on me in the afternoon. What can I say? The poor boy needs a break.

Unfortunately, I have a very bad day. On the way back from the bathroom I get to coughing so hard, I can't catch my breath. I get sick to my stomach and my legs give out. As I land on the floor, I hear my arm crack. Then everything turns black.

Awful Marion stops over to find me curled up in the hallway, screaming and moaning like I've just fallen through the roof. She calls an ambulance and tells them to pack me up and send me to the Cities to see Dr. Scrub Suit. Of course they haul me to the local hospital instead. My right arm is broken, and I'm in so much pain they finally give me a shot of something. It makes my head so weird that I do not argue when Awful Marion raises a stink about sending me down to the Cities to Dr. Scrub Suit. Next thing I know, I'm back in the ambulance and on my way to get cured.

From here on, things get pretty mixed up.

I meet Dr. Scrub Suit after they've pinned my arm and trundled me off to a hospital room where I can look out over an alley and a bunch of dumpsters. He's followed by a pack of Junior Scrub Suits. He stands at the foot of my bed with a clipboard and talks to Darryl and Awful Marion. I hear him going into the same lingo about how we can do this and we can do that and there's a twenty percent chance of this and a ten percent chance of that.

No one pays much attention to me. I feel like I'm back in Miss Johnson's third grade class where I'd raise my hand and wiggle and yell, "Miss Johnson! Miss Johnson! I know the answer." She never called on me, not once. I think she was mad at me for threatening to cut off her favorite Cynthia's hair.

Darryl signs all the papers. For two days they put me through more tests than the fertility doctors could imagine. They X-ray me, cat scan me, clean out my innards and drain as much blood out of me as they can find. I've got an IV hanging that pumps everything except what I need—something for the pain. I'm so weak I can barely whisper, and I can't get out of bed.

Along about the third day, one of the Junior Scrub Suits comes in all by himself. He looks scared so instead of talking to me, he talks to the window.

"Cynthia," he says, "we're concerned because you are undernourished. We're going to put a tube down your nose and try feeding you through it."

Like hell, I think. No one is putting anything down my nose.

I shake my head and say, "No."

"But we have to do this." He says to his clipboard.

"No," I say back to his clipboard, as loud as I can. I sound about as ferocious as a mouse and all the effort makes me break out in a sweat.

He backs out of the room.

Photograph copyright Michelle Rau

A while later Dr. Scrub Suit marches in with Awful Marion and Darryl. He tells everyone but me why it's necessary to put this tube in. I tell him to go to hell. Darryl looks like he wants to run. Awful Marion acts like she's on another holy mission.

"Now Rocky, you know this is for the best," she says, looking adoringly at Dr. Scrub Suit.

It takes awhile, but they finally wear me down. When I finally say, "Okay," Dr. Scrub Suit nods at Awful Marion and walks out the door.

A nurse comes in to hold my head while the Junior Scrub Suit jams this tube down my nose. It feels like someone is poking at my sinuses with a fork. My eyes water and I cough and gag. The veterinarian was nicer to my old cat, Harley, when he put him to sleep than this guy is to me. I start to cry, then I start to cough.

"I do not want this," I croak.

"Now Cynthia, you gave consent."

They push and shove and finally get the tube down. Then they pour some stuff into it, and I feel like someone is blowing me up. I throw up the rest of the day.

That night, when no one is looking, I pull the damn tube out. The next day, they put it right back down. The nurse clucks and ties my good arm down. In her best kindergarten teacher voice she says, "Honey, this is so you do not accidentally pull it out again."

Now I know I'm in prison.

And god I hurt. I'm tied down, hooked up so I can't move, and every inch of my body aches like nothing I've ever felt before. I'm reduced to sniveling and moaning and even begging.

When one of the Junior Scrub Suits comes in, I plead. "Please, can't I have something for the pain?"

She looks at her clipboard and scrunches her eyebrows together and moves her lips for awhile and finally says, "If we give you any more, it might affect your breathing."

"I do not care," I weep.

"You do not want to become addicted," she replies.

"I do not care," I continue to weep.

She backs out of the room.

They start pouring the pesticides into my veins again. I wish I wasn't so dumb with words so I could describe how awful it feels to hurt and throw up and never sleep and know that you can't get out of this.

I beg Darryl. "I want to go home."

He looks so tired and worn down. He shakes his head. "Doctor says this will shrink the tumor."

By now, my skin is turning yellow and dry and flaky. I do not give a damn about the tumor. I want to go home, but I'm too weak to fight.

Nighttime is the worst when Darryl leaves and I'm all alone behind curtain number three. I have this ache in the back of my throat, like when you want to cry and you just can't get it out. I lay and shiver. Nothing warms me up. I try to think about my garden and the motorcycle but I can't. I wonder what happens after I die. Will I stay in this bed forever? Maybe that's hell. Will I just be gone—poof—no more Rocky?

In the middle of all this darkness, I start to cry. A nurse comes in. Instead of standing by the foot of the bed she comes right up to me and strokes my forehead. It feels like what Mom used to do when I was sick.

I keep crying. Instead of talking, she sits on the bed and keeps stroking my face. It's the nicest thing anyone in the hospital has done so far. Finally I stop crying.

"Can I have something for the pain?" I ask.

"I'll see what I can do."

When she leaves, I figure I'll never see her again.

In awhile, a Junior Scrub Suit comes in with the nurse-angel. The scrub suit fusses with his clipboard and says something about how I'm already getting a lot of morphine. Nurse-angel shuts him up by asking me how bad my pain is on a scale of ten. No one has asked me this before. I say, "eleven."

Junior Scrub Suit looks at me and at his clipboard while nurse-angel stands next to him with her hands on her hips. I can tell the poor guy is terrified and trying to figure out whether he should be more scared of nurse-angel or prescribing more pain stuff.

Finally, he says, "Okay," and walks out.

All night long the nurse-angel works with the IV and asks me how the pain is. Dawn is coming through the window when I finally say to her, "It's a three," and promptly fall asleep.

God, it feels so good not to hurt. I do not care that I'm groggy. I dream about my snap peas. I need to get home to tie them up. I wonder if Darryl has planted the tomatoes Selma sent over. For the first time in ages, I feel peaceful.

Darryl comes in sometime in the morning. I'm mostly asleep, but I know he's there, holding my hand. When I wake up, I ask him if he remembers that trip to Sturgis. He laughs about how we ate at the Road Kill Café. He's still convinced that the hamburgers were made out of ground squirrel.

I tell him something I've been afraid to say before, "Darryl, when I die, I want you to cremate me."

His face starts breaking up, but he doesn't say to me, "Oh come on, you're going to get better."

"I want you to put some of my ashes in the garden. Maybe if you get them in the corner by Selma's something might finally grow there. And then I want you to take the rest out to South Dakota and just scatter them into the wind."

I feel so much better getting that out. We both cry, and he kind of crawls in through all the damn tubes and tries to hold me.

Before I fall off to sleep, I ask him one more thing. "Promise me you won't let me hurt anymore." My voice is thick. When I open my eyes I can see Harley, the old cat, curled up on the end of the bed. He's all white and shimmery.

Everything feels so sweet until Dr. Scrub Suit and his pack of Junior Scrub Suits sweeps in. He stares at his clipboard and then at me. I can barely keep my eyes open, so I can't see much of him, but I can hear him.

When he leaves I can hear him right outside the door. His voice is high and strained like he wants to kill somebody. "Who ordered all this morphine? That's enough to kill her."

I do not care. Darryl doesn't care. Why should Dr. Scrub Suit care? But he does. Next thing I know, people are rushing in fiddling with the IV, adding this and that to it.

Darryl asks what the hell is going on and someone says, "Little too much morphine. We're giving her something to counteract it."

Well, whatever they do, it works just swell. Within an hour of Dr. Scrub Suit's visit, I'm in agony. I can't imagine hurting any worse than this and still being alive. I'm sweating and gasping and thrashing.

Darryl marches out in the hall and starts yelling, "Nurse, she's in pain. Somebody do something!" I hear a low voice trying to calm him down, but he keeps on yelling. Finally a very firm female voice tells him that if he doesn't quiet down, they'll have to call security. Doesn't he know there are sick people here?

Poor Darryl, I've never seen him look so defeated. He comes in, looks at me and the tears pour down his face. I can't even reach my arms out to him because one is in a sling and the other is tied up.

I look at him and see all my agony on his face. I whisper, "I'm dying. Help me."

He stands there for a long time, like he's trying to make up his mind about something. Then this determined look settles on his face. He leans down and says, "I love you." I know he means it because he never says it to me.

He goes over to the empty bed next to mine and pulls out the pillow. Then he unties my wrist so he can really hold me. I know exactly what he's going to do. For just a second, I'm scared. Then I think about the motorcycle and the wind blowing my hair around and the wide outdoors.

He puts the pillow over my face and pulls me to him, holding the back of my head as hard as he can. I can't breathe. For a moment I struggle, even though I do not want to. He holds me tighter. He's rocking me like a baby.

The world is going dark, but I can feel the wind on my face. When I open my eyes those telephone poles are whipping past me and I can breathe in the smells of the ripening corn. Now I'm floating somehow in that room. When I look down I see Darryl holding this poor, scrawny-looking bag of bones. He's humming to himself and swaying.

So, as I said earlier, I'm pretty sure that I'm dead now. But I can't leave until I know that Darryl is okay. He's so damn honest. If a nurse comes in and asks him what happened he's likely to say, "I smothered her."

Somehow, I get real close to him—close enough to whisper—even though I do not make any sound.

"I love you Darryl. You did the right thing. Put the pillow back. Tell them I died peacefully in your arms. Just tell them that."

And I keep saying it until he lays the bag-o-bones that used to be me down on the bed and puts the pillow back.

He turns on the call light and holds me, or what used to be me, until a nurse comes. He says, "She died so peacefully."

He cries, the nurse cries, and I float through it all praying that Dr. Scrub Suit doesn't walk in and either try to resurrect me or accuse poor Darryl of murder. If he does, I'll figure out some way to haunt him for the rest of his life.

It's time to go now. I'm seeing a bright white light ahead of me—honest. It's warm and comfortable like the mid-May sun pouring down on my deck. I look at Darryl one last time. God, I'm going to miss him. I'm sailing down that road on my motorcycle with Harley, the cat, on my shoulder and everything is peaceful. I think I'm on my way to heaven. ♥

Numb

By Roberta Hower

You sat there
face buried
in your hands
tears flowing
from your eyes
gasping, sobbing
hair black
as your clothes
daylight
pouring in through
The Waiting Room Window

Peering
through the doorway
I had followed you
at a distance
nervously, yet quickly
unknowing...
being there...
numb
and not yet knowing
why
or what I possibly
could do or say
to make it better

A few minutes ago
you stood there
at his side
watching
in disbelief
and shock
trying to be hopeful
with tear-laden eyes
as we tried
to revive
his silenced heart

He looked to be
"about 10"
"an alter boy" you said
"a good student"
You couldn't understand
why he did it
What would make him
tie his tie so tight
and take that step

Buzzers and alarms ringing
Nurses and Doctors
skilled hands
working quickly
Their minds analyzing:
Drug-Shock-Drug-Shock
Compression...Compression

Squeezing the ambu bag
Whirling oxygen
And medicine around
Artificially to a
Body and mind
That didn't want to
Anymore

Watching
with anticipation
We saw
the unchanging
straight line
on the monitor

And then...we stopped

He had died...
in spite of our prayers
in spite of our skills
in spite of our medicine

You left
and I followed you –
because someone
needed to follow you
and ask
"What can I
do for you
Father?"

And you cried
as I touched your shoulder
feeling numb
and not yet knowing
what more
we could have done...

The Butterfly of Healing

by Joan Stehle Werner

As nurses, we hear many stories. This is the story I would tell, if there was any nurse to hear. A story of healing, and of a butterfly.

It was a bluebird day. The kind of day when the sun bobs occasionally behind and between the clouds, the breeze softly blows, and the bluebirds would have been singing, had there been any nearby.

It was the summer of 2000, and I was up north high on our old aluminum extension ladder, staining our family's old log cabin. My brothers and I had been trying to bring life back to this old, now nearly decrepit cabin, which had lain fallow since my father's death in 1984. One brother had begun the year before by painting the trim and repairing the septic system. But, with fifteen years of ignoring most maintenance, there was a lot of work to do. This was my seventh trip to the cabin that summer, and my painting job was nearly finished. The first four trips up, I had been accompanied by my kids, husband, mother or dog, but these last three trips were with myself, alone. I was determined to get this staining job done before school started.

So, I had cleaned, sanded, caulked and now was applying stain on the logs, the final step. I massaged the logs with liquid brown, and with every stroke I found myself in a near reverie of memories. I remembered the early days at this very cabin, swimming, canoeing, playing cards, watching hummingbirds, and being scared by an occasional bear sighting on the peninsula where we were located.

Mainly these memories focused on my father, his gentle manner, his wisdom, and his love for me. I could actually see him cleaning the boat, splitting logs, painting and fixing the dock, and bringing fish up from the lake. I thought of my dad's loving yet occasional hugs, made all the sweeter by their infrequency. And over these last three trips to the cabin alone, I grieved for him like I had never grieved before. I talked to him, told him how very much I missed him, and how empty I had been after he died. I asked him how I was doing in my quest to renew his beloved cabin, and sought his guidance in my endeavor.

Photograph copyright Palmer W. Cook

So, with each brush stroke, memories wafted through my consciousness. My reflections wandered until they settled on a particular day in March of 1984. On this notable day, I had gotten up to the squeals of my new baby boy. I had fed him and bathed him, drying his lovely curly hair. Soon I would be leaving to go to the hospital, to the hospice unit where my father rested. He had been placed there after a tortuous three-month odyssey of suffering, brought about by his severe case of rheumatoid arthritis, septicemia, seizures, and various other traumatic medical events. He was on a respirator and, in reflection, I believe he had managed to stay alive until he was sure that my baby boy and I were all right following a difficult pregnancy and birth.

As I was dressing my little son, my husband came in from warming up the car for my drive to the hospital.

There was still over a foot of snow on the ground and the driveway was caked with ice and matted snow, a typical day in March here in our locale.

Yet, this particular morning he bounded in the house, exclaiming, "look what I found in the driveway! Right on the ice!" In his hand was a beautiful live butterfly, with velvety black, blue, and yellow wings. It tenderly lifted its wings a bit as I held it in my hand, marveling at the presence of this tiny, unexpected guest in the midst of what was still, for us, winter. My son giggled at the bright new visitor. And the three of us sat almost mesmerized by the butterfly, in deep puzzlement over its presence in our driveway.

My memory of the time involved escapes me this long hence, but it was within fifteen minutes or so that our phone rang. It was my mother calling from the hospital. Dad had died.

Another stroke of the thick brown brush and I remembered my life following this March day. I never grieved deeply for the loss of my beloved father at that time. I worked like I had never worked before, filling each day so full of university and nursing school activities that I didn't have time to feel. I believed I needed to be strong for my family, especially for my mother who was completely lost at the prospect of living without Dad. And I separated from my inner knowing, until years later, the fact that my Dad had visited me just after his death, as the butterfly, whispering that he was fine, and flying high.

And so, these last three times up north I had taken the time to grieve. I would sit by the lake in the evening and talk to my father. I told him about the sixteen years that had passed since he left. I told him about his grandchildren, now two boys aged 14 and 16, and how proud I thought he would be that they had grown into good human beings. I apologized for not taking better care of his beloved cabin and added that it was almost as if we couldn't bear to be there without him as the hub of our activities. I told him how I never thought he would die, since he seemed so well able to do everything else he ever set out to do. I told him how hard it had been for me to finally accept that he would never be coming back. And, I told him how much I had loved and still deeply love him. And, I cried over losing him like I had never cried before. I told him that after many years I had now come to know that the butterfly was his message to me, a message from beyond, confiding that he was happy, blessed, beautiful, and better off.

Back to the present, high on the rickety ladder, I was finishing up the last few logs. My brush and my arm grew tired, and I longed to be done. The rich, thick, brown liquid went on like a blanket, filling in the nooks and crannies with its veneer of thick protective warmth.

With these last few strokes of the brush I found myself wondering if my father would approve of the staining job. Had I done it right? Was it acceptable in his standards? Would he say, "good job"? Though I was tired, should I give it a few more strokes? "What do you think, Dad?" With these questions at the forefront of my mind, I caught a flitting movement in the periphery of my vision. A flutter, backed by the lake in the distance and the towering birch trees. I paused to briefly focus more clearly on this intrusion to my memories and questions.

Nearby, just out of reach, flew the butterfly, black, blue, and yellow. The same butterfly. I had my answer. The butterfly, here and then gone in a flash, whispered "Good job."

The message is for us as nurses to listen. To listen to stories of healing, and to marvel at what may not seem possible. Through listening, we can participate in the wonder and awe of the healing power of the universe, and of the many ways this healing manifests itself, both for us and for our patients. ♥

The Extraordinary Ordinary

Third Visit

Poem by Karen Roberts
Photograph by Tracy Rasmussen

On my third visit, I notice a battered leather purse
hanging from the hall closet doorknob.
It is scuffed, dusty and black,
a style not seen in years, but back now; retro chic.
He has no wife now, no daughters, no friends.
Alone, he is eaten away.
Cigarettes draw life from his lungs daily as he once drew
"the smooth satisfying smoke" from them.
He walks a last mile for a Camel,
relying on our kind ministrations to ease his pain and loneliness.
We reminisce about life, work, family and community.
His beloved wife died 26 years ago in the fall, on a crisp day,
while he worked in the fields.
Just back from town, groceries still in sacks, she lay on the floor.
"It was fast, though, they tell me." His eyes are full.
On my way out, after pain patches, laxatives, and other topics
he thought never to discuss in his lifetime, I stop.
"Whose purse is that?"
"It's—was—my wife's. She always hung it there, when she came in.
I just never got
around to moving it, I guess."
I touched his hand, understanding.
He is not alone. She is with him, always.

Automatic

by Julie Ann Fitch

With a sigh,
The negative pressure unit
Vacuums oxygen
To its sticky sacs,
Exchanging it for carbon dioxide
At the finely regulated capillary membranes
The CO2 dissolves warmly
In the winter air
From the now laughing mouth
Of the child.

Charge

by Enid A. Rossi

The wind hisses across the grey
water, creating black ripples.
Fluffy white geese sit smoothly on the ruffled surface,
their necks tall.

I lie in my hospital bed slowly
burning inside. All around is white scurrying,
deciding what should be done for me.
No one asks what I want.

The cool water breathes fresh and clean.
Grey-brown ducks spread their wings and glide to a
stop, dipping their heads in the ripples.

The burning rises from my feet spreading
upward with heart pounding and mind pulsing,
"You need to stay another week. Your doctor won't be
back from vacation until Monday."

Phone my son. I am signing myself out of this hospital,
"I will be home today!"
I feel light. I can see all around. My arms stretch out
as if to catch the wind.

I'll decide when to glide to a stop.

My Mother Doesn't Jog Around the Lake

by Joanne Calore Turco

My mother doesn't jog around the lake.
She walks up and down, back and forth, on one side only.

"Why?" I asked one morning after she returned.

"You can't see as much from the other side.
No flowers, weeds, ducks, or bugs.
One day a grand turtle dragged her scaly shell to shore
And basked in the sun.
I could see the smaller turtles in the water behind.
To catch the early rays.
Farther out on occasion an egret slips silently along,
Then disappears—I scan the surface to spy where he will
re-emerge. Families of ducks bob for food, bills down,
tails up, Over and over, then gather like sentinels in a line
and slide gracefully away."

"You just watch the ducks?" I queried.

"No, I like to mull things over too ..."

"I thought mulling was to simmer cider and cinnamon on a
brisk fall night ..."

"It is— I let my thoughts simmer and bubble," she answered.

"So you walk and think and watch the ducks?"

A sly smile crept across her face.

"Yes," my mother said,
"I like to get my ducks all in a row."

Camilla

by Mary Louise De Natale

The simplicity of life

The beauty of life

The vision of life in this one flower.

Life With You

by Maria Theresa "Tess" P. Panizales

Everyday as I pass by, I get the glimpse of life's beauty,
how you have survived it in facing life's struggles,
unknowing how you stand when you stumbled.
It bothers me how you maintain that glitter in your smile.

As I say, "Hello," and you gave back same mumbling words;
I cannot discern, how much courage you have,
in order to face life's reality . . . the ebb of life.

As I do my care, I imagined how active you have been;
how you nurtured a family, showering them with love.
Today, you seem to be at your caregivers' mercy.
Relying on them, not knowing if they're empathetic to you.

Sometimes I would like to decipher your thoughts,
your eyes may speak of your feelings.
But I want to hear you . . . listen to you . . .
I wish I could do more as a person.

You did help me grow, you meant a lot,
you taught me to be stronger, to be more humane,
to be able to unmask reality, and see life's struggle as
BEAUTY . . . while I'm still young.

For Paul: Your (Wheel)chair

by Susan K. DeCrane

Simple in form
Unchanged through the years
It hugs your body
And becomes an extension of your being
Freedom, power, livelihood
Does it give these things to you
Or you to it?

Its lap holds memories
And the smell of cigarettes and stale aftershave
The wheels contain the adventures of the years
Dried beer and mud
From the many canyons of the past

Like a pair of old shoes
That have grown more comfortable with age
The dreams of what might have been
Worn away like the treads of a tire
Peace and acceptance now
The fuel for your travels.

Nurturing Life Through Horticultural Therapy

by Jackie Carlisi and Patricia La Brosse

Since the beginning of time, there have been relationships between people and plants. The relationship encompasses rituals, holidays, births and deaths, sustenance, shelter, medicinal, and clothing. It is a well-known concept that people around the world realize the therapeutic benefits of working with plants and nature. Humans tend to gravitate toward botanical gardens, arboretums, parks, flower shows, garden clubs, conservatories, and places of natural beauty as a means to self-nurture including healing the mind and spirit. Traditionally these benefits are self-initiated but many people are not able to facilitate this process on their own behalf.

During and after World War II, it was noted that working in a garden promoted a curative effect for soldiers in a Veterans Administration hospital. Since that time, the recognition of the healing aspects of person-plant relationships has evolved into the treatment modality known as horticultural therapy.

Mr. Claude Girourd says, "It reminds me of when I was growing up at home."

Horticultural therapy involves plant and plant-related activities that are aimed at improving the social, physical, psychological, and general health of participants. It focuses on the value of the process rather than the end product. Individuals who have been diagnosed with developmental disabilities, mental illnesses, and physical disabilities have enhanced their lives by simply working with plants. Other special populations such as older adults, adult and youth criminal offenders, and substance abusers have found horticultural therapy improves quality of life.

Much has been written about the science and art of nursing. The science of nursing encompasses all the scientific knowledge and technology available for education and *practice*. The art of nursing refers to the ability to use the profession's body of knowledge in service to people in a way that has meaning for both the recipient and the nurse. Humans are viewed as bio-psycho-social-spiritual beings with which nurses enter into an interpersonal relationship for the purpose of assisting them toward an improved health state and a sense of well-being. Some current theories include a view of the nurse as a healing, therapeutic presence as s/he encounters and engages in opportunities to improve the quality of life as viewed from the perspective of the person, family, or community served.

The essence of nursing is caring, which grids the relationship between nurse and care recipient. Caring can be viewed as bringing all we know and all we are to this

Mrs. Leola James said, "I didn't think my hands would work."

relationship and being truly present while we work with clients to promote health and the quality of life. As the nurse enters the client's world, many circumstances may present that enable caring through creative interventions from which both will benefit. Horticultural therapy can be of significance to nursing practice in that it can provide an avenue for self-expression as well as demonstrated scholarly activity through transdisciplinary collaborative research.

We generated the idea for a collaborative research project involving research in horticultural therapy following a luncheon hosted by the dean of the College of Applied Life Sciences at the University of Louisiana at Lafayette. We secured funds from the local Festival des Fleurs de Louisiane and conducted a 20-week investigative study with residents of a long-term care facility. Weekly horticultural therapy activities were designed with specific therapeutic goals. One-hour sessions were structured to address one or more of the following: Sensory stimulation; memory stimulation; enhancement of fine and gross motor skills, including improved hand/eye coordination; socialization; and creativity. The researchers facilitated each activity by demonstrating and providing supplies. One led the group activity and the other offered therapeutic presence to engage the participants and to apply the nursing process. Weekly field notes recorded individual behaviors and overall group process. Some of the participants and their comments are pictured.

Horticultural therapy provides an opportunity to self-nurture through the nurturance of plants and engaging in plant-related activities. The research participants experienced the opportunity to create, nurture, enhance self-esteem, and express their uniqueness through activities such as making botanical note cards, propagating plants, painting terra cotta pots, and creating dish gardens. This art form fostered trust and self-disclosure with the group, facilitated holistic communication, allowed the research to be present in the participants' world in a way that would promote health and quality of life, and provided a new and innovative experience in the mutuality of caring. ♥

Seven participants proudly display their decorated grapevine wreaths:
From left to right, bottom row: Mrs. Leola James, Mrs. Maydel Dubois, Mrs. Mabel Lewis, Mrs. Gladys Johnson, and Mr. Joseph Parker, Second row is Mrs. Juanita Solomon and Mrs. Catherine Bellomo.

About this project, Mr. Parker said, "When we started, I didn't think I could do it—but I did it!"

Behind the Mask

by Norrie L. MacIlraith

Emerging from behind the mask used professionally in the operating room as a perioperative nurse, I have found a multitude of ways to express my artistic creativity using the guise of character masking. "Behind the Mask" is now a code name of my small, home-based business from which ideas are conceived; costumes that may include masks are designed, and construction is carried out to completion.

The story has a beginning, a middle, but, at this time, no ending, as it is evolving and ongoing. It is often said that creativity begins during childhood when daydreaming is encouraged and the imagination unlimited. Hopefully, the foundation is laid for lifelong enjoyment. Children often play "dress-up" with old clothes kept in a trunk, drawer, or worn-out box. They can become anything or anyone they wish as a good portion of the fun is choosing what to wear while portraying their characters.

Historical Background

I personally remember doing this growing up. The trunk was out in the garage. Neighborhood friends would be over and we would play for hours. All types of roles were acted out from "doctor and nurse," comedy, magic shows, favorite stars, and, of course, reading and making up plays. The outfit/costume was extremely important and had to be just right!

Then came the music and dance lessons, each lending its own form of costume for performance. Enter into the mix not only conceiving the design for costumes, but the actual making of them. (Yes, I learned to sew.) Once the designer was born, friends and others wanted their outfits made, too. While growing up, this talent was extended to include learning many applied handwork techniques I could incorporate into the costume making.

When I entered the nursing profession, I had no idea how my talents might be utilized. As a student on rehabilitation rotation, I designed clothing for patients so they could look nice in their wheelchairs but be able to physically handle their needs. My peers "in training" wanted help with personal clothing and for costumed activities—parties, of course!

The nursing profession was evolving as I gained experience and began exploring a variety of ways to teach my patients and provide interventions in their care planning. My love for characterization through costuming

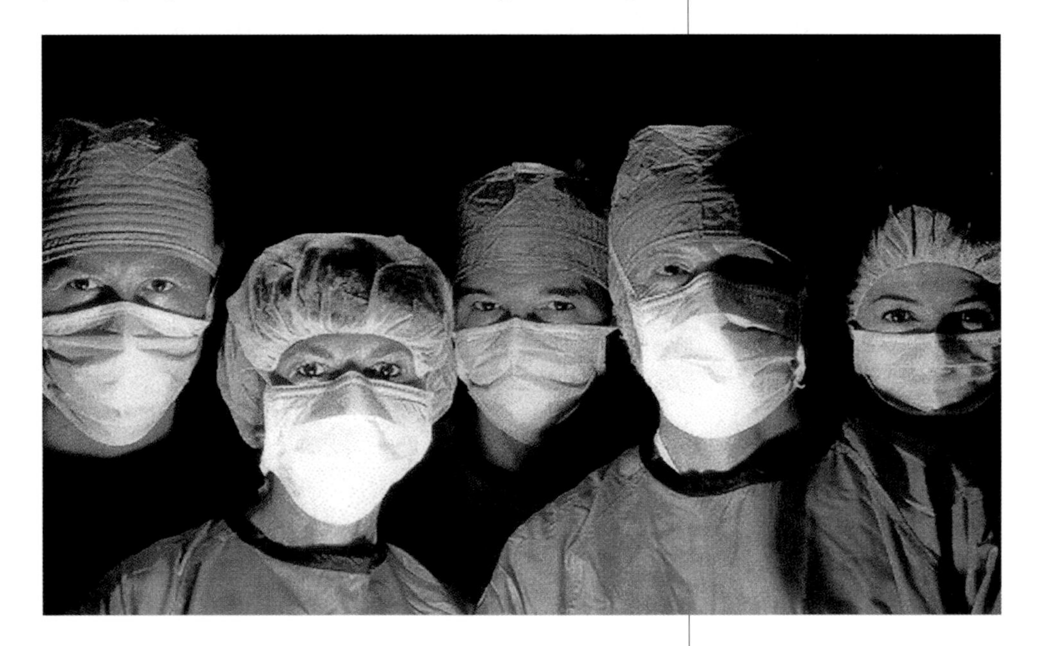

and masking brought with it change in delivery of my care. Children were introduced to stuffed animals, hand puppets, and clowning. They were encouraged to be one of the characters and tell me what they felt. Teens and adults were often involved with role-playing to express feelings and learn about their surgery. Role-playing has been instrumental in teaching professional staff how to listen, interview, and talk with their patients.

Over the years, adding the mother role, I became involved with my daughter's activities and a volunteer costume maker for her performances in dance, theater, and forensics in addition to annual Halloween costumes (see above). It was from this ongoing activity that my small business took wing as other people asked me to do their costumes for them. And so today, what began in childhood as fun and daydreams has turned into a second career commanding all the fun and excitement only creativity can bring.

Exploring the Applications

By some standards of definitions, costumes are nothing more than clothing. This is true when we look back over the ages and recreate bygone years of Rome, Greece, Medieval, Renaissance, Civil War, Victorian, Roaring 20s, and even into the 1950s, 1960s, and 1970s. But costumes are more than that. They set the mood, are part of the scenery, create emotion, and allow the wearer to step out of self and be another for the observer to enjoy. The simple act of donning a mask gives rise to self-confidence, self-expression, and a means to achieve wellness.

Dressed up. We all seem to know that people enjoy getting dressed up whether acting in a theater play, performing arts such as dance or music, having a costume party, or for a special event like Halloween. Costuming, whether seen as a simple prop or as an elaborate portrayal, allows individuals to act differently than they normally do and thus allows a role to be executed. This role-playing provides a major intrigue to the observer as well as participants. There are not age barriers or limitations.

"Behind the Mask." This may simply be a figure of speech without actually wearing one physically. The imagination creates what will be and holds that idea in mind for the characterization. Other forms may be used, such as puppets; hand puppets; face paints; hats; and other props, including briefcase, cane, shoe box, and telephone.

Collaboration. Often, there is a team approach in costume execution. Ideas stem from brainstorming sessions with individual clients, theater boards, production staff, school officials, teachers, public and private organizations, and merchants in determining a reason for the planning and execution of a given costume. The channels of communication are always open and changes are inevitable.

Research. Just as an actor wants to know as much as possible about the role s/he will play, a costume designer must be sure that the creation is correct. Research is conducted regarding the period of time, types of fabric used, original patterns for construction to be authentic; these must be found and reconstructed for proper fit. Assurance that the costume fits with sets and scenery must be made, as, ultimately, costume blends in to become scenery – and is manageable by the wearer. Note-taking and updates are extremely valuable.

Talent. Talent is an innate form of expression that just is, or may be learned and developed over time. Exhibited in a variety of ways, talent in making costumes encompasses an artistic license to create. For the individual so inclined, this is a real challenge and can be mind-boggling. Included is an eye for color and design, a visualization of how things can or should be. This is coupled with the dexterity of eye-hand coordination, and of using tools, machines, and a multitude of gadgets. Manipulation of fabric takes time and patience as do the accessory additives in trims, embroidery (hand or machine), and craft application. Individuals must learn about construction, sewing, handwork (knitting, crochet, embroidery, tapestry, tatting, and lacework), a variety of craft applications and must keep abreast of what is emerging as new to use or know how to revise the old.

Professional Interventions

Role-playing is often used in the classroom to assist the health-care provider in learning how to interview and interact with clients and teams. Medical, nursing, and social services programs find this form of instruction invaluable because each student may sit in chairs and focus upon the feelings that role may bring. Children respond to role-playing best when used to allow them to express how they feel. Small props, such as hand puppets or stuffed animals, may be available so that the child may begin without saying things in the first person. Observation with professional interjection provides a beginning conversation later because children often will talk to the prop object. Explanations of coming to see a doctor or undergoing procedures or surgery and talking about something that happened to them are made easier through this type of play.

Therapeutic wellness can be enhanced through costuming. First, ask how do you personally react when dressed differently from everyday? Feel that energy? Stepping out of your mold and becoming another in a different light can be uplifting, be invigorating, take the edge off, reduce everyday stress, and, in addition, be FUN! Over a period of a few hours, spirits can rise. First there is the planning and choosing of the costume/outfit and the anticipation of what is to come, see, and do. Once into the activity, think about what you can be and how to execute that image. When complete, remember the good time, what was shared with others, or how feelings were communicated. Being "behind the mask" opens doors for individuals to come alive, throw away old feelings, explore new avenues, rethink change, and try new approaches to bothersome problems. Try it! This may become your greatest adventure.

* * * * * * *

Previously, I said that the story is evolving and ongoing. What I do know is that, for me personally, being able to apply my creativity through costume design and construction is extremely rewarding. As long as there are ideas to be developed, deadlines to meet, and a cross-section of client temperament stimulation, I shall look forward and arise to the occasion. The challenges are there as an individual and a professional as I truly love being the creator of illusions "behind the mask." ♥

Family, Friends and Memories

by Cathleen M. Shultz

Quilting, a centuries-old art, was part of my formative years. Grandmothers, great-grandmothers, aunts and family friends quilted. These women introduced me to quilted treasures from their homes in Ohio, West Virginia, and Pennsylvania. Most of the quilts were functional and used when the winter's bitter cold and cool, budding springs prevailed. Others were stirring collections of colors and patterns.

There is nothing quite like sleeping in a bed with hand-made pillows and feather tick mattresses, layers of quilts, hand-crocheted pillowcases, no central heating, and rain lightly tapping on the overhead tin roof of the family homestead. The thoughts bring feelings of comfort, like being bathed in the past. The farmhouse, built in the 1830s, sits prominently on a rolling hill. Inside sleeps my grandparents, great-grandparents, some cousins, and siblings. Grandma Addie let me choose the six quilts we placed on the bed; I was 10 years old. The selection was from a closet full of bed coverings. She talked about each one, who made it, what the fabrics represented, and whether the quilt was a gift or the result of a church or 4-H quilting-bee. As her hands lingered on the bedcovers, I was intrigued by the colors, patterns and textures. Clearly, I'm hooked.

The following years became a collection of women's quilting stories that were generously shared. My husband, Sam, patiently visited quilt shows, the Quilt Museum in Paducah, Kentucky, quilt exhibits, Amish communities, historic homes, antique stores, auctions, quilt stores, and more with me. Patterns and quilt books were selected for my quilt library. I joined a quilters' guild where I live in Searcy, Arkansas; several master, nationally known quilters

Photograph by Jeff Montgomery

live in the area. Annual trips to the American Association of Colleges of Nursing in Washington, D.C. provided some time to explore national museums' quilt holdings.

Progressing from making blocks to connecting blocks into patterns, I frequently turned to sewing and quilting to express creativity and feel comfort from the creative act and human connections. Each quilt holds memories of moments in time.

The pictured hand-made quilt represents the last quilt that my dear friend and "Arkansas mother" Auda Grady and I made together. Small cloth pieces, intricately connected stitch by stitch, form this quilted art. The wedding ring pattern is a traditional favorite. This particular pattern was made by Auda's grandmother. We spent many Sunday afternoons, following church services, cutting and quilting over 2,700 pieces. We talked and shared and spent hours together and apart to make our special quilt. Sadly, she died suddenly about two months after the last stitches were drawn. I miss her presence. Viewing this quilt brings memories of our relationship, and the times of sipping hot tea, sewing, laughing, and sharing together.

Each of my hand-made quilts has connections and memories. Some quilts are inherited, some made together with women of talent and depth, some are gifts, and all are cherished. The gift from my grandmother, through her mother and grandmother, began in the farmhouse on a rainy evening long ago.

My ancestors fought in the American Revolutionary War and immigrated from Sweden, England, Scotland, and Germany. They came for American freedoms and opportunities. Ancestors since, including my father, uncles, brother, nephews, and niece participated in military engagements to ensure liberty. What a gift they gave me as part of their family, and quilting came with this heritage. My 14-year-old niece, Amanda, wants to learn how to quilt. It is time to pass the quilting legacy and memories. ♥

Photograph by Jeff Montgomery

One Gone On

by Anthony Walker

Nursing found me, and only recently, art has found me too. Creating art has become a wonderful part of my life. It gives my spirit time to explore who I am and what I believe. It takes courage to put art out there for the world to see. It has become my choice to live the life of the nurse and artist—the one complimenting the other. This is the story of my discovery of my art; I offer it here to serve as an inspiration to others as they explore their artistic selves.

One day, I found discarded blocks of marble dumped in the woods and had an epiphany. A powerful feeling of belonging came over me. Placing my hands on the cool, rough stone put me in contact with the earth. To me, unhewn marble is like bread—it has a smell and a texture and a magic in it. It was baked and formed when the earth was created, and I felt as if it would, indeed, become food for my soul. I knew that a finished piece of sculpture, smooth and highly polished, could become a thing of beauty. I wanted to create art from stone. Perhaps this desire was borne of a need to satisfy a hunger or an urge to create something from nothing. I was not taught this concept. It was inside me.

I felt as though this was something I was meant to do in my life, I would become a sculptor. Had the marble sculptor been inside me all along? Perhaps all that was needed was the opportunity. It was as if the marble was placed there—in that spot, in those woods, along the path I chose to take that day—just for me.

As a nurse, I take great pride in the excellence I bring to my work. I have found that I must strive for balance in my life in order to be the best I can be. Practicing hard as a nurse is a very rewarding part of life, but is not my entire identity. I like to think of myself as a tree. Nursing is the trunk that gives my life meaning and satisfaction, and it supports my home and my family. My love of art is just one of my many branches. It is a part of my life that gives me joy, fulfillment, and a creative outlet. By engaging in art, my mind is always engaged, and I am more at peace. Now, I am able to give more of myself to the patients and families I care for, because my artistic self enhances and fulfills me.

One Gone On by Anthony Walker

Sculpting helps me to manage the stress of my work with clients. It can be a therapeutic tool to heal the spirit of both the patient and the nurse. *One Gone On* is just such a sculpture. I created it in 1999 as a way to express the sorrow and loss of my sister, Kathy, to colon cancer at only 31. In the sculpture, a maternal figure is seen cradling a pea pod which to me is symbolic of the womb. One of the peas, Kathy, is missing, leaving only myself and my three remaining siblings. This is not a sad sculpture; it is a tribute to Kathy's life. She has only gone on ahead of us to our next life. I loved my sister very much, and it was a difficult journey toward accepting her death. My art helped soothe my spirit and give me peace.

As a nurse, I am confronted on a daily basis with the fact that we are mortal. In time, another one of us will "go on." That realization forces me to live truly in the present. Tomorrow is not guaranteed. My response has become to find joy in today and appreciate that my art might outlive me. In time, the limestone marble will disintegrate in the rain and weather. It too has a lifespan, but for now it remains as a symbol of the time we all were together.

An Unfolding Life

By opening myself up to the task of making art, I have found a way to know myself better. By accepting my art as "good enough" to share with others, I have found a way to like, and even love myself a bit more. By understanding myself and loving myself, I have opened the doors to being more joyful. By being more joyful, I have become a person more able to enjoy and celebrate the uniqueness of others. By celebrating others, I become a beacon of hope and an anchor for those in need. By helping others as a nurse, I can begin to heal the world one person at a time.

I want to celebrate my originality, and I want my art to be unlike anything done before. As a self- taught marble sculptor, I approach the creation of art with a naiveté and almost child-like joy. I honestly do not know how other artists work with stone. One thing that is probably very unique is my use of discarded surgery drill bits to carve detail in my artworks. Surgery drill bits are single use items that are discarded after each case. I have the hospital's permission to recycle the hardened carbide steel and diamond coated burs used in otolaryngology and neurosurgery cases. These discarded tools of the medical trade become the tools of this nurse-sculptor's toolkit.

In my art-work, I use a hand-held electric rotary drill. The scrubbed and sterilized drill bits carve into the limestone marble with ease, and the tips last a long time. I use them as a painter uses a brush or pen. My colors are created through the use of texture and shadow. And, even though each sculpture begins with my ideas, sometimes the vision changes as the stone reveals its own ideas while I sculpt.

Gallery ID8,
Baltimore, Maryland, USA

An Influence of Art

I think my art has brought me closer to what Maslow called self actualization. My wife Melinda, also a nurse at Johns Hopkins, and I have had the good fortune to be able to create a space where other people and their art-work can be celebrated. We opened an Art Gallery in Fells Point, Baltimore, in 2003, that we called Gallery ID8 (ideate, verb, to form an idea). It is a place where people can share their ideas and a sense of belonging. Each voice, each person, and each new direction the artist strives for can be valued here. It is a place that is outside our striving to meet our basic needs. We hope it will inspire others to reach beyond the ordinary tasks of living.

Delicate Artistry: Nursing of Children

Basic Needs

by Carol A. Williams

Maslow's hierarchy of needs is one of the first theories the artist remembers learning as a student nurse. The theory describes the necessity of having water, food, clothing, and safety as the most basic human needs.

Children in Russian orphanages have the most fundamental needs. The artist knits woolen socks and sends them to the orphanages to help meet those needs. The socks are knitted especially with children in mind—bright colors, stripes, and patterns.

On the high end of Maslow's hierarchy is the need for self-actualization. Art is a means of obtaining self-actualization. It allows the artist freedom to discover oneself and to share that person with others. Fiber arts come in many forms; knitting is one of those forms. Creating the wool socks for the orphanage children allows the artist to express caring and share in a creative form.

In knitting the socks, needs on both ends of the hierarchy are met. The socks serve an additional purpose in that they bring people of two cultures together. The poem is a reflection on the art of sock knitting and how the art form bridges both cultural and human needs.

Basic Needs

Basic need —
Winter in Russia
Orphanage children with bare feet.

Basic need —
To reach out and share with others
The art of knitting, the art of caring.

Needles click . . .

Strong primary colors breaking down old barriers between peoples,
Establishing a fragile trust.

Wool fibers knit into

Patterns,
Stripes,
And Cables,

Crossing cultures
To warm feet through caring hearts.

♥

Original art by Megan Hoffmann, RN, BSN

"I love art, and I'm always looking for ways to incorporate it in my practice. I have grown a special love for drawing cartoon-like pictures to be used on our floor in signs, educational materials, and dry-erase boards. I almost always draw a quick rendition of each patient's face on his or her Styrofoam cup. It's amazing the warm reception I have had to adding just a little piece of myself to what I do!"

Rena Dee™ Connecting Children Around the World

by Helen Currier, Kimberly Daughtery, and Heather Robertson

Rena Dee is no ordinary girl. Rena is, in fact, a 16-inch muslin doll that, on her first tour, traveled to more than 10 different pediatric dialysis/transplant units in hospitals in England, Virginia, New York, Indiana, California, Missouri, and Texas. Rena Dee has now visited four continents! Today, she serves as an ambassador for children with end-stage renal disease (ESRD) and as the inspiration for Hope™, Rena Dee's newly "born" sister ambassador doll for children facing HIV/AIDS.

Rena Dee was created in response to pediatric nephrology nurses pleas for a unique support-group approach for ESRD patients. Some programs were so small that a school-age child might never meet another child facing a similar situation with the same disease. So, Rena Dee was born, with the children painting her body and drawing her face and hair on. She provides an opportunity for children on dialysis to share secrets, tips, and strategies to cope with ESRD. Each host hospital stamps her passport and offers their patients the chance to add their own personal touch to the diary.

Rena Dee represents wellness and preventive rehabilitation. Rena teaches kids that it is important to keep in touch with friends and shows them that it's okay to be different, for this doll has all green features. Children had that insight! (Adults couldn't have planned it better.)

In October 2002, Rena Dee accompanied a NASA mission specialist, whose son is a liver transplant recipient, on the space shuttle Atlantis's mission to the international space station.

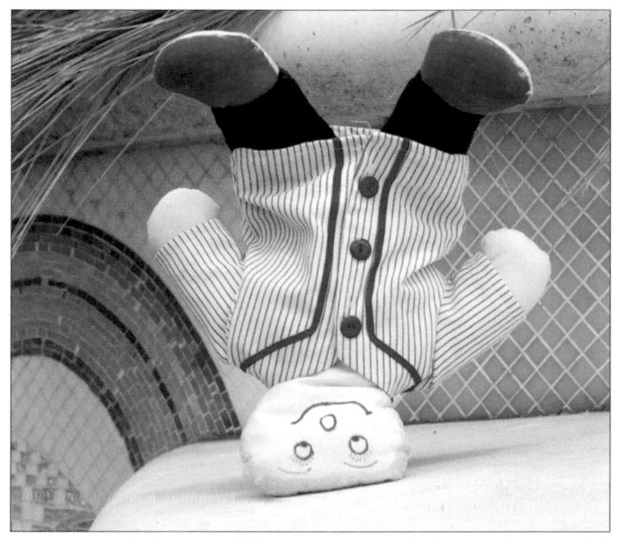

Rena Dee's ready for anything!

Rena Dee showing off her "catch."

A note about the authors: We are essentially Rena Dee's mothers. Kimberly Daughtery was the child life specialist on our renal team. She is currently working in a supervisory capacity at Heartland for Children in Florida. Heather Robertson was in the marking department at Texas Children's Hospital. She has since completed medical school and is doing an obstetrical residency. Helen Currier is currently assistant director for the renal/pheresis group at Texas Children's Hospital in Houston, and has been known to introduce herself as Rena Dee's mom.

If you are interested in a scheduling a visit from Rena Dee, she can be contacted at renadee@texaschildrenshospital.org.

Unfolding Artistry Through Relationship: The Story of Faiza

by Sandra J. Lynch

Editor's note: Ms. Lynch received the 2003 Award for Excellence in Caring Practice from the American Association of Critical-Care Nurses for this extraordinary exemplar of professional nursing care of a child.

My first glance, my first memory of Faiza was this: A wisp of a child, a tiny toddler, tucked snugly in a red wagon, propped and positioned to allow her a clear view of her world. Born with a congenital small bowel defect that left her unable to digest properly, she had been sustained on IV hyperalimentation. Despite providing crucial nutrition, her bright orange skin announced to me that she also suffered irreversible liver failure. I was well versed in the care of adult and pediatric patients as staff and charge nurse in a university-affiliated solid organ transplant unit. However, Faiza was only the second pediatric patient in our hospital to receive a liver and small bowel transplant. Her arrival signaled a new era on our unit, and I participated actively by taking on the role of transplant liaison.

It was through this role that I first met Faiza and her family. Faiza was born in the United States to newly immigrated Somali parents, both of whom spoke only minimal English. As part of my role, I was responsible for initiating patient and family teaching and gathering patient data in preparation for the transplant—a difficult and arduous experience, especially for kids. Despite her appearance of poor health, her face lit up with joy at the attention she received from the nurses. I was immediately captivated by the extraordinary strength of her spirit, strongly evident from that first day.

Because combined abdominal organ transplants are rarely available, especially in the size needed for Faiza's small body, it turned out to be another six months before a donor liver and bowel transplant became available. Following transplantation, and despite a complex recovery process, Faiza continued to demonstrate a strong inner spirit that carried her through this difficult surgical experience. It was during her early recovery process that I became acquainted with Faiza's mother, Rho. It became clear early on the source of Faiza's resilience. Rho had learned early that life is a very precious commodity, for she had escaped her war-torn home in Mogadishu, Somalia, only the year before. Rho's journey to the United States had been fraught with danger. Culturally and politically, people from Somalia in general have a deep distrust for people not of their clan; the recent war had intensified this distrust. Trust was therefore a quality Rho had learned to guard carefully and which, for her, had to be earned. Rho's survival through this difficult past had depended upon her trusting the right people.

In this context, earning Rho's trust was difficult and challenging for all involved in Faiza's care. Nurses, especially, were not to be trusted, and we discovered early on that if you were "fired" by Rho, you were in good company. Despite the cultural and emotional challenges, I decided to become Faiza's primary nurse, knowing that the key to excellence in caring for Faiza lay in the ability to create a trusting relationship with Rho. I quickly developed a deep respect for Rho, who, despite being surrounded by a foreign culture that she did not trust or understand, was willing to allow her precious child to be cared for by us if it meant a chance of her child surviving. As a mother myself, I easily understood her fierce desire to protect Faiza.

I knew it was important to better understand Rho in order for us to properly care for Faiza. Toward that end, I learned all I could about the Somali culture and recent history. I discovered that, as a Muslim woman, Rho keeps herself covered with the exception of her face and hands, to protect her modesty. I came to understand the Muslim practice of prayer five times a day and provided the family with complete privacy during prayer as much as was possible. This was a difficult but important task in our busy, university-affiliated hospital and involved coordinating numerous procedures, medications, and assessments around the rhythm of prayers.

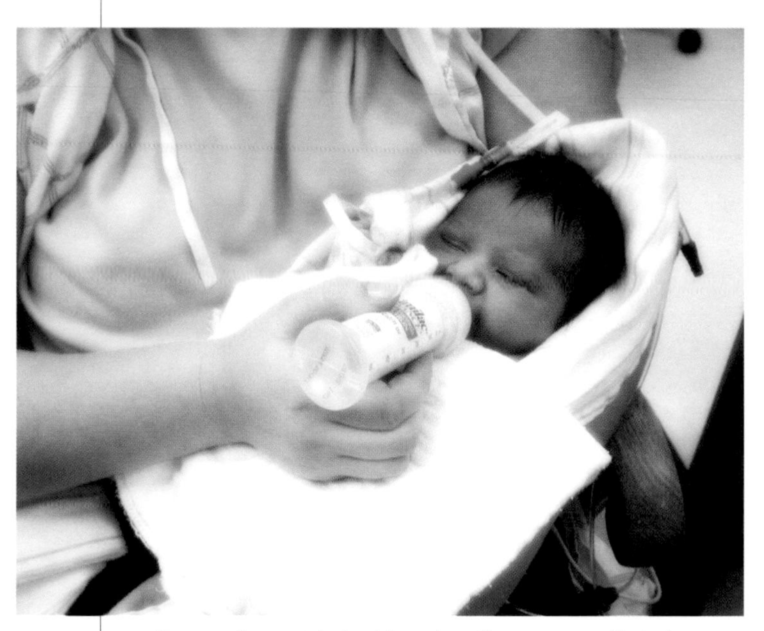

Photograph copyright Jyn Meyer. http://jynmeyer.com/design/.

I remained open to Rho's requests for herself and Faiza. I took time to hear all of her concerns and fears. I supported her right as Faiza's mother to be involved in every aspect of care. I taught Rho continuously, and she became familiar with all of Faiza's medications and their purpose as well as how to take them, when to take them, and how to observe for side effects. Because Faiza was highly immunosuppressed, I also emphasized the importance of cleanliness and sterile technique to protect Faiza from infection. Rho developed impeccable technique and also made sure that anyone having contact with Faiza was just as careful.

I became her strongest advocate on our unit, educating other health care staff about the importance of culturally congruent care and this family's unique needs. Rho became less and less adversarial as all of us began to hear her voice. I supported Rho's role as Faiza's strongest advocate and noted she was not afraid to speak out on her child's behalf. I spent many hours assisting Rho in understanding our hospital culture and the wider American culture. In return, she taught me much of her rich Somali culture. Over the weeks, months, and eventually years spent caring for Faiza, Rho and I learned that, despite being raised in two very different worlds we had one very important common ground: We were both mothers. In that part of ourselves, we understood each other perfectly and, within this understanding, we opened a sacred space where we could unite in our humanity.

I cared for Faiza and her family in a variety of roles for several more years after her transplant. When she was first discharged, I was her transplant coordinator. Later, I practiced as her primary nurse in home care. I remained her main in-home caregiver until Rho felt comfortable and competent to care for Faiza without outside assistance.

Over numerous hospitalizations, I continued in my role as Faiza's primary nurse, having the privilege of caring for Faiza and her family, many of whom were non-English speaking. I preserved cultural customs and managed language barriers when teaching and providing support, communicating caring and respect with each encounter.

This relationship deepened and broadened this past winter when Faiza was admitted for her final hospitalization. Faiza had once again developed terminal liver failure. Due to severe coagulopathy, Faiza's medical doctors were unable to attempt a liver biopsy for diagnosis. Rho was informed that her daughter's only chance for survival was to receive another liver. Rho was horrified. She confided in me that she felt as if every procedure and aspect of care was only adding to Faiza's pain. Rho's deepest desire was to protect Faiza from further pain.

On one remarkable day, Rho asked to speak to me privately. After being certain we could not be overheard, she asked, "Can I be sent to jail if we stop now?" I was astounded! My heart broke that she should be carrying such a fear. She worried the doctors would take Faiza away from her if she refused treatment. I spent much time with her and Faiza's father discussing their rights, and both were very clear that they had watched their precious child suffer for too long, seeing also that Faiza continued in severe pain. Rho asked if there was a way that they could let Faiza die while treating her pain. As teacher and advocate, I explained to the family how Do Not Resuscitate (DNR) plans are made and supported their right to make this request. They wanted so much to spend Faiza's last days in a comfortable place where they could all find peace. I assisted Rho in writing down the family's specific desires for Faiza's care, and a conference with the medical teams resulted in initiation of the DNR order.

I facilitated and coordinated a new plan of care based on hospice principles. The health care team collaborated to treat Faiza's unrelenting pain and created an end-of-life plan of care that was culturally congruent and supported Muslim beliefs and practices. Faiza's family remained at her bedside for several weeks preceding her death, where I, too, spent many off-duty hours. During this shadow-time, as we awaited the end of Faiza's life, Rho requested if I would be the person to remove all of Faiza's external appliances (Hickman, GT, and ostomy device) after her death. Coordinating with the staff nurses on the children's unit, every detail was arranged in advance to reduce the pain and stress to both the family and health care team. Faiza's family had worked so hard to provide this beautiful child with a meaningful life; it was my deep desire to facilitate her and her family with a peaceful, meaningful death.

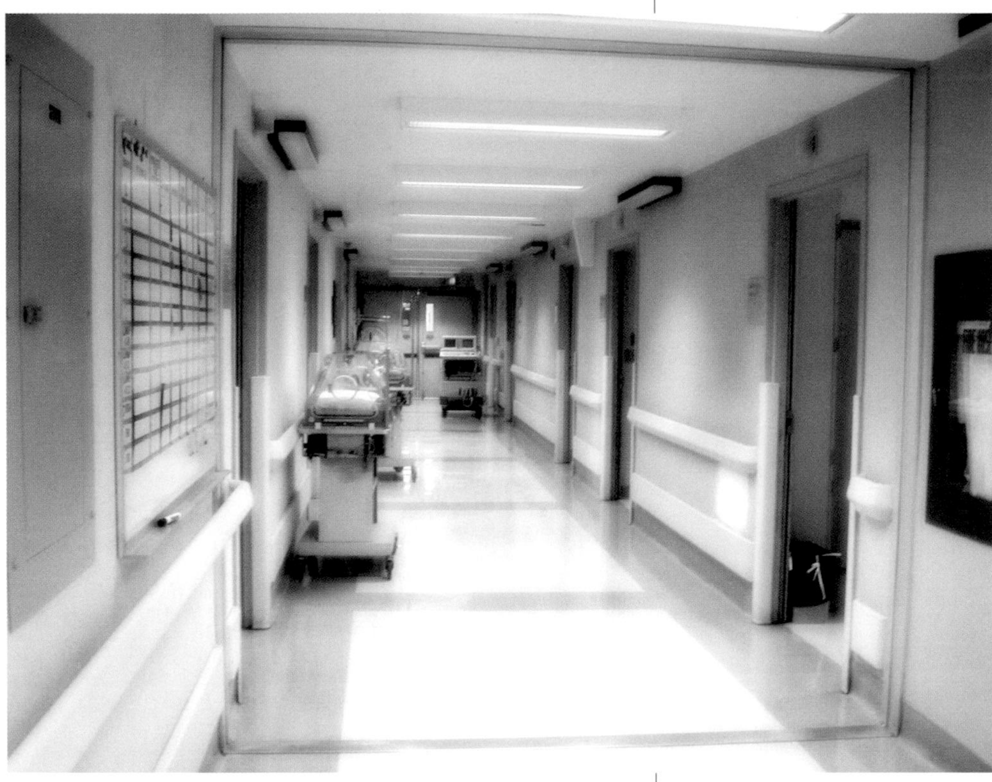

Photograph copyright Jyn Meyer. http://jynmeyer.com/design/.

Faiza died peacefully and quietly early on a Sunday morning, in my presence and within the loving embraces of her family. As I gazed at her through my tears, I was blessed to discover the quiet expression of an angel. Faiza's face actually glowed and a tiny smile once again lit her lips. Sweet Faiza, she always loved attention. I envisioned her laughing with the angels.

After respectfully removing all of Faiza's external appliances, symbols of our earthly attempts to cure, Rho invited me to join her and Faiza's female relatives to complete the washing and preparing of Faiza's body. This was an intimate and powerful cultural ritual, and I was deeply honored to be included. The loving way in which these women prepared this precious one's body has helped in my own healing as I go through my grief journey after losing Fiaza, this beautiful child.

Assisting Rho and Faiza through this incredible journey remains one of the most powerful and important experiences of my career. Fighting for this family's right to a peaceful and dignified death for Faiza has been one of the most special experiences of my life. I feel that my most important role as a nurse is to advocate for families and their rights and to fully empower families in the care of their children, providing culturally congruent care, support, information, respect, and indeed, love. ♥

Nicholas

Remembering Eva

by Kathryn Gramling

Nicholas is graduating from "Busy Bee."
In yellow gown and mortar board.
He is an animated, race-car loving 5 year old boy
Whose "Mommy is in heaven."

Nicholas has his brother, Jeffrey,
Grammy and dad,
To help him grieve and feel safe.
He doesn't want for anything except that you know
His "Mommy is in heaven."

He asks the barber.
He tells the electrician
Reminds his aunts and uncles.
And then he goes happily about his world
Knowing they know
"His mommy is in heaven".

I think of the words in
Eric Clapton's song:
"Would you know my name,
if you saw me in heaven?"
And I wonder.

Is this wonderful child,
Building a safe place for his mother and his love.
Is he making sure you and I will know her name
When we get to heaven.
Or is he making sure her name
will not be forgotten while we walk this earth.

Breast cancer killed Eva two years ago.
It did not kill her spirit or love.
Nicholas is making sure of that.

Mother and Child in Amsterdam
by Catherine Fraser

Song for a Baby, Lost

by Sandra J. Lynch

Elijah, you may have been just one
   tiny drop
Upon this earth
   But you touched the heart
         deep within ...
your deep brown eyes.
Pools of gentle, sweet softness,
   you touched me
with a blessing.
   Sweet, pure Elijah
You are God's holy baby
You dance with angels
   and your laughter rings through the heavens
I hear your voice
   Mingling with the sound of a
Bird song.

   Thank you, Elijah.
Sweet baby Elijah, you are forever
   A song in my heart.

ER Echoes

by Bonnie Raingruber

Rippp...
The sound of scissor
slicing sleeve and pant
showing flesh, showing heart
showing the red-blooded stab
from a knife fight at Del Rio High.

Ahhh...Ohhh...
Sternal press and pain
voice like a loudspeaker o'er head
"Talk to me, wake up
our tubes go in next." I whisper back
"Don't get blood on my new tennis shoes."

Urppp...
Salt-water sounds replace
coffee ground emesis from an NG tube,
an IV is in, threading
my mind's eye with morphine.
My life's blood leaves.

Zippp...
The sounds of my world
are silent now.
This black plastic shroud
is sleeping bag until
my mother views the body.

Shhh...
Another helicopter is landing.
Sirens still rattle your world.
I go to a lighter land.
The warmth has me
for the first time in 15 years

Moving Image

by Mark Clarke

For years he drove the
mobile medical clinic
down the back roads,
out to the farm workers,
used up all his medical skills
trying to heal their wounds.
Then one evening,
overheated, with one tire going flat,
out on Agua Frias Road again,
he watched the sun go down,
Sutter Buttes turning back to gold,
he figured it all out.
Big as a billboard,
he repainted the van
to look like clouds,
and added the bright faces of children.
He threw out the medicines.
Now he delivers more useful things:
Popsicles, cool water on hot days,
sturdy gloves, thick socks,
paper and pencils, crayons for the kids,
and scraps of poetry written
in their native tongue.

Sailing

by Helen Currier and Charles Tapley

The setting is a pediatric chronic hemodialysis unit where late afternoon treatment times can allow for a child's full attendance at school. Still, the first treatment hour is dedicated to school work and learning activities. On occasion (well, frequently), teens can be found complaining about school work. This afternoon's complaints centered around writing the *dreaded* poem.

Thus, we took them on a guided writing exercise. We steered the patients (students) away from poetry product and technique. We began instead with imagery and drew inspiration from the recently unveiled Sail Park at Texas Children's Hospital. The park contains colorful sail forms above flowering plant beds and evergreen ground cover. The canvas sails are mounted on lightweight masts and boom forms designed to rotate 360 degrees on their perch atop raised beds atop "wave" walls. The teens identified the park as a metaphor for patients facing chronic illness. This park, designed to welcome the imagination, enchanted our young "mariners."

Taking this metaphor to the page, the dreamy and enchanting repetition of a pantoum's fixed form was introduced to the patients. A pantoum is a Malayan poetry form written in quatrains with whole lines repeated in an interlocking pattern (1234 2546 5768 7381) creating a kind of circle.

A rich discussion was facilitated where senses were drawn upon and the pantoum *Sailing* was shaped. *Sailing*, the poem, is a metaphor for pediatric patients facing a life of chronic illness but who resist being defined by the illness. It is also for those who nourish their spirits.

Photograph courtesy of Paul Hester.

Photograph courtesy of Paul Hester.

Sailing

by Helen Currier

Shiny masts and signal flags
Feel the gentle breezes
Grasses dance with the bejeweled waves
Touching the water

Feel the gentle breezes
See the sails change course
Touching the water
Healing the spirit

See the sails change course
Sea flowers attract winged creatures
Healing the spirit
Texas Children's Hospital

Sea flowers attract winged creatures
Grasses dance with the bejeweled waves
Texas Children's Hospital
Shiny masts and signal flags

Charles Tapley is the architect of Sail Park at Texas Children's Hospital. Paul Hester is the photographer of the four Sail Park photographs. Helen Currier is assistant director for the renal/pheresis group at Texas Children's Hospital in Houston.

Midnight Thanks

by Mary E. McBride Majkut

Oh, God
I hugged my son tonight.
He was asleep in bed, so warm and settled.
Oh, how I clutched him and whispered to him
That I loved him so.
He, in his sleep, reached out and hugged me.
And I held on for dear life
As I felt the tornado of Life's injustices
Whipping at me and
Tearing at my heart.
And yes, I held on to a dear life.
My son, Matt, is eighteen;
A high school senior
Accepted at colleges this month
Picking out his prom tux this month
Working the extra hours this month for
Tux, summer clothing, gas money.
So predictable, so safe.
But Angie did not go to her son tonight
And hug him in his warm bed.
She came to the ER
After her eighteen year old son, Josh,
Drank a bottle of lamp oil.
Sweet, bright, Josh arrived in the ER
Throwing up, thrashing, bewildered.
Bonnie took him. I couldn't do it; I knew him.
Then Josh decompensated
And I had no choice but to assist.
I paralyzed Josh as the doctor intubated him
And we sent him out into the star-filled night
By helicopter.
And I cannot help but to think
As I sit in my bathtub bathing in my tears
Washing off the night's wrath.
I realize that it could be any parent, any child.
It could be me. It could be Matt.
How Angie had cried
Trying to make sense of it all.
What had she missed, she wondered.
And I wondered, too.
About me, about Matt
As I hugged him
And held on
And thanked God
At midnight.

6

In the Process of Becoming a Nurse-Artist

"I didn't find art; art found me."

-Christina Impoco Nieves

In the Process of Becoming a Nurse-Artist

by Christina Impoco Nieves

Editor's note: Christina is a nurse-artist from Massachusetts. She was awarded the 2002 and 2004 Pinnacle Award for Media: Arts from The Honor Society of Nursing, Sigma Theta Tau International. Here we present Christina's journey to nurse-artist and showcase a number of her works of art as a testament to her unique story.

"I didn't find art; art found me." This is my usual answer to the question of how I began my journey toward art. Pondering these words always opens up a meaningful, internal exchange as I reflect in detail my work with art.

Child's Play

Who wouldn't think that being an artist was the most wonderful thing going? If asked at any point in my life if I wanted to be an artist, I suppose I would have jumped at the opportunity. However, I never saw that opportunity. Neither did I ever see myself as particularly talented or gifted as a visual artist. Like many children and teenagers, I enjoyed arts and crafts and poetry writing, and—less commonly—I became a fairly accomplished classical guitarist at a young age. However, when I chose to pursue nursing, I quickly dropped my sense of creativity and plunged myself into the world of science.

Once I reached adulthood, I viewed my level of artistic talent to be around that of a child at 10 or maybe 12 years old. This is, coincidently, the time in life when many people discontinue their artwork—whether that art is drawing, singing, dancing, or other forms of art. Adolescence and young adulthood are a time when people become keenly self aware and acutely concerned with the

Paraclete I
Charcoal on paper

The Best is Yet to Come
Acrylic on canvas

world and their place in it. Drawing or singing or dancing becomes only for those who are good at it in a competitive sense. The rewards—praise from friends and families—goes away then in the typical pattern associated with "growing up," and the artwork that was once of paramount importance as a literal vehicle of growth and development is now considered lofty, frivolous, and child's play. The development of mental faculties and acquisition of social competencies then frequently subjugates artistic self-expression to a secondary level of importance. Similarly, adults are rewarded for left-brain prowess and affirmed for intellect, wit, and wisdom. Brainwork is more highly prized than heart-work, and most adults remain in a thinking and reasoning realm where they continue exercising only that logical and scientific mind. This is especially true in the health care arena where exceptional mental aptitude is required and is prized as the means to achieving success.

However, like the dutiful dog in Pavlov's laboratory, we are still running to the bell to find our rewards! Positive reinforcement is not wrong, but I believe the positive reinforcement for scientific thinking and achievement has sent nurses the erroneous message that the creative processes and humanistic self expression through the arts are of a lower order and therefore less important and should only be pursued in adulthood in order to receive adult rewards like financial compensation and verbal accolades. While such rewards are admirable, they should not be the sole criteria determining whether or not nurses should pursue artistic endeavors.

Your Gift Will Make Room for You

My experience with art begins within the context of Proverb 18:16 which says, "A man's gift maketh room for him, and bringeth him before great men." With no formal training as an artist, I began to draw. I drew as a spiritual exercise. I drew as a means to make sense of images presented to me—images I saw on the inside. Words, prayer, music, events, thoughts, and feelings all stimulated internal images and fed my need to create through art. Importantly, the more attention I gave to this practice the more available it became to me. Increasingly, I noticed these images presenting messages for me to convey, both for myself and for others. Each time I engaged with the art through dialogue, journaling, or just remaining present, the imagery "spoke" back to me. One may argue that the act of creating art as a reflexive response to inner stimuli is cathartic and that catharsis in and of itself is known to possess curative value. However, catharsis alone could not explain the phenomenon I was experiencing. This was not a one-time discharge of pent-up emotion, now lying static on paper as catharsis would suggest; this was a dynamic exchange taking place within me.

Changing

Interacting with the art subsequently caused real change in my life. Through art, I began to discover my true self and my deepest heart's desires; indeed, even my integrity. I found the ability to make sense of past and present events through the lens of art. Creating and interacting with the art gave me a voice, an awareness of my own inner thought patterns and tendencies. I gained clarity on spiritual dilemmas that were normally non-discursive and beyond my ability to articulate. I received direction, inspiration, and vision in many areas of my life. I later found I could utilize art to aid in understanding and healing physical symptoms I experienced. Through art, I discovered a relationship between my inner and outer beings and the existence of an inextricable shared bond between them. Art had brought authenticity to my life; I became more congruent, stable, and whole.

Art became for me an avenue of healing my body, soul, and spirit. This felt odd. As much as I would describe myself as a spiritual person, I was also (as a nurse for many

Blue Series
Acrylic on paper

years) scientifically-based. In that sense, I would have preferred to experience something more conventional and validated. At this time, I had not even heard of art as a therapeutic modality, so dabbling in this felt uncomfortable. Yet, the fruit from my art exercises was undeniable and pleasantly rewarding. Rather than dismiss this experience simply because I did not fully understand it, with encouragement from a trusted spiritual director, I continued to pursue the work.

Art as a healing intervention sounded strange and felt to be in direct antithesis to the more widely-known and trusted scientific method of healing I was accustomed to in my practice. I certainly believed in the value of non-traditional forms of healing. I also believed in God and that one could receive divine healing. Yet, as I nurse, I saw and engaged in activities that were very clinically based.

Over the years, I had acquired this understanding of the vital relationship between spirit, soul, and body on both a personal and professional level and began to feel frustrated with a practice that appeared to exclude access to the whole being. Art was a healing catalyst for me. Might it not provide an opportunity for healing in patients as well? I came to believe through my own experiences that art, as a healing modality, could be utilized as a nursing intervention on all planes of existence.

Blue Series
Acrylic on paper

Trying to Make it Fit

As my experiences through artistic expression deepened, body-centered care began to lose its appeal to me. As an intensive-care unit (ICU) nurse, this was devastating. My change in focus was profound and caused the thrill of ICU work to lessen along with the deep sense of satisfaction I had once experienced in my work. I found myself becoming increasingly more concerned about the state of a patient's inner being. I wanted to facilitate healing on the inside.

Over the years there has been a huge movement toward more holistic nursing practice within the overall profession, but I believe that collectively we remain far from achieving this goal. Our attempts are well meaning but sketchy and fragmented at best. We attribute spiritual care to the diseased and the dying and soul care to mental health patrons and those with disrupted coping mechanisms. Care of the body remains supreme, blatant, and obvious.

I made various attempts at trying to develop a more holistic approach within the confines of my professional nursing practice in the ICU. However, giving even more consideration to the psychological and spiritual needs of my patients was not the answer. I had always been astute in this area, and for the most part there was no change in my level of enthusiasm. However, I saw little place for the inclusion of art in my practice. And so I began the long journey of trying to find my place within nursing.

My quest has led me down many paths. To this day, however, none has completely allowed me the opportunity and freedom to implement the arts as a recognized therapeutic intervention within the domain of nursing. The usual and immediate well-meaning counsel from most friends and acquaintances in health care has been a suggestion to change my practice focus to psychiatric care. Among the many career paths I've considered, the mental health field has had the most persuasive allure. It would seem a logical place to explore. First, much of the theoretical basis for why and how art heals is grounded in the vast arenas of psychiatry, psychology, and spirituality. Second, I am absolutely fascinated with the inner dynamics of being and how my work with the arts attests to the guiding tenets of these fields of study. Yet, much like body-centered care, the focus is also narrow and non-holistic, targeting the mind and excluding vast other realms of the soul, spirit, and, of course, the body. Here too, spiritual care is secondary and often occurs as an unintentional byproduct of accessing the soul.

Perhaps, I was not going to find where I fit in nursing. Frustrated, I considered pursuing my practice in other fields, including psychology and pastoral counseling. As I systematically evaluated each choice, I found myself saying over and over again, "It's not just psych and it's not just spirit." Each of these seemed relevant to my desire to bring art to the clinical arena, but I felt that to pursue my effort from a framework other than nursing, would be leaving an enormously valuable part of me behind. I believed my nursing background more than qualified me to engage intimately with patients/clients through art. Nursing combined with my ever-growing work as an artist would be a perfect fit. But where?

A Return to Education

Determined to realize my vocation, I entered a master's degree program at the University of Massachusetts at Amherst. My passion and goal was to combine both the worlds of art and healing into one integrated practice. I believed my best chance at doing this could occur as a nurse practitioner. After all, I would have more autonomy and would be practicing with patients who, for the most part, were able to communicate. This vision did not seem to materialize. I quickly found out that I was going to be involved in primarily practicing medicine on some level and not accessing this psycho-spiritual realm with art that I so enjoyed. I did not want this exclusionary focus for my life's work. I recall throughout my studies wondering if it was too late to leave and become an art major. Was this really what I wanted for a career?

My favorite course was my master research project which I called, "A View of Emerging Spirituality of Children through Letter Writing." For this project, I appraised several letters written by children to God that I found in the book *Children's Letters to God* by Hample and

Anger
from the series "I Grieve," Sculpting on canvas

Depression
from the series "I Grieve," Sculpting on canvas

Marshall. It was wonderful! I got it! I was finally able to appraise spiritual thoughts and soulful lexis through the art form of expressive writing. I was hooked.

Mentors: A Critical Step

Working with Professor Jeanine Young-Mason, RN, EdD, on this project allowed me the opportunity to appraise this inner life that I so deeply desired to interact with. The qualitative-style research Dr. Young-Mason discussed seemed a great match for what I enjoyed and was actually necessary to properly articulate its truth and value. Her own journey and passion in realizing the vital relationship between the arts and health care has been a source of inspiration. Dr. Young-Mason and I collaborated on several art projects. These collaborations became the basis for my work titled "Metamorphosis: The Road to Recovery," for which I was awarded the 2002 Regional Pinnacle Award for Public Media: Art and also the 2003 International Pinnacle Award for Public Media: Art from Sigma Theta Tau International.

Finding someone of a like mindset was crucial for me in the development of my identity as a nurse-artist and the continuation of my quest to integrate the arts and healing. I knew of no one else involved in this effort. The landmark work by Peggy Chinn and Jean Watson called *Art & Aesthetics in Nursing* (1994) had not yet been published, and it was not until my last few semesters of graduate school that I became aware that there was even a discipline called art therapy. I decided it best to complete my graduate studies and became determined to later develop a practice incorporating the arts and healing.

Transitioning After Graduate Studies

I held a variety of nursing positions over the next few years, including practicing in community health, teaching, and nurse practitioner work in emergency medicine. For me, nothing has been quite as rewarding as my work with art. I decided to stop putting the major focus on finding the right career path and continue to create art, right were I was.

Nurse-Artist or Artist-Nurse?

I continued to create art that was meaningful to me—art that expressed what I was feeling and experiencing in everyday life. One winter, while enjoying a long stretch of time off, I gave myself permission to work on some pieces I had been visualizing for some time. These images formed the basis for my first gallery exhibit and have been profitable in reproduction. I called the series *The Process* as it aptly conveyed my life over the last few weeks and months. My artist statement attests to this:

> *The Process* is a series of works spanning the last several years of my life. It is an incomplete collection, incomplete in that it is as a series of windows opening at various points to reveal glimpses of an ongoing journey.
>
> *The Process* for me as an artist is an illustration of my spiritual walk with God. Each picture, born of a new thought, a new fear, a new disappointment, or a new experience, reveals the intimate exchange of Spirit and Life between me and The Almighty. This exchange is dynamic, ever flowing, moving fully through the deepest spectrum of human emotion. It is from this place that each piece of art is conceived. Be it in the form of a familiar character from scripture or a nameless figure, they are the visual manifestation of the lived experience, of a sacred relationship.
>
> Your individual interpretive response to these illustrations may be quite different from my own. And that is how it should be. For that is the inherent beauty of art: the ability to uniquely stir and stimulate inner movement. I hope only that you remain present to feel and listen to how each one may speak to you. For that indeed is the secret of "The Process."

Transformation

Creating "The Process" was literally and figuratively a defining moment for my work as an artist. First, to promote the work required I communicate who I was and what my artwork was about. Articulating this endeavor was crucial because doing so was a means of validating its relevance to my life and signifying the transformation taking place within me. I began to see myself as an emerging artist. It also became the basis for creating a portfolio, developing advertising and marketing strategies, and initiating a business plan. These business concepts were foreign to me, but I quickly utilized resources from the public library and small business groups, and I joined a local artist league for support and guidance.

Now, with encouragement from family and friends, I decided to look for venues to show and sell my work. As I had developed a personal attachment to much of my work, I found parting with the originals difficult. By collaborating with a graphic artist, I had several images reproduced which allowed me to keep the originals and permitted mass production at reasonable cost to the consumer.

My first opportunity to show my art came from a local hospital that maintained a small gallery. I took two framed reproductions for exhibit and waited. Within a few weeks, I received a call from a patron inquiring about purchasing the piece titled "Little Faith." To my surprise, she informed me the piece she had seen on the wall had already sold and that she wanted to order two of them. She shared with me a recent personal difficulty and how the artwork had seemingly captured the experience of it. She said it gave her hope. I was thrilled! The shear fact that another human being found enough meaning in my work to want to own it was both humbling and inspiring. I am forever grateful for the many such interactions clients and patrons have shared along this journey. They are always timely, spurring me on as I continue this venture. Seeing art as an avenue for healing was fast becoming a reality.

Little faith
Charcoal, pastel and ink on paper

Exploring a variety of media such as charcoal, inks, paints, and pastels provided me the tools necessary to interpret process into imagery. My art embraced themes of soul, spirit, and elements found in the natural world. I attributed my life experiences, personal quest to know God, and background in nursing as avenues of connectedness with the human condition, a distinct inspiration for my artistic expression. While continuing to develop both a body of work and my artistic skills, I began inquiring, internally and through the literature, about the

"I attributed my life experiences, personal quest to know God, and background in nursing as avenues of connectedness with the human condition, a distinct inspiration for my artistic expression."

connection between art and healing. Precisely what was it that made art therapeutic?

As an artist, I found I possessed a gift of healing. I believe artists are entrusted with the care of another's soul, speaking spirit to spirit, and "deep calling unto deep" (Psalm 42:8). My work as an artist was consequential. The healing potential of art appeared to lie in its power to communicate. While preparing for an upcoming exhibit, I contemplated this revelation through the use of poetry:

Art communicates ... love, joy, sorrow, pain,
beauty,
hopelessness, helplessness, grief ...
and hope itself,
disgust, rage, passion, horror,
and every range of thought, feeling, and emotion,
spiritual expression, religious expression,
oppression,
obsession,
political views, history, freedom,
dreams,
family, culture, ethnicity,
the natural world around us,
the wonder of birth and pain of death.

Art communicates through ... line and form, value, composition,
color,
shadow, texture, tone,
in use of space,
in abstract thought,
in hauntingly realistic imagery,
in bizarre symbolism.

Art communicates by ... educating, warning, admonishing,
confrontation,
motivation,
stimulation of thought and action,
it is evoking, provoking, revealing
and cathartic.

Awakening
from the series "Metamorphosis the Road to Recovery," Charcoal and pastel on paper

Decision
from the series "Metamorphosis the Road to Recovery," Charcoal on paper

I have seen what can happen when one encounters art that is most meaningful. It moves people in countless ways. I have seen strangers weep, confess hidden pain, and share private joys. People talk to the art, walk away from the art, or remain solemnly silent before it. I have seen people overcome with the presence of God and those with psychiatric disturbances appear lucid and able to connect in the moment. My gift as an artist-nurse began to touch more lives than my practice as a nurse alone ever could.

I began to read. I read everything I could find pertaining to art as a healing modality. Literature from the art world, humanities, psychology, psychiatry, and spiritual practices indicated a place for art as a therapeutic intervention. My experiences with art, personally and professionally, confirmed this. My work reflected this inquiry. Still, I wanted more. What about other art forms? Were they just as effective? What of my experiences with expressive writing, classical guitar, and poetry? Surely, there must be a purpose and deeper meaning to all art forms besides entertainment.

Metamorphosis

The maxim "art imitates life" could not ring more true. As a self-proclaimed seeker of truth, I was passionate about self-discovery and concepts that govern the inner being. Once again, my artwork reflected this notion. I wanted to tackle head on my own inner turmoil. I craved authenticity. The series, "Metamorphosis: The Road to Recovery" was birthed within this environment.

Metamorphosis is a series of twelve pieces of art that illustrate and interpret the 12 steps of Alcoholics Anonymous as I understand them. Utilizing fairly rudimentary images of the human form and the life cycle of the monarch butterfly, I attempted to capture, through form and symbolism, the resulting spiritual growth and recovery process that can occur as a result of incorporating these concepts into daily life. This reflected the internalization of "Truth" for me and the subsequent emergence and manifestation of the changed, surrendered life.

Associated images surfaced as I spent time with the 12 steps. I understood that this imagery was significant. Comprehending its relevance, along with purposeful integration of such knowledge, would appear to be a crucial link in the pursuit of greater self-awareness. I am extremely indebted for a deeper acquaintance with the works of Carl Jung whose assumptions speak to the value of interpersonal relationships maintained within ourselves through imagery.

Each picture began as a basic figure lacking detail and gender identity and progressively took on a more defined form and structure. This reflected the idea that addiction knows no boundaries, age or gender. Addiction is an all-encompassing, life-draining entity which shrouds the individual in darkness. Value and color represent the presence of spirit and life; light and darkness, liberty and oppression, movement of thought, focus and energy. These are coexistent polarities germane to the pathway of sobriety.

Sharing With an Unnamed Public

Originally, this was a collection meant for private reflection. However, as I began to share the pieces with others who had come to the knowledge of recovery, their responses fascinated me. Interacting with the imagery appeared to foster a sense of insight and awareness as to the experience of addiction within their own lives. I decided to share "Metamorphosis" with others.

Opportunities for exhibit and lecture presented themselves. I began to speak with various health care personnel regarding the possible use for art in health care. Many doors opened for me as a result of my work with this series.

During my experience with "Metamorphosis," I began to see the need to incorporate an appreciation of kinesthetic awareness and the value of working with other art forms. I noticed people often had a need to express themselves with gestures and movement when interacting with the artwork. Sometimes songs, clichés, or poetry would come to their minds. Each expressive art form seemed to hold intrinsic value for specific needs. I realized this knowledge was necessary for my practice and soon entered a certificate program for healing with expressive arts.

What Is Expressive Art?

The expressive arts involve utilizing various art forms such as drawing, painting, sculpting, music, movement, dance, and storytelling for recreation and self-discovery through the creative process. We express our inner life by creating outer forms. To experience the arts in this manner simply means to express outwardly that which is otherwise, often, unspeakable.

The expressive arts allow us to be in touch with our innermost truths. Whether in metaphor, realistic imagery, movement, music, or sound, the work becomes more meaningful and substantial, and is an expression of the innermost self. Expressive art is not about creating artistically accurate work but rather work that is a part of us. It is often said that expressive artwork focuses on process rather than product. It is therefore accessible to every nurse and patient. Utilizing the arts in this fashion fosters self-awareness, creativity, and spontaneity, and may offer unparalleled insight into the inner life.

Education in the expressive arts has been extremely valuable in actual clinical application and appreciation of client interactions. The theoretical framework for

Forgiveness
from the series "Metamorphosis the Road to Recovery," Charcoal and pastel on paper

expressive arts has roots in the fields of: art, psychology, psychiatry, spirituality, and mind-body theory. The works of Carl and Natalie Rogers, Carl Jung, Shaun McNiff, Roberto Assigioli, Jacob Moreno, the Bible, and many others are integrated in my understanding and practice of the expressive arts. I remain partial to the existential-humanistic philosophies, which remain interwoven in my eclectic approach. I agree with a quote from John Bradshaw (1992) whose work also has been profoundly influential to me. From his book *Creating Love*, he states, "While I stand on the shoulders of giants, I take responsibility for my interpretations of all of the sources I have mentioned." I possess deep gratitude for those who have laid such rich foundational truths on which I may continue to build

Equipped with greater comprehension of the working dynamics of expressive art, I created a series of five sculptures titled, "I Grieve." This effort was first and foremost an outpouring of my soul, exploring the depths of my own grief within the context of Dr. Elizabeth Kubler Ross' work with death and dying. In this series, denial, anger, bargaining, depression, and acceptance became concrete realities, taking the form of corresponding human faces twisted with emotion. This work reflected the shared human experience of grief, loss, and the process of dying. It mirrored and paralleled the contorted countenance and anguish in suffering of body and soul.

Sharing this work with individuals and small groups permitted me access to an inner world both to understand and to facilitate an

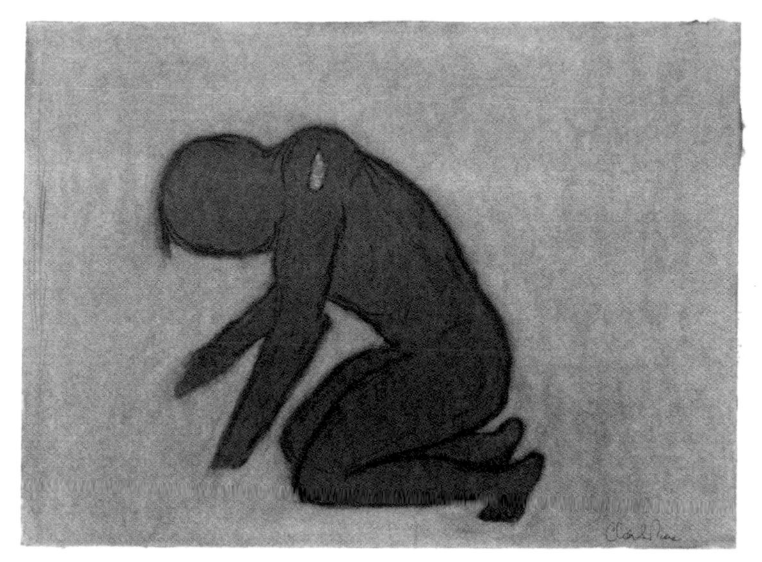

Humility
from the series "Metamorphosis the Road to Recovery,"
Charcoal and pastel on paper

individual's method of grieving. Once again, participant response was fantastic. I received the 2004 National Pinnacle Award for Public Media: Art from Sigma Theta Tau International for my efforts with this series titled "I Grieve: An Application of the Expressive Arts to the Grieving Process."

Seize the Day

Developing expertise with the expressive arts has been the most gratifying work imaginable. Workshops, lectures, writing, and consultant work with therapists involving clients from all over the world have been the outcome of my work with the arts. While opportunities have been sporadic, new doors seem to present themselves as I am able to pursue art for my life's work. I am hopeful such prospects will include developing art and healing programs; completing several unfinished book manuscripts for eventual publication; teaching others around the globe how to access their inner world through art; and continuing to create, exhibit, and sell my artwork.

The continual recognition from the world of nursing for my work as an artist and expressive arts facilitator has been an incredible honor and continues to provide the impetus to continue my advocacy for art within the domain of nursing. Although I have been fortunate to experience a significant level of success, frequent frustrations, scarcity of funding, and disappointments incurred along the way often seem to outweigh my achievements. Focusing on these setbacks obscures my view of the future, causing me to feel—and therefore be—stuck. This happens repeatedly.

Thankfully, I came across the work of author Saul Bellow (1996). Bellow's attitude possessed a peculiar similarity to my own philosophy and yet seemed to hold the key to my impasses. In his literary classic *Seize the Day*, Bellow pens the words of Dr. Tamkin. Tamkin, a pivotal character, is describing his life's work to Wilhelm, the

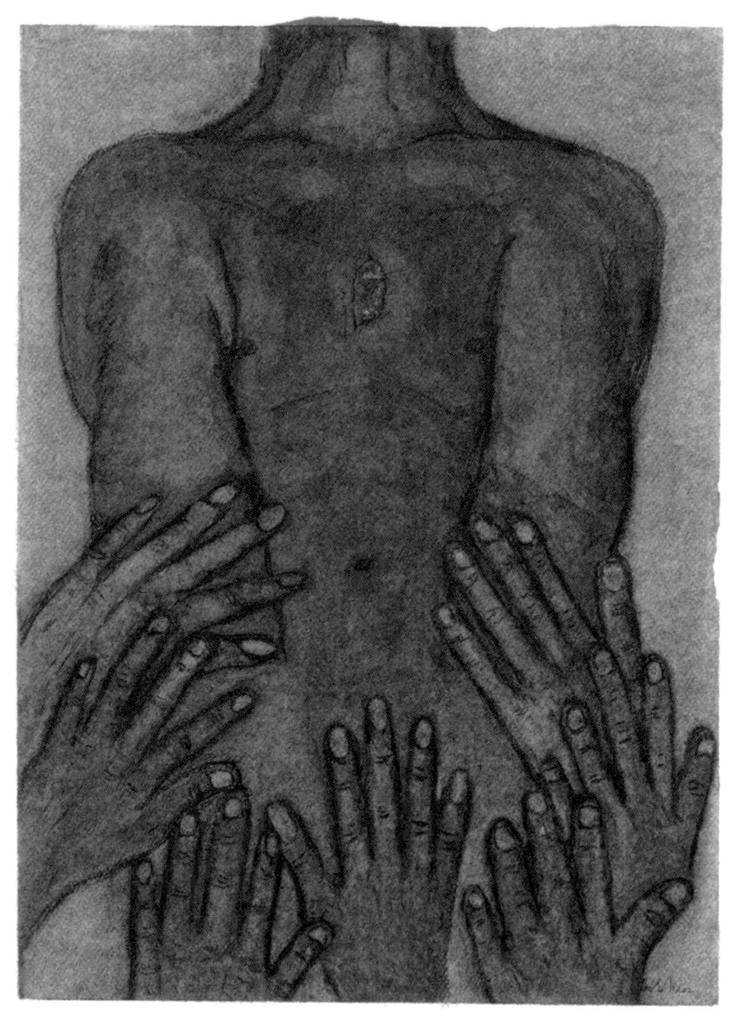

Restoration
from the series "Metamorphosis the Road to Recovery," Charcoal and pastel on paper

book's protagonist. Dr. Tamkin suggests the primary objective or highest calling is the passion found in sharing his gift. Monetary gain appears to be a secondary but inevitable byproduct of such a perspective.

"With me," said Dr. Tamkin, "I am at my most efficient when I don't need the fee. When I only love. Without a financial reward. I remove myself from the social influence. Especially the money. The spiritual compensation is what I look for. Bringing people into the here and now. The real universe. That's the present moment. The past is no good to us. The future is full of anxiety. Only the present is real, the here and now. Seize the day."

Bellow accomplishes with words what any great artist achieves on canvas. He beautifully illustrates the heart of the matter, thereby illuminating the way. This ever-so-slight shift in perspective is liberating. The answer to Tamkin's success is found in the diligent business of sharing the gift and staying present with each opportunity, in the here and now. This viewpoint is freeing, causing me to agree with Bellow that: "Only the present is real, the here and now. Seize the day." ♥

Surrender
from the series "Metamorphosis the Road to Recovery," Charcoal on paper

Acknowledgements

This chapter is dedicated to the memory of my mother, Joyce Impoco, for her life and "the gift." And to my husband Raul Nieves who through example has taught me the beauty of living life fully present in the moment.

REFERENCES:

Bellow, S. (1996). *Seize the day*. New York: Penguin.

Bradshaw, J. (1992). *Creating love: The next great stage of growth*. New York: Bantam.

Chinn, P. & Watson, J. (1994). *Art & Aesthetics in Nursing*. Boston, MA: Jones and Bartlett.

Hample, S. & Marshall, E. (1991). *Children's letters to God*. New York: Workman.

Scripture references from *New American Standard Reference Bible*. Chicago: Moody.

The Passage

by Christina Impoco Nieves

The Passage, 1998, was created through the media of charcoal and colored pencil. This image was inspired by the life and loss of my mother-in-law, Modesta Nieves.

Early summer of 1998 brought along the devastating diagnosis of pancreatic cancer to Modesta. In the months to follow, we, the family, as well as Modesta, prepared for her passage in this little room, until her death in the early fall.

Being honored to speak at her funeral, I wrote, "We watched as you struggled to release yourself from this moment in time, into eternity. As a caterpillar in cocoon transforms into chrysalis and finally emerges in the fullness of beauty and liberty as a butterfly, so did you." In the weeks following her death, these words and subsequent image took shape within me as "The Passage." The little room and people appear to be shrouded in death and sorrow as represented by the deep tones of charcoal. Life manifests as a colorful butterfly. An angel, barely visible, releases her to continue on her journey.

My work on The Passage has been healing to me in accepting the death of this dear woman. My perception of death has been made somewhat more hopeful as I am able to perceive it as a difficult but natural part of life's journey. This in turn has translated into a greater ability to minister hope and presence to those experiencing the painful transition of The Passage.

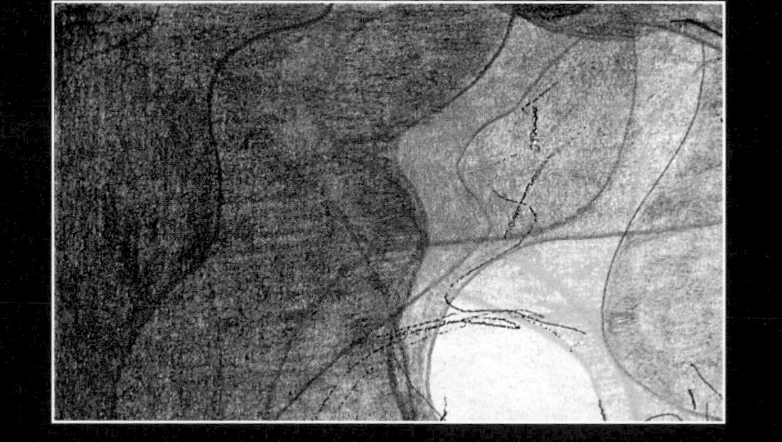

Reflections: Nurses' Interiority Unfolding

After the Battle: In a Room Where We Have Tried to Save a Life

by Jeanne Bryner

The curtain is pulled and it is time
to lift the oxygen from the nose
be careful of the hair's cilia.

I hurry to turn off hissing
of hoses and machines.
I have been here before

Wetting a white cloth for the face,
sliding down the jaw's crease
and landing in a neck

Filling slowly with lavender.
I am lost in a glacier
of glistening spittle and the mouth

Surprised in an "O."
I am afraid of the undressing
how the arms straighten

For a gown of blue flowers.
I have been here before
washing the hands of a man

And thinking of my children
on busy August days.
Falling, falling. There is not time

To clean out all the palms hold.
The black wheels turn as I
wipe gel from the rib cage

And trace a burn mark on the chest.
I want to kiss it. I want to kiss it.
Once, long ago I would know where

To gather roots for a poultice,
how to kneel and be forgiven.
Another face enters the room, a woman.

Together we roll this trunk
these four limbs. I have been here before.
Sour breath of warm stool mushrooms

Inside the buttocks. I hear the sound
of running water and throw
the body's mud away. A final sigh

Or moan comes after this.
It is the wind and not a complaint.
There is a strange land ahead.

Here, take this pillow, for its dreams.
I am afraid, so I talk about rain
and a trip we may take to Scotland

How the grass is tall there and the music
pure. The man's journey has started,
and I'm looking to see if I can tell

Anything about the road. I have lost
something in the business of heart scribbles
and paper strips curled upon this floor.

I toss them like confetti.
Once, long ago the needles were swords
and the man was a knight, maybe a king.

His blood meant battles for a god,
for honor, a country.
His spirit is a hawk circling.

I have been here before, crying
picking up heads on the moor
knowing it is done.

A Lesson from the "Phantom"

by M. Cecilia Wendler

It was a hectic sort of day, one that began ordinarily, with my name on top of the list of nurses "floating." Staffing other units during time of fluctuating census is a common occurrence in acute care, and as a registered nurse on a surgical ICU, I have come to view these days as special opportunities for growth. It was in this unlikely situation that I would discover the lesson from the "Phantom of the Opera," the true meaning of compassion and the importance of the aesthetic link in nursing practice.

I had been reflecting for days following my attendance at the "Phantom of the Opera," the Andrew Lloyd Weber opera whose Twin Cities run had found me in the audience on three different occasions. I was engaged in a lively inner exploration of the meaning and nuances of this important production, learning lines and discussing at length its imagery and implication. Many of my friends and nursing colleagues had also attended, creating fascinating conversation at work and at home. But it was a patient, her husband, and a day of "floating" that gave me a fullness of understanding of the true meaning of the work.

I had been asked to help out on the medical ICU that day, a welcome assignment to our "sister" unit. It was a very busy place that day; the morning passed breathlessly as both of my assigned patients underwent interventional cardiology procedures. Soon it was midday.

The charge nurse requested that I assist in providing nursing care during lunchtime break periods. I approached one nurse in an isolation room who gratefully indicated she was more than ready for lunch. As the nurse peeled off her isolation garb, I was offered this terse report: "She has a weird fungal infection; she's dying. We just got the Do Not Resuscitate order. The husband has been in denial, but now he has finally agreed. By the way, he's dysfunctional. He doesn't like much of anyone, so just stay clear of him. Actually, you don't have to do anything in here; I'll be back in 45 minutes." And she was gone.

As I gowned, gloved, and masked for contact and respiratory isolation, I remembered the music from "Phantom" and the ballroom scene: "Masquerade! Paper faces on parade, Masquerade! Hide your face so the world will never find you." I smiled to myself at the metaphor—and then I entered the room.

The room was darkened, the shades, pulled. My patient, a young woman, lay chemically paralyzed and massively edematous. Eight IV pumps infused pressors, sedatives, paralytics, and painkillers; a Swan and arterial tracing added glow. The room was cluttered with the evidence of a prolonged hospitalization: two sets of pneumoboots; several wash basins; support stockings washed of their soiling yet again, now, hanging to dry; a cooling blanket; extra linen; trash filled, even overflowing; and the monitoring screen smeared with some unknown substance. The hiss of the ventilator filled the room. But the moment that stopped the sense of time passing was the first instant I saw the husband.

He, too, was gowned, gloved, and masked. He sat on the edge of a chair too small for his hulking body, hands crossed over that of his wife, his face buried in the bedclothes. He did not look up when I entered the room.

"Oh, my..." I thought, "where can I begin?" The computer screen flashed for the patient's current vitals. An IV bag was nearly dry. There was enough cleaning to attend to, to fill two hours of time. And all I could do was to look at this sad man.

It is always a deep challenge to come into an intense situation such as this when there is no relationship established. But I wanted, very much, to reach out to him, this husband, and this soon-to-be widower, to let him know I could see and understand his pain. What I could not seem to do was to find the words that would help me to meet his inner self.

At that very moment, the finale of the "Phantom" replayed before my eyes. In my head, I could see Christine, the heroine of the opera, laying on the stage. She had just expressed her hatred of the Phantom, who demanded Christine choose between the death of her lover or an eternity spent in darkness with the Phantom. In that instant, Christine finally perceived the anguish, loneliness, and pain of the Phantom's loveless life and performed a miraculous act of compassion. She stands, fully upright, caresses his horrible face, and sings: "Pitiful creature of darkness; what kind of life have you known? God give me courage to show you, you are not alone." And then she kisses him. Fully. On the mouth.

At that moment, that timeless instant, I, too, knew what to do; a voice in my head said clearly and simply: "Choose compassion." I approached the figure of the bent-over husband, placed my hand gingerly and lovingly on his shoulder, and whispered to him: "Sir, would you accept some comfort from a stranger?"

The result of my touch and those few words were transformative, for him and for me. He stood fully upright, all six-plus feet of him and wrapped his massive arms around my shoulders. He buried his face in my arms and he cried. And he cried. And he cried. And all I did was—*hold him.*

I accomplished nothing in terms of physical care for that patient for those few short minutes. But I bridged the gaping chasm in the life of this young husband, father, and soon-to-be widower, by recognizing his suffering and compassionately offering myself to him. Our time together was brief but rich and powerful, and I am certain that the experience was as life-renewing for him as it was for me.

I am convinced that the secret to longevity in bedside nursing is in full openness to the experiences that confront us every day. The renewal of self—preventing the overwhelming loss of the nurse's being-in-the-world, while witnessing suffering, struggle, and death—lies not in the "doing" of nursing but in the "being" of nursing. We cannot be afraid to kiss the Phantom, because, when we do, like the Phantom, we can finally and forever leave behind the safe mask of professional separation and engage openly in the compassionate caring that distinguishes us as nurses. ♥

Sunshine and Shadows

by Sharon R. Hovey

The HeART of Nursing is expressed in the simple but elegant beauty of this adaptation of a traditional Sunshine and Shadows quilting pattern. Health and illness are reflected in the gold-flecked navy triangles—our human fabric of health contains scattered episodes of illness. These navy triangles are repeated in the design and depict the "sameness" of those for whom we care. The shaded triangles represent the diversity and uniqueness of those individuals, families, and communities cared for by nurses. The color and size variety of the shaded triangles portrays various developmental stages of the human experience. The mountainous climb of life is ever ascending—expressed with the upward direction of each multicolored triangle. The yellow-gold center offers warmth and renewal for the human spirit. Framed in gold, rich in color and symbolism, this creation provides distinctive expression, enjoyment, and peace. ♥

Reprinted from "Miniature Quilt Ideas" handout, 1996, p.41.

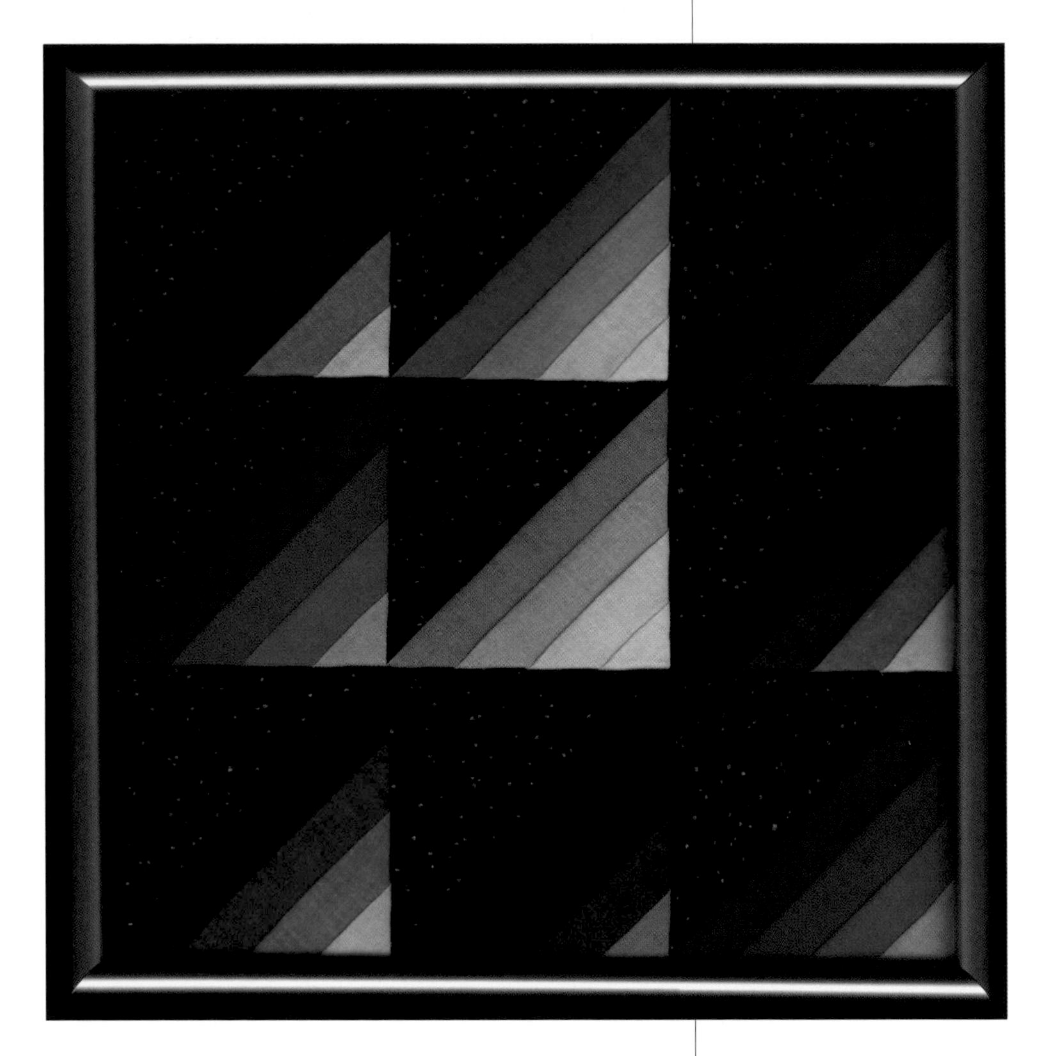

Reflections from 25 Years of Nursing

by Deborah B. Borawski

The English professor dying with
hepatic cancer
He had commanded English literature,
Shakespeare, Chaucer, Dickens.
In his cold gray pallor, had command
of nothing…
(My first patient to die.)

The three year old, on a ventilator,
whose parents had tried to keep quiet
by giving her Nyquil…
every hour.

The young Muslim man who had
slit his own throat
because his family had been shamed.
Did he have the same God I did?
He held this *Koran* on his chest
all the time.

The well-to-do businessman,
who wore gold rings
and whose heart was
so weak from infarctions
that we were afraid to let him lift his arms
lest he fibrillate.
It happened.

The wheezing, rasping,
emaciated TB patient
Demanding and angry,
helpless and frightened. Isolated.

The young Hispanic mother
who labored all night
and suddenly her placenta abrupted.
The baby died,
the mother bled out.
We lost them both.

The alcoholic who we've detoxed
again and again.
He's amorous with a 0.40
and begins to fight as he comes down.
No family, except a sister
who won't take him home.
He can play country music and sing.
Used to play professionally.
What a waste.

The teenager who tried
the little black seeds
that grew our behind the barn,
on a dare from his buddies.
Crazy; out of his mind.
We tied him down; tried to pump his
stomach;
Then he vomited all over me.
I knew this kid.

The old lady who was told
she would have to wait
until she finished eating
before being put on the bedpan.
She messed the bed
and then cried.

The woman who was always in
the hospital.
The staff hated to take care of her.
She was always on the bell,
wanting something,
anything just to get you in there.
We didn't have time for her.

The perfect preemie that wouldn't
breathe.
We took its picture for mom and dad.
I wrapped it in a blanket
and took it to the morgue refrigerator.
The security officer was with me.
I couldn't cry.

The grandfather who didn't come back
to the house on time.
His grandson found him
Under his tractor in a ditch.
If only someone had gone with him…

The institutional patient with
tertiary syphilis who chases me
waving my own umbrella,
because she thought it belonged to her.
I had keys. She didn't.
I got out.
She died there.

The First Day Fell Like a Blow

by Peggy Flauta

The first day fell like a blow.

Not your first day, oh no—
you had been there,
(and I avoided you and yours with a mother's dread)
Secretly,
Desperately,
I hoped that you would die
before I had to look in your mother's eyes

and feel her pain...
hunger for breath that does not come
But you lived,
or, rather, grappled with death...

And the first day came, and went.

The second day came
And lingered
And suffered;
red blur in cruel, muted tones
mingled with (my) pain and (my) fear
Still, you made it.

I left in that strange daze...
Feeling hurt
And angry,
Life-drained.
It was dark outside, still dark
(I hadn't seen the sun in two days)

I couldn't know "why,"
find "purpose";
but felt a pressing need to profit from this
horrible experience

If
the Life drained from me
and the Love I gave
helped to sustain you, then I say:
"Take it.
I give it willingly
and gratefully..."

Your beautiful eyes,
and the adoration in your mother's eyes,
are worth
a few nights' sleep.

Driving in Circles: A Metaphor for Life

by Frances R. Vlasses

In my town, many mothers like myself spend many hours driving car pools, driving around town, picking up, dropping off, talking, meeting, the comings and goings of daily life…snippets of mindless actions to world rulers. None of this is on the 6 o'clock news. Why should it be? This is just REAL LIFE: the hidden work that happens by thinking, caring, loving, listening, hugging and sharing our ways through the stories of a child's triumphs (passing the test), a teenager's trials (getting cut from the team), a husband's jungle since he, too, gets driven to the commuter train.

A sociologist could study the contents of our cars and know us. We have a variety of supplies, varying by age and life cycle: handiwipes, juice boxes, pacifiers, sheet music, golf clubs, Band-Aids, old French fries, tissues available for all who enter here.

Our family signature can be found in our tape collection. Beauty and the Beast, lots of sixties stuff, Van Halen, philosophy of science, measurement in nursing research, nursing articles. Obviously this is the car of a doctoral student mom with a 9- and 14-year-old music lover and a 60s kind of dad, hidden behind a tie. This husband and wife inhabit their twenty-year-old first marriage with their standard two children. They are curious beasts in the 90s. The "average-ness" of this household masks the conundrums caused by this configuration.

At first glance, my driving in circles has no meaning—a mindless task: "delivering" the children, a task easily criticized by some as early socialization to yuppie life. But what all the car-pooling mothers know is that what you see actually blurs the truth. For in these tasks, like so much caring work, is the essence of a woman's life. For as you know, the dropping off and picking up is only the vehicle for the hearing, talking and connecting that is the making of meaning for this family.

I imagine myself as not much different from my ancestors: cave women who gathered and dispersed food and nurturance to children; being among other women—keeping the dialogue going as the tasks of life take place, evoking meaning from the landscape. Yet slowly she goes. She learns and teaches—how to intersect, interpret, get what is needed without excessive intrusion, all the while taking in the voices of children, friends, nature. Maybe developing a philosophy of man that didn't get written—arms and hands are for other things. Some would later derisively call this common sense or caring.

The philosophy tapes connect me outward to the non-Mom part of me, the doctoral student world. In my work life, I have also been known as hard driving, yet I find myself driving in circles in this part of the nursing world. Sometimes I am driven to pursue an idea; sometimes the ideas just entangle themselves in the circles of my mind.

I drive on in both lives but wonder how meaning is created in this second world that only I experience. A world where I circle the library, the exams and the "hoops": the paradox, which defies any type of logic. For example, on dissertation topics: "You must feel passionate about it," I am told, "or else you'll never get it done." And "It is not your life's work." Does anyone else see the irony in this?

Where, exactly, does one find a problem that one cares deeply about and yet will be easily abandoned upon completion? Many have, I am told by those who say how much they *hate* their dissertation and never publish any of it.

But back to the driving.... There is little or no meaning in these tasks (a scary thought), but activity alone is meaningless. The meaning waits to be created. Where I go for this is significant, back to a place where I could be about the business of care, and in that process, being cared for—a practice home.

Yes, I return to a place 800 miles away where what I saw, did and heard made "sense" to me. Where clinical nurses made sense of their work through a shared struggle with illness, bureaucracy and complex personalities. At Grace Hospital I learned many ways of making sense of the troubles I saw, and it was nurses who helped me find my way of making sense. I understand now that it only makes sense in my practice home. Some say if it makes sense in practice, it makes sense.

And I can use this practice home now, to help me make sense when academia comes crashing in, trying to distort my world with competition, "objective" logic, and other alienating rules of order and control. Lest I too become beaten down by the humdrumedness of driving in circles and accept someone else's reality for these tasks, I accept a nurseworld I saw in practice as my "conceptual framework" for creating work systems and practice environments that give meaning to the work of care, the work of nursing.

The community of caring that I found among nurses at this hospital helped me to create a reality from which I now question my student world, and to which I often return (sometimes like a psychotic patient). Many here try to tell me I imagined this experience at Grace (a delusion?), a practice home. But I know it is real, for I hold it in my mind.

It may be gone now, I don't know. I know it once was. I carry it with me. IT causes me "trouble." It makes me not fit, because it is the way I make sense of the nursing world, and others object to it. It is a little like having an address on the other side of the tracks.

Communities of caring can exist, if in no other way than through shared struggle, a commitment to similar values for caring, and an acceptance that we may go after these values in very divergent ways. Find it in you, wherever you keep it—your practice home—for it helps us to make sense, and so we can help others make sense of it too. Maybe, some of us just drive car pools, are just a Mom, just a nurse. Not me, not us, those of us who are part of caring communities. We know how to find the meaning in jobs just like these. ♥

Adventuring Toward Renewal

by Michele Burkstrand

Adventuring—leaving my ordinary life and engaging in a broader exploration of the world—is both a platform and a theme in my process of artistic exploration and inner renewal. Through the lens of my cameras, and away from home, I see and experience a new life, and gain perspectives that energize and ground my personal life and my nursing practice. The product of these adventures —the photographs—provide a visual reminder of these wonderful times, energizing and informing others as I tell the associated stories.

Majestic Morning

I have been a nurse for over 15 years, and even though my job as a nurse is very rewarding in and of itself, I never really thought about how I keep engaged in the difficulties of patient care year after year. As a bedside nurse or as a charge nurse in a busy, university-affiliated surgical intensive care unit, it is not uncommon to have to make decisions that dramatically affect patient care or outcomes. The context is intense, and no days are the same. Because of the demands of this environment of patient care, it is especially important to plan for and engage in renewal activities. When I realize that I'm beginning to lose focus, I know it is time to plan another adventure, in order to renew my energy and refresh my attitude.

Sometimes all I need to do is take a day off, organize and prioritize my personal life and then I feel like I can focus on my practice anew. Other times I need to revitalize my inner self by doing something creative and totally different. I have done crocheting, needlepoint, and ceramics off and on for many years, but when I need to really jump-start my "attitude," that is when I need to take time for me, through photography.

Growing up, my family would take trips either in or out of state at least twice a year, and that is where my love of travel started. When I was about 13, my parents gave me an inexpensive camera to use on one of our trips and that's when I discovered the joys of photography.

Now, whenever I go out of town, for a day or for weeks, I bring along my camera. Even a short trip results in many photographs, because I take numerous pictures. I play with the camera, trying a different approach; I'll take two or even three shots of one subject, trying a new filter or a different angle, to create a different feeling or mood. I've discovered I can take chances with my photography that I cannot take

A Bouquet of Color

at work. I can linger, experience, and work to capture the feeling that the moment creates, in a way that is entirely different than the unfolding demands of critically ill patients. The photographs become both a memory captured and a visual point that allow me to tell the story of the moment once I've returned home. When I later share my best photographs with my friends at work, it creates both an artistic sharing of the moment passed and allows others to enjoy a "mini-vacation" as I tell the story of the picture. By showcasing the pictures to others, I can relive the trip over and over again, savoring its pleasures.

A recent trip to Kenya provided many opportunities to photograph the unique flora and fauna of Africa. One of the first mornings there, I glimpsed this aged, bull elephant in the foreground of Mt. Kilimanjaro, and I was humbled and honored to see this majestic sight. It puts into perspective how small we are in "the big picture" of the world. This photograph reminds me that even the littlest kindness that I offer as a nurse can have great meaning for a patient. When the patient feels good, that is the best reward for me, and it makes me feel like I made a difference in the big picture of the world.

After joining a photography club a couple of years ago, I started to realize that I never noticed how beautiful flowers and plants are. I never took the time to stop and really look at the details of design and texture of plants, and after doing so I see how delicate and intricate they are. Patients, too, can be very complex with their diagnoses and health problems; yet we need to remember that they are also delicate and intricate in the context of their lives. Beautiful flowers and complex people are both very interesting and unique in their own ways. The brilliant colors of these African flowers, against a primarily brown landscape, highlight their beauty beyond words.

When I return from these adventures, I re-engage in my nursing practice with vitality and a sense of peace, eager to share the photographic memories and stories. This sense of renewal and focus helps me to remain enthusiastic about the difficult challenges of the care of patients… until it is time to travel again. ♥

African Poinsettia

Going from Knowing to Unknowing

by Catherine Fraser

Healthcare is stressful for both professionals and patients who face a variety of unknowns. Creativity as aesthetic and personal knowing can help with managing fear and the mysteries surrounding health and illness. Nurses and other healthcare professionals can use the creative process as a means of self-care. Clients can use creativity to increase awareness and self-understanding of biological and psychological processes like birthing, healing, disability, and dying. The ideas and my images broaden the concept of creativity and increase the appreciation of how life experiences provide a foundation and vehicle for practice

I have reflected on my experiences as a nurse, art therapist, and artist. My way of understanding, my way of synthesizing and understanding experience is through creativity and image making—or art. I am interested in expanding the concept of creativity, whether through social interaction and art-making or interpreting an experience.

Going from Knowing to Unknowing
by Catherine Fraser

From Knowing to Unknowing

This image was made with acrylic paint and watercolour crayons. The words "going from knowing to unknowing" encapsulate my theme. The left side of the image depicts analytical concepts and measurable knowledge. The figure on the right represents a being at the threshold of understanding and not understanding. The right side is the quiet, meditative, non-verbal, visual, mysterious place of gestation and creativity that is waiting to unfold.

The images "Joy of Being in the Body" and "Sharing Moments" depict the importance of being in our bodies and connecting with self and others. I did these images (2 of 29) while recuperating from surgery. Engaging in this activity helped me cope with the pain and enhanced my sense of well-being and healing.

In art-making, a person uses art materials, is open to the flow, and incorporates intuitive and aesthetic knowing and layers of meaning. In this process, a person is called to pay attention and may not know at first or fully understand the meaning of the experience. Over time, the meaning unfolds. The visual is another way of knowing, experiencing, and being.

As a discipline, nursing has focused on tasks and scientific knowing. More recently nursing has gained a wider focus that includes other dimensions of knowing such as intuition and imagination. Incorporating all ways of knowing into nursing practice and experience is important for improving client care. We often deal with medical tasks that relate to physical and emotional bodies. But it is also important to address people as spiritual beings that are multidimensional. Three of those vital dimensions are the aesthetic (appreciation of beauty), the creative, and the mysterious or unknowing. Unknowing is that which relates to the mysterious—to awe and forces in this world much larger than ourselves.

Nurses deal with knowing and unknowing in relationship to birth, life, and death. Nursing and the creative act take courage, faith, and trust that the expressions of knowing are intended. Events like the Severe Acute Respiratory Syndrome (SARS) outbreak of 2003 brought home to me, in a concentrated way, the importance of self-care and dealing with the unknown.

I believe art-making and creativity is healing and has great value in my practices, in client self-expression, and for workers' self-care. It is important to bring all types of knowing into our practices—especially aesthetic, personal knowing, and creativity.

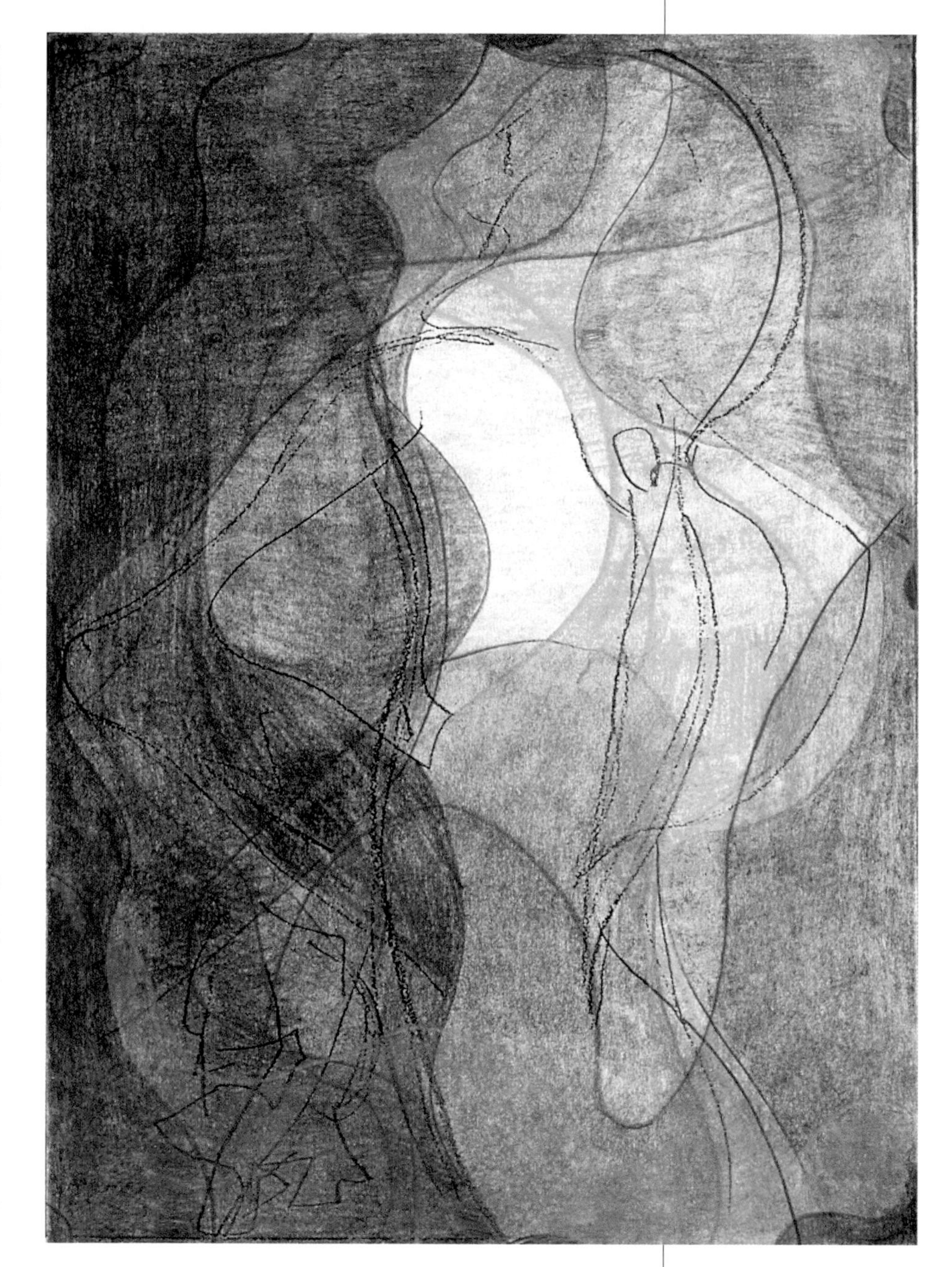

Joy of Being in the Body
by Catherine Fraser

Sharing Moments
by Catherine Fraser

Grief*

by M. Cecilia Wendler

It is a slow swim upward,
This return to the surface

Enough time has passed that
I am surprisde when, ambushed
once again,
by my quicksand loss —
It sucks me under,
Threatens to envelope me —
Especially if I fight it.

I learned long ago, as a child, that
the way to survive a plunge into quicksand is
simply
to
STOP.

Breathe slowly,
Move with agonizing care,
Reach out:

For a branch
For a friend
For an anchor.

Grasp tightly.
Then.
inch forward,
slowly,
until,
muddied,

You pull yourself free.

**Dedicated to the memory of Joe Taft*

What Lies Within

by Tonia L. Marine

One of the many lessons I have learned in my career as a geriatric nurse is that, many times, death is not the enemy. The hardest, darkest shifts I have spent are the ones where someone is in the process of dying and cannot seem to get there. I go home after an 8- or 12-hour shift in tears because I know the cycle needs to progress for this person. He (or she) needs to move to the phase of life which is death, but his body betrays him and he seems suspended between life and death, unable to move on.

In my mind, these times of dying are like the night of winter solstice: long, dark, cold, and seemingly never-ending. It becomes hard to believe that there will be light, or death, at some point. When I work with a dying person, I struggle to maintain comfort for the body that is present, and wonder where the spirit is at that time. I, like many others, assume that the body and the spirit hear me when I speak, but neither can respond. What does the spirit see now? The beauty of another side of the cycle of life? The light in the darkness?

The aurora borealis represents this time to me. A time when the spirit can see, with wisdom, both sides—life and death. This is a time when there is incredible beauty even in the darkest and longest of nights.

This pattern, called northern lights, is usually worked entirely in white. However, I chose to interpret the aurora borealis more literally, creating a representation of this phenomenon we sometimes see in the night skies of Montana. The needlework, and the variegated, undulating light it represents, serves as a reminder to me that there is beauty in dying, communication even through silence, and light even at the darkest hour.

Northern Lights by Tonia Marine

Only One Ocean

by Mitzi Grace Mitchell

This poem uses the metaphor of the ocean. Some believe that life on earth came from the ocean. Individuals can be seen as part of the ocean of humanity. Instead of seeking to label them, one can seek the essential humanity of each. Just as the ocean is intrinsically and naturally one, humanity, too, despite our labels, is also one. Once the humanness is seen in each person, his or her unique meanings, needs, hopes, and concerns can be sought. Without this understanding, one cannot get beyond the labels. One aim of nursing is to go beyond the labels and to see the fundamental humanness of each person.

Only One Ocean
We call you Atlantic, blustery and bleak.
Blood-warm and exotic, is Indian we say.
Pacific, is next, vast and unending.
Icy and frozen, we label you Artic.
Antarctic, we say is distant and desolate.

But fish do not name what they swim blithely through:
Birds do not say what they skim swiftly on.

For there's only one ocean,
always in motion.
Whatever the name,
you're always the same.

Warm moves to cold,
solid to vapor.
Only one ocean,
changeable and changeless.

Only One Ocean by Rosemary Mitchell

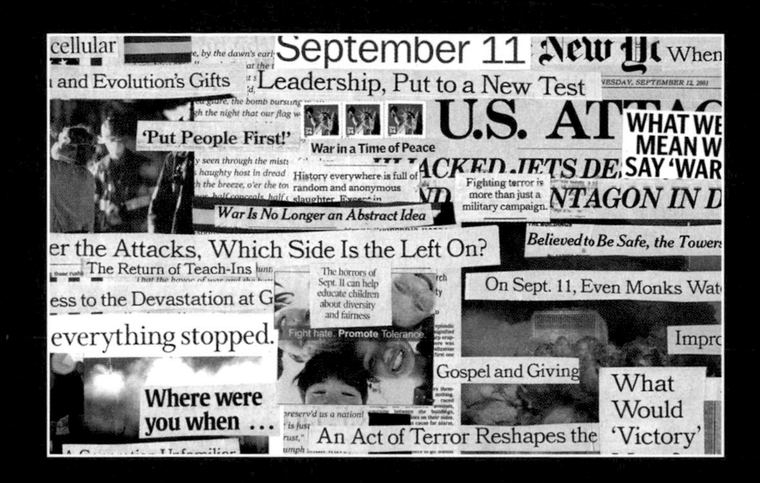

The Other is Me

Past the Signs*

byJulie R. Tower

I watch your chest move up and down
But it is not your own.
Your eyes are fixed with no response,
Your limbs but stiffened bone.
Your pulse is rapid, your pressure low
And ICP beyond belief.
I wish the nurse in me would go,
Would ignorance bring relief?
My stomach is tied all in knots
But you seem to rest in peace,
Past the signs that are telling me,
You'll soon crash, you, my brother, I see.

* *In memory of Joel Tower*

In Dependence

By June Heider Bisson

A different place,
A different space,
A different lonely.
I close my eyes
Take me home to my bed.
Separated,
My bed and I, living in difference
In between is waiting, left hanging,
Waiting;
    to go to the bathroom,
    to get a comforting sip of tea
    from my cup, that fits my hand.
Waiting for someone to pick up my remote
    from the floor
    to wait,
    for breakfast that's cold and
    not what I ordered
    Separate,
    I
    from
    mine,
needing, and not being needed.
Am I anyone?
Does waiting have a voice?

Through the Looking Glass

by Mary R. Benkert

Reflections, they can show you an image of yourself, another or place, or they can send you into deep introspective thought. My inspiration for this piece of stained glass came from a very personal nursing experience from within my own family. Over the years, this piece has gained more meaning to me in how I have shaped my professional nursing career. From its reflections, it forced me to see images of myself in my role as a nurse and to re-evaluate how professional and personal roles can be blurred, but from that a stronger, more supportive role can arise.

My desire to learn the art of stained glass became realized several years ago, when I took a class, which focused on the foil versus leaded technique of creating stained glass artwork. I loved it immediately and went out to buy my own supplies, so that I could continue to create this type of art on my own. For some time, I had been creating a leaded project in my mind, with my father in mind. I kept putting it off, since I didn't know how to do a fully leaded project, but it stuck with me. After my father was diagnosed with malignant melanoma, and I was planning a trip back to visit my parents, I knew that this project would be realized and would be brought back as a gift for my parents. It would contain etched and clear glass bevels that could reflect the sunlight from the window, where I had envisioned it would be hung, and it would contain the same dark green colors that matched the somewhat recently painted living room that my parents had updated together.

Being a total novice at the leaded technique, but using already cut bevels, I thought it would be easy to piece together without an exact plan as a guide. I thought, "This is a linear project, no rounded pieces, no glass cutting of the bevels; it should all fit together without any difficulty." I was surprised about halfway through when my linear, easy project was not square and didn't really fit the way I thought it should. I felt a sense of urgency to have this piece "just right" and to have it completed for this trip home. With much frustration and adjusting of the outer pieces to make it "fit," it was completed. It looked not bad for a first try, but I could see the imperfections it contained. It was hung in the living room window I had envisioned, for all to see.

With that visit home, I saw my father recuperating from a second surgery and receiving interferon injections from my mother. I saw him going to work every day, as he always had, but this time, looking nauseous every morning. I saw him doing everything else he had always done, but with a little less enthusiasm. It was in the plan, since I was the nurse, for me to take over the injections while I was visiting, to give my mother a break. I received the instructions from my mother as to how to give the injection, not really listening, because I was the nurse. We argued over technique, and I proceeded to give my father probably the most painful shot he had ever received. I assisted no more with injections.

I was home again that winter, after my father ended up in the ICU, when the melanoma had spread to his brain. My approach to the hospitalization, nurses, plans for rehabilitation, etc. was purely clinical. My father was just another client that needed discharge planning, coordination with the head nurses when care didn't go smoothly and talking to doctors about the plans. I was in control of these issues and could handle all of the medical situations that arose. This was my job, because I was the nurse.

When my siblings, my mother and myself would return home after our "shifts" of visiting at the hospital, we would sit by the fire in the living room. I would look at the stained glass piece in the window, reflecting sun or streetlights, and I would remember "healthier" times when my father made the fires and served us crackers and cheese before dinner.

I was back again that summer for the last month of my father's life. By that time, the front section of the living room had been converted into a hospital room, with hospice aides arriving twice daily to assist with activities of daily living. My siblings, mother and myself all took turns sleeping on the couch near my father's hospital bed, so we could attend to the feeding pump alarms and administration of medications. By that time, all members of the family had become quite adept in the nursing skills needed to keep my father comfortable. I no longer was the only nurse in the family.

My mother had kept my father's hospital schedule exactly the same when he came home. Cares and medications had not been "grouped" to allow not only my father, but also my mother, a long stretch of time to sleep at night. After clearing the threat of any medication interactions with the hospice nurse, I adjusted the schedule to a more compatible one for home care and home sanity. This one act, because I was a nurse, made a difference in all of our lives. My mother didn't have to be up at 11 PM, 1 AM and 6 AM; she could get a little more sleep and feel a little more refreshed to start the day over again.

That living room was the focus of life for all during those last few months. After my father died, we planned the final touches of his funeral, and we entertained guests after the service in the living room. It was and remains the focal area for my family's social interactions (both pleasant and unpleasant).

I was initially inspired by my father's illness to create this piece. I wanted him to proudly display my piece of art in a particular window in the living room for all to enjoy. There had been that sense of urgency to initially complete the project, even with its unequal, not "square" edges. I now know why that unknown sense of urgency existed. As I look at the glass, I see reflections from the past and present. I see how I was the nurse, not the daughter or sister during this time period. I see how that was my role and my method of coping during this difficult time. I see the mistakes I made in being "too clinical," but I also see the differences I made because of that role. I see how we all came together and apart as a family. I see tube feedings, medications, diaper changes, nights spent on couches, but also the coming together of family and friends.

That was over six years ago, but the stained glass piece remains in the same spot today. When I return home to visit, the family still spends time in that part of the living room. I look into the glass and reflect with more maturity about that time in my life where personal and professional roles became unclear. I now have more clarity as to why my nursing role overshadowed all other roles in this situation. Life isn't always perfect or the way you want it to be. There often is no exact plan to follow to help guide how all the pieces should fit together. It's not always "square," but that's OK, sometimes others don't even notice those imperfections. I will always have that "looking glass" as a reminder that it is time for reflection and OK to do so, when I admire it hanging in that window in the living room. ♥

Supplicants

by Joanne Calore Turco

Not so silent supplications
Midnight prayers from bedside breaths.

Take his pain, make it mine
Bring her peace, I will struggle.
Swap our bodies, rest our souls.

Missives hurled towards heaven's ears.
Does anyone hear?

Catharsis

by Josephine McCall

When I was a tender age, subjected to a father's rage,
Sure it was something I had done, maybe girl instead of son.
Anger boiled within my veins, then guilt for feeling—Such a shame.
Father's one you do not question. What he does is law, no flexion.
But then I think and remember Mother. (I cried some tears, as did my brothers.)
Pulled her out across the floor, slapped her face, her robe he tore.
Baby sister in her arms—he didn't care who he harmed.
So many years within my past, perhaps I had found my peace at last.

Until a child too young to fight, subject too, without a flight,
Recalls the fear that once I held and pulls out feelings I once felt,
Knocks so gently on the door behind which strong emotions store
And bids me deal with this again and realize what a war it's been
To fight my way and have a life and realize this was unearned strife.
These things I see buried deep, intended them always to sleep.
But looking in these deep blue eyes, I could not calm her tiny cries
Until I faced what I went through and came to grips with my own truths.
Then with compassion I did share and give to her total love—I cared.

Termination

by Josephine McCall

Draw the shades
Dust the tables and shelves one more time
Stack the books and run your hands across the desk
Touch your memories and think of brighter days gone by
of successes more than failures and
hope that was given to many
where none had been before

Turn off the lights and cross the threshold
Close the door with a steady and firm hand
Stand on the patio and take a deep breath

Creating Connections through Quilting: The Friendship Quilt

by Jeannie Zuk

The Friendship Quilt for a Cure started as a collaboration of nurses in the School of Nursing at the University of Colorado Health Sciences Center and grew to include additional staff and faculty from a variety of university departments. Quilting has long been known as a creative outlet for both the quilter and recipient of the quilt, providing healing, remembrance, and connection. Each of the contributors to this quilt had been touched by breast cancer in some way and wanted to use the art of quilting to convey a sense of caring to others. The squares in the quilt reflect the individual talents and personalities of each of the contributors. One of our members was diagnosed with breast cancer the month we gathered to plan the quilt; other contributors were survivors themselves, while others created quilt squares in honor of dear friends and family. The quilt is a visible and tangible representation of what nurses do best—provide care, comfort and support.

Whenever the quilt was displayed, viewers were compelled to reach out and gently touch the individual squares, running a hand over the surface of the quilt. Some of the squares were admired for the skill of the quilter, while some squares elicited tears because of the story that went with the creation of the square. Nancy's square, "Ellie's Star," pictures imagery used during chemotherapy treatments: heat radiating from a star coursing through the body, killing cancerous cells. Emanating from this star, cool, blue rays flow, signifying health and healing. Another square shows a running horse, Magic, who helped breast cancer survivor, Rosemary, believe she

Contributors to the quilt: Denny Webster, Jeannie Zuk, Nancy Holloway, Rosemary Corrigan, Sue Hagedorn, Dianne Padilla-Gutierrez, Susan Epstein, Virgil Rice, Saichai Puapan, Paula Pahl, Susan Geddes, Gay Hull, Kay Vaughn, Robbie Dyer, Susan Lawrence and Bernadette Sullivan. Photograph by Scott Arnold.

would see the next spring. Even the wooden frame that holds the quilt tells a story. Crafted by Virgil, the frame was donated in memory of Deborah, an artist, mother and friend. Deborah was pregnant with her third child when she was diagnosed with breast cancer. Virgil adopted Deborah's children after her death, and the quilt frame commemorates Deborah's life, her spirit and her gifts.

The finished quilt now hangs in the waiting room of the Breast Center at the Anschutz Outpatient Pavilion, University of Colorado Health Sciences Center, Fitzsimmons Campus. We created the "Comfort Care Fund" and raised over $5,000 in support of underinsured women receiving breast cancer treatment at the Breast Center. This fund will help women who travel long distances for chemotherapy but cannot afford overnight accommodations in the area, as well as women who cannot pay for a meal during their long treatment sessions. The quilt resonates with viewers, and many people have spent quite awhile contemplating the squares, immersed in their own thoughts. The circle of caring continues as stories about breast cancer are formulated when witnessing the quilt; the quilt became an engaging and relational process with the individual viewers. The art of the quilt enabled connection with individual women and allowed us to feel that our quilting made a difference in women's lives. The quilt represents nurses caring through action. ♥

The Faces of Oklahoma City

by A. Lynne Wagner

The face of hatred explodes on the calculated morn,
destruction of innocent lives, victims of distant cause.
The face of the building disfigured beyond recognition,
inner structures exposed and twisted in pain.
The human face, bloodied, staring,
inner spirit not yet comprehending,
protected by action to save the savable and count the dead.
The face of caring smiles and soothes
the human form under concrete slab, not yet a tomb.
The helping face responds with courage and
extraordinary strength,
risking life in unstable building,
enduring the seeping pain of human loss.
The face of horror tries to make whole
the body parts strewn among the building parts,
testimony of human fragility,
amidst the immortality of their story.
The face of youth banished from earth's life,
too early, too soon to make their mark,
except in the hearts of mourning family.
The faces of evil or God or clown,
all called up to explain, to cope with this tragedy
of man gone awry.
Which mask will be worn on the morn?
Which face will face who?
The face of hope springs up with song,
empty church pews fill,
empty words find meaning.
The God face promises a better tomorrow,
but when will the hurting stop?
When will the evil face say, "I'm sorry"?
When will the grieving face say, "I forgive"?
When will the clown face laugh?
When will the healing face build new lives?

The Lady Who Sang

by A. Lynne Wagner

She came to us in that crack between night and day,
when the world yawns together,
some yearning for sleep,
some stretching to consciousness,
but somehow connected in the dawn's shadows.
Sirens heralded her thrashing arrival
and swirling red lights magnified her mania.
Her world was alien to our sense of time.
She laid on our stretcher,
but resided somewhere we could not go.
Unapproachable, nameless, ageless,
we simply called her "the lady who sang."
and tattooed her records as "cubicle seven."
She smelled like day-old garlic,
her body tattered as her clothes,
both harboring unwelcome life that jumped at us
as we removed faded cloth to treat her wounds.
All the time she sang a tune unknown
with words that made no sense,
except to give a rhythm to her writhing soul.
As I bent to place pillow beneath her head,
just once her eyes met mine,
a small window inviting me in.
I went and saw her fear, understood.
I listened, heard her words in jumbled song.
Then gently said, "What a lovely sound.
You must love to sing."
She quieted for an instant
as I waved away the doctor
who had come to sedate her.
"I will stay and listen to your song
until you go upstairs
where another nurse will move to your rhythm.
We have a clean bed for you to heal your wounds."

Bonded now, yet separate, her cautious smile,
framed by blackened teeth amidst her melody,
ridiculed our presumption that our clean sheets
could bind her wounds so deep.
We never met again, but this her gift:
In our brief encounter
when two worlds overlapped,
I stepped beyond my shell and knew life more
Than all my books could tell.

First published in Wagner, A.L. (Summer 2000).
Connecting to nurse-self through reflective poetic story.
International Journal For Human Caring, 4 (2), 7-12.

Homeless, not Helpless, in Seattle

by Grace C. Jacobson

The homeless are a growing community of concern, not only to nurses but to all involved with health. Found in small towns as well as high population cities, some gather in groups, others are solitary. All are individuals. Care needs are basic: food, shelter, medical and dental provision, security, and love. Survival in any holistic sense requires all. Reality of obtainment varies drastically across our country, as does a modicum of welcome, acceptance and help.

Dignity, self-assurance, a sense of balance seems apparent in the man portrayed in this painting. Fortified against the chill Washington air, his body seems compressed by at least four bulky layers of faded, worn clothes, an overlarge, perhaps stuffed cap...and a sack, to tote his worldly goods. Tape secures his pant legs from drafts. Pausing outside a church he squints against the sun, facing the photographer with composure. "How is your day?" he asked, and "Yes, you may take my picture." He did not act offended or angry, defensive or ashamed. He did not strike a pose, she did not request it. "I asked to take his picture because I thought he looked like Santa Claus," my daughter said. "He was nice to talk with, although we didn't say much. And then we went our separate ways."

A human interaction, with mutual respect. Isn't that what we should be about? And if we can help provide for needs, shouldn't we? We can do this individually or as a group through legislative activity in our nursing organizations... in our communities and our country.

This picture provides a reminder of needs, but also of strengths. Church is a symbol of compassion, often a provider of food, for body and soul. The sun is bright and throws shadows: of cross...one to bear or one to guide? A crown of thorns almost is clear across his chest...or is it smudge and wear? The body shadow... bowed shadow... bowed in supplication, or hung in despair?

We make of shadows what we wish... But for the man and so many others like him, we must open our senses to recognize how and where we can assist. He is homeless, not helpless nor hopeless. He is a fellow human from whom we can learn and with whom we can share. ♥

Painful Lessons (Parts One and Two)

by Peggy Flauta

Nurses learn tough lessons from patients. That suffering is draining; administering healing in some situations costs us more than our time and effort. It requires spirit and strength to care about patients who are confronting death or enduring a painful life. I have always tried to provide compassionate care, balancing my patients' physical and emotional needs. It wasn't until I found myself "on the other side of the bed" that I realized just how deeply pain and suffering touches the very core of belief systems and that the usual coping methods need to be modified to accommodate this physical and spiritual upheaval.

I found myself humbled by pain and insecurity. My feelings overwhelmed me; at the same time, my inability to be creative kept me from expressing them as I usually have, in journaling, or free-verse. I turned inward. In the midst of despair, I found a voice for iambic pentameter. I wrote sonnets. The rigid structure of the sonnet became my focus during long, sleepless intervals.

Fourteen lines.

Ten syllables to a line.

abab cdcd efef gg.

This became my focus, like breathing in labor. Not sonnets for reading but sonnets for writing, for occupation. Providing concentrated diversion when the clock refused to move from 2:00 am to 3:00 a.m. Along the way, my nurses cried with me.

Painful Lessons, Part One

This the door I did not dare to open
Of pain and fear, of general despair
Pervading my spirit, now to weaken
Asleep, yet not completely unaware
Of windows spread with sheets of tears for rain
Immobilized, forever I stand still
Weighed down and held by broad, consuming pain
It needs a room of nothingness to fill
What empty, cobwebbed room is this I find?
Is it a place reserved inside my heart?
It is; the narrow, hollow, lightless kind
Lest I become accustomed to the dark
I call to God who lifts the heads of men
I sob and beg and fall and rise again

Gradually, I became able to turn outward again. By Grace, this pain could be managed. Once the pain had been dealt with, there remained the healing to be done. I had the after effects to deal with. The loss of control; the doubt. Depression lingered even after dramatic physical improvement. Pain had taken months out of my life, perhaps years out of my nursing career.

Ancient wisdom teaches, "A merry heart does good like a medicine." I began to laugh at what had happened to me, find the humor in it. I wrote "Top Ten Lists" and goofy limericks for my nurses. Much the way a child laughs at some narrow, frightening escape, I laughed heartily and protectively. And still I wrote. Now, satire.

Painful Lessons, Part Two

I'm one of those ambulatory services nurses who covers five areas, but all I really want to do is staff the recovery room. There is a cartoon character on the wall in our kitchen with a caption that says something like "Every day is Monday!" I forget what the character is doing, but he is obviously miserable. I'm the nurse who changed the caption to read "Every day is Pain Clinic!" expressing my discomfort working the pain clinic. So, naturally, I ended up getting assigned to staff it for about a month. A few years later, it got worse. I end up as a pain clinic patient.

Let me first say that I was not dissatisfied with the care I received. My nurses were concerned and experienced. The anesthesiologist who cared for me was the ultimate professional. He was thoughtful, knowledgeable, and well-respected. He had skills with needles like no other. I had no quibble with him. So what was the problem? My problem was with one tiny—actually lengthy—aspect of his practice. Needles. Funny, right? A nurse afraid of needles! Now I don't like to complain, but really, has anything changed since medieval barbers?

One of my favorite procedures is the Stellate Ganglion Block, which in Latin, means, "star clustered stymie, as in stoppage of normal mental function and breathing." I arrive, and one of my nurses asks: "Are you here to be pithed?" (I manage a weak laugh.) I tell my doctor, "My shoulder and forearm are absolutely killing me, and I haven't slept since the first of June." (It's then October.) He smiles, and I swear he says: "Here, let me stick a nine-inch needle in your neck, about a millimeter from your trachea. Don't swallow, don't move, don't say anything; it will just be a little bit longer, lay still, don't breathe, it'll only take a minute! Now, tell me, does that hurt?" What, no leeches? Of course it hurts!

Everything that anybody does to you while you are in pain hurts. Your husband kisses you, it hurts. Your children talk to you, it hurts. Your dog curls up next to you ... well, actually the dog curled up next to me actually helps sometimes. But imagine even seeing a nine-inch—okay, three-inch needle—that is about to be "placed" in your epidural space. You'll have to trust me on this, "placing" hurts!

Pain is the hottest topic in hospitals since Kevorkian. Everybody is talking about pain. They are studying it, competency-ing it, and QA-ing it. All this is hand-in-hand with the IV Conscious Sedation Modules, Post-tests, and Reviews. What I want to know is: Why can't the procedures I need be done with IV Conscious Sedation? I know, it sounds suspicious to me, too. Payback. I try to schedule any dental work I might need for the same days as my pain clinic visits. I figure, why waste all that adrenaline?

When the pain gets really bad, and I'm so worked up that all I can get down is chocolate-covered tylenol with codeine, I reach for that business card with the pain clinic phone number on it, and you know what? Suddenly, it doesn't seem that bad at all. That pain clinic card sure works for me!

So what's my real point?

It's this: Encourage your patients to cry out in their trouble and help them find a voice for the despair they are holding inside them. Storytelling is a powerful outlet that crosses age and culture lines. Some will want to write down their stories. Some stories you will want to write out. Listen to what suffering means to your patients and give it significance. Then, teach them to laugh again. Laugh together. Learn these painful lessons together. ♥

"Kate's Story" Private Collection

by Lea Barbato Gaydos

Kate is married, the mother of four, and has been a hospice nurse for 11 of her 20 years in nursing. She told me this story.

> It was Saturday. My dad was painting a house ... I went to my music lesson as usual. It was a long way from where we lived. And always, my friends and I would stop for fish and chips after the lesson. But this particular time, I had this extreme urge to get home as quickly as I could ... I had no idea why; I just had to get home ... there was my dad coming up the street, and I saw him drop ... drop dead. And then, when I was 17, my mum died from cancer. I helped nurse her ... I lost my family at 17.

One of the consequences of these deaths was the loss of what Kate called "her birthright." Kate is from "down under" (Australia), and in her world, her parents' educated tradition and her own school qualifications ensured her right to go to university. Their deaths and her belief that she needed to enter the work force as soon as possible disallowed her this heritage. It was not until she was in her 40s that she was able to return to school and reclaim her birthright, represented in the painting by the books and the open birdcage, (because going back to school set her free). Kate considers herself a Warrior Woman, so one of the changes she requested after the rough draft was presented was to cut off the long flowing locks I had drawn on the central figure. She believes the short hair more accurately represents her self-image as a Warrior Woman.

After the loss of her parents and separation from her sister, she buried her grief "under the carpet" until she began working with dying patients. During the making of her Life Journey Portrait, she said, "I realized that if I was going to go on with hospice nursing, I had to deal with my own pain ... I felt a terrible sadness that I could not get over. If I hadn't ended up in hospice care, maybe I could have gone on for years and years and not dealt with it ... I am totally in touch with my feelings now. I know who I am within. I am in a position to help others through their pain because I know what emotional pain is all about. I can be present. Authentic."

Artist's Statement

Most of my work is telling the life stories of people through visual art. I call these "Life Journey Portraits," and, although I execute them, I really see them as being co-created by the person whose story I am telling along with myself. And thus, each piece is unique and expresses not only my aesthetic but theirs as well. I use three different media: pastel, egg tempera, and etching. The choice of medium depends on the elements of the story, the way it is told to me, and the person's aesthetic.

Other pieces of my work explore the great mythic stories such as the hero's journey and universal human experiences like memory and loss. I have been very influenced in my work by Carl Jung, Joseph Campbell, my background in psychiatric nursing, my studies in cross-cultural anthropology, and the art of the Italian quattrocento (especially the frescoes of Florence), Byzantine iconography, and the symbolist painters.

I am most interested in exploring those things we know about ourselves, both individually and collectively, and those things, not so apparent, that lie below the surface and influence us in unexpected ways. Whether I am using the tools and skills of art-making or nursing, the purposes of the psyche and the spirit are consistent themes in my work. Though these purposes are often expressed in abstract terms, I love the irony of making them manifest in the human form and so my work is both figurative and representational. I believe I am also drawn to human form because in my work as a nurse I have touched and found beauty in many different expressions of human anatomy.

My work is both contemporary and ancient. It is contemporary in that I work with old media in new ways, including the use of computer imaging. I use contemporary theories of the psyche and new knowledge about traditional societies to create a visual, metaphorical language. It is also contemporary because it is interdisciplinary, a new and fast growing phenomenon in a world flooded with the blurring of boundaries in many fields. It is ancient in that my concerns are those that have interested human beings for millennia. Who are we? What are we doing here? What does it mean to be human?

The feminine foundations of this work are evident in that it is based on the development of relationships, synthesis, and caring. It is also a curious combination of language and visual art. Both language and art-making are required to create the images. This work is both secular and spiritual. It is secular because the images reveal the real stories of real people trying to understand and live their lives as best they can. It is spiritual for the same reason.

24" x 36" pastel on board

Cage of Pain

by Priscilla Mackenzie Kline

Chronic pain …
… is like being in a cage
limited … penned in … cut off from reaching.

If only I could be let out … freed for a brief time …
a moment or two … to see clearly again
unhampered by bars
to feel fully, free of the chain that limits range of movement
to feel whole, free, with full choice.

Sometimes the chains, the pains, are momentarily forgotten …
until brought up short by
an aggravated twinge …

to be free … to be unhampered …

this would be bliss.

One moment of soaring free would help …
might even allow a return to limits, shackles,
the comfortable known boundaries of
the cage of pain.

But not to feel this freedom wears one down,
renders one preoccupied, narrowed, cramped,
searching … even frantic.

Maybe it's only possible to soar from pain
with one's imagination …

still bliss … the power of one's mind.

Designing a Memory Quilt

by Elizabeth Lada Morse

For many years I admired quilters. Quilting, it seemed, could be experienced in many ways from functional to creative expression of art. Quilts have three layers—a top layer with machine or hand-sewn pieces of fabric that create a pattern, a middle layer that provides the warmth, and a backing. Designing and creating the patterns of the top layer generally have the most variation, although choosing the batting (middle layer) or backing has also received much attention from quilters.

After my husband, Mitchell, passed away, I decided to make a memory quilt and use his ties as the design material. This was a healing project that allowed me to work through some of my grief after his unexpected death from a heart attack at only 49. The ties exemplified who Mitchell was. The patterns of the ties included traditional patterns as well as his special interests.

The Design Image

I thought about the design for weeks and had sketched out some ideas on paper, including the size, the pattern on the top layer and what story the quilt would tell, and to whom. As I was thinking about the design of the quilt, I began to prepare the material to be used. Disassembling the ties was tedious work, and it allowed me to think about the colors and textures of the fabric and how it might be used. Ties are patterned and cut on the fabric grain bias, which allows them to drape nicely when worn, it also makes it difficult to work with since it stretches easily. This was something to consider as I thought about the shape or pattern I would cut from the fabric. In disassembling each tie, I was reminded of the life that Mitchell and I shared.

I decided on a heart shape for the fabric of the ties and then tested various sizes and heart patterns. I played with the idea of using the colors of the fabric to create an image of the letters MVM—Mitchell's initials. How many hearts would be needed and the spacing of each color along with the overall size of the quilt was considered. Whether to

use the fabric from each tie more than once was also a consideration. The ultimate size was shaped by a 7 x 7 = 49 pattern, and it was able to accommodate two of the three initials.

The design held much symbolism. There were 49 six-inch square blocks cut from his white shirts. He was 49 years old when he died. Each square contained a heart cut from a different tie—a subtle message to make each life experience a unique one. The heart shape was used to demonstrate love and the fact that he died of a heart attack. The letter M, for Mitchell, can be seen when tracing the blue hearts and the letter V, for his middle name Vaughn, can be seen when tracing the red hearts. The placement of the "Big Dog" heart is at the center of the quilt—he shared his space with Newfoundlands. The edging of the quilt is made from suits and resembles a matted and framed picture. (The matting is light gray, and the frame is navy which speaks to his traditional values.) The back center of the quilt has a picture of Mitchell with birth and death dates. The title of the quilt, "Businessman with a Big Heart," is machine stitched along the back border.

Analysis of the Design

The design and completion of making the quilt accomplished what I had intended. It allowed me to tell a story of Mitchell. I showed the quilt (wall hanging) in a quilt show in Connecticut and called it "The Tie That Binds." It was also on exhibit as a demonstration of healing art at the 2003 biennial convention of the Honor Society of Nursing, Sigma Theta Tau International. During these exhibitions, I discovered that many people have unresolved grief. The wall hanging gave them an opportunity to think about how they might address resolving their own grief. The quilt now hangs in my office where it provides me with many wonderful memories and comfort when needed.

Homage to New York
by Cathy Peters

Editor's note: "Homage to New York" was awarded the Sigma Theta Tau International Nursing Art Media Award for 2003.

Homage to New York

by Cathy Peters

Throughout my career in nursing, I have been honored to participate in the most poignant events in people's lives. I have observed, listened, and learned. One of the most vivid experiences of my career was the opportunity to assist in New York after September 11, 2001.

As a Red Cross volunteer, I participated as a member of a multidisciplinary team. For weeks, our group triaged and counseled dozens of individuals. Our clients included workers from lower Manhattan and families and friends of deceased victims. I was a privileged witness to this extraordinary historical event. Although there was phenomenal physical destruction, I was more deeply moved by the people and their stories.

Creating the collage seen here was an act of hope and of healing. "Homage to New York" measures 24" by 36" and is featured in the "Virtual Union Square" exhibit of the museum of the City of New York. Nursing practice, spirit, and philosophy are woven into the amalgam of perspectives represented in the work. Examples include text and images featuring a nurse tending to volunteer workers, another moving supplies, a stethoscope taking the pulse of the American flag, and emphasis on kindness and the value of human life.

"Homage to New York" also represents the diversity of experiences that are the heart of this world-changing event. The horrors of September 11 can educate us about fairness and tolerance, which are essential ingredients in building successful relationships.

Through the process of cutting, pasting, and layering newsprint and magazine images, I literally pieced together the experience in a way that was meaningful to me. Unexpectedly, the work became a vehicle for sharing what I had experienced with nursing colleagues and students, in formal presentations and small group discussions.

I encourage colleagues and students to process their clinical experiences through the arts and humanities, as both a source of inspiration and renewal.

Peaches

by Mark Clarke

I have felt the final flutters of a dying heart,
my hand on the chest of an old, old man with emphysema,
a patient who decided to die in the hospital
rather than have his family find him down and dead at home.
I have attended enough deaths to learn
that death is a transition,
not a simple now-you-are-on-now-you-are-off event.

I often feel my own heart flutter for a few beats,
then pound its way back into rhythm with the world
reminding me: one day it will finally get to stop and rest.
What will the trigger be?
A little curdle of blood damming some crucial artery?
If it comes soon: sixty-miles-an-hour down Highway Ninety-nine
into an overturned truckload of fresh picked peaches.
Imagine spiralling into all that golden sweetness,
one more thing of this delicious world to taste.
It doesn't frighten me too much,
I have been careful to taste all I can, while I can.

Blood and hot peaches,
sticky and rich with the scent of life and decay.
The golden coal in my heart slowly fading
to almost nothing on this side of everything.
Don't touch it, you'll burn your fingers.

Photograph copyright Colin Maykish

Preparing Others to Nurse: teaching

Blending the Art and Science of Nursing

by A. Gretchen McNeely

Description of the artwork

The crocheted bookmark, which itself represents "knowing" through reading, and the doily are visual representations of the fundamental patterns of knowing first described by Carper (1978). The solid border on the bookmark represents White's (1995) sociopolitical context for nursing. Each of the ways of knowing is depicted by a different color: Purple (empirics), peach (aesthetics), white (ethics) and green (personal). Women's ways of knowing (Belenky et al., 1986) are also included and represented by the color blue. The varigated crochet thread was used to show the interrelationship of the patterns; none alone is sufficient. The four areas of the discipline of nursing (clinical practice, theory, research and education) are incorporated into the design features of the doily, represented by the single doily with four distinct sections. The white and peach mats also emphasize the separate structures in their four-sided design. Finally, the frame that holds the doily presentation together represents the sociopolitical context within which the "ways of knowing" in nursing are learned through education, studied through research, conceptualized through theory, and utilized through practice.

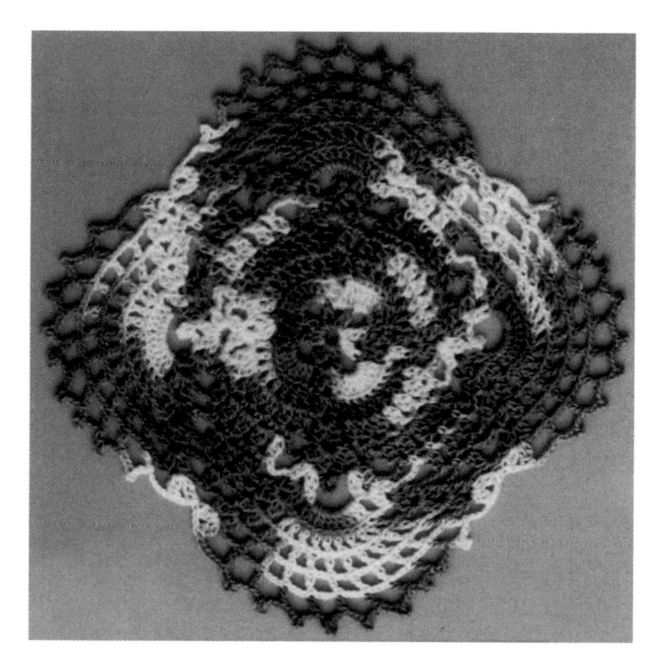

Inspiration

This work was created in the fall of 1996, when I co-taught the "Ways of Knowing: Aesthetics" content in the Theory Development course in the Family Nurse Practitioner program at Montana State University. I was role-modeling an assignment the graduate students had been asked to do in which they were required to communicate their understanding of "ways of knowing" in a visual/aesthetic format. It has been said that a "picture is worth a thousand words." The students were asked to use their "creativity to present one or more of the fundamental patterns of knowing in nursing" as originated by Carper (1978), defined by Jacobs-Kramer and Chinn (1988), and critiqued by White (1995): empirics, aesthetics, ethics, personal knowing and the political-social context for knowing. Gender variations as presented by Belenky et al. (1986) could also be included.

How incorporated into practice

I have used this work in teaching graduate students to visually interpret the ways of knowing content. My students have been very creative in the assignments and have, without exception, exceeded my expectations for them. The framed, crocheted doily is hanging in my home, and I make bookmarks for each of my students, which I give to them along with the explanation of it at the end of the semester. ♥

REFERENCES:

Belenky, M.F., Clinchy, B.M., Goldberger, N.R., & Tarule, J.M. (1986). *Women's ways of knowing: The development of self, voice, and mind.* New York: Harper (Basic Books).

Carper, B.A. (1978). Fundamental patterns of knowing in nursing. *Advances in Nursing Science,*1(1), 13-24.

Jacobs-Kramer, M. & Chinn, P. (1988). Perspectives on knowing: A model of nursing knowledge. *Scholarly Inquiry for Nursing Practice: An International Journal*, 2(2), 129-139.

White, J. (1995). Patterns of knowing: Review, critique, and update. *Advances in Nursing Science,* 17(4), 73-86.

A Tribute to my Mentor

by Sharon A. Brown

I was but a fledgling nurse.

My nursing knowledge was limited, and not well versed.

Your standards were HIGH…

Your expectations GREAT…

You inspired me to see, nursing was my fate.

Education and wisdom, you provided.

Mentoring and coaching…it never subsided.

As I reflect upon my achievements,

it becomes evident to me,

that, because of YOU,

I am a better ME!

Cross Stitching: Lessons Learned

By Diane L. Stuenkel

Stitching and nursing education? An unlikely mix. However, the process of learning to cross stitch—from potholders on my grandmother's front porch, to eventually being selected to stitch samples for a national stitching publication—may offer some clues.

Lessons learned from cross stitching

1. When the floss gets tangled, the stitches are uneven, and more stitches are being ripped out than put in, walk away. There is wisdom in doing things (stitching, writing, studying) when one is "in the mood."

2. Large projects take time. Completing a large cross stitch piece, a nursing care plan, or any large project, requires breaking it down into a series of small, manageable tasks. For example, working on the angel's wing tip or a ribbon.

3. Details count. Adding a pewter metallic thread for one stitch—the clasp of a purse hanging from a perambulator—caused the framer to remark on how that one stitch really "made" the piece. The art of nursing lies in teaching our students to think creatively when individualizing care.

4. The back should look as neat as the front. The piece will look better and lay better if it is done correctly. A good, solid nursing background may not "show," but it provides a foundation for nursing practice that will serve our future nurses well throughout their careers.

5. It takes practice. One does not move from novice to expert—whether in stitching or nursing—in a flash. While keeping my hands busy, stitching has afforded me the time to reflect on my nursing practice. Reflection can help us learn from mistakes, identify strengths and weaknesses, and formulate an action plan for the future.

These "lessons" can be applied to nursing education. Assisting students to develop reflection and self-evaluation skills may facilitate their movement along the novice to expert continuum. Encouraging our nursing students to develop time management skills, pay attention to details, and to think creatively will serve them well as nurses and as life-long learners. ♥

Co-Creating Change

by Linda Jerzak

Co-Creating Change was created as part of a leadership course, which was one of the first graduate level courses I was to take in pursuit of an MSN. The challenge that catalyzed production of the painting was to create a work that represented or symbolized the student's conceptualization of leadership in nursing.

Having been, at that time, a nurse for over 20 years, and a women's health nurse practitioner for 10, I felt that I had a pretty good notion of what leadership in nursing was all about. After all, my nursing career had included not only patient care, but also teaching innumerable classes, serving on boards, chairing committees, leading groups, facilitating workshops, mentoring nursing students, and starting a women's health clinic. In addition to all this, I was a parent to two teen-age sons; clearly a phenomenal leadership challenge!

Participation in these professional and personal activities had all focused upon facilitating change and growth in people and within systems. For the most part, and from all objective measures, the changes had been positive and the projects deemed successful. However, the change for which I was most grateful was the one least tangible or measurable. It was that change and growth that had occurred *within me.* I was a very different person from the shy and tentative BSN graduate of 20 years ago. My life in nursing, caring for others, had strengthened, enriched, opened, and enlarged my being. I felt an expansion of self at my core and was grateful for the participatory opportunities and the many individuals I had known that had (mostly unknowingly) facilitated this personal growth. The mutuality of change, then, was also clearly a facet of leadership.

As the course progressed, I encountered ideas that offered expression to the nebulous clouds of knowing, drifting just out of mind's reach. The words articulated what I recognized as the truth of my leadership experiences. "Yes! That's it!" I found myself saying. "Of course! I've always understood, but didn't have the words to express..."

The symbolic representation emerging from my new understanding demanded tangible expression. I doodled ideas in my notebook during class. Paint and canvas were easily accessible, as my husband is an accomplished artist. His considerable talent has always been intimidating enough to keep me from picking up a brush myself, in spite of his encouragement. However, this image was so clear! Surely, this painting demanded birth and was indeed soon born.

Co-Creating Change says, with acrylic on canvas, what I could not articulate nearly so succinctly in words. Simply put: that leadership, growth, knowledge, wisdom, healing, and health are all co-created by human beings. We each, by bringing our unique energies to share, enrich all within our circle upon the earth. As such, we are much more than the sum of our individual selves, and our co-creations are much more than any one could be capable of alone. Change is inevitable, though often frightening. Together, as us, we can face into the spiral of change with faith that the apparent chaos will yield to self-organization and new growth. Knowledge, illumination, and the light of day naturally yield to wisdom, reflection, and the darkness of night. All of existence cycles back upon itself, losing itself to new expression.

Co-Creating Change now hangs above the desk in my office. It is the visual expression of my understanding of the art of nursing. ♥

Co-Creating Change
by Linda Jerzak

The Dance of the Discipline

by Carla A. Bouska Lee

The Goal

Educate the person wholly;
Teach the task fully.
Coach the heart carefully; Embrace the soul gingerly.

Alas, the art and science of transformation is delicate.
The methods complex and intricate;
The goals sought exquisite;
Performance here only a visit.

Dear teacher, cherish the discipline and
Prize the gift of each human being,
As the arduous journey is forged in search of meaning,
Each learner rings his own chime
To reach the ecstatic peak and greet the sublime.

The Process

Crisis and change know:
Out of the storm comes calm and serenity;
From entrapment rises creativity and consonance;
From myths/mysteries and confusion emerge clarity and synchrony;
From tension and stress evolve precision and perseverance;
From wrongs, with study or forgiveness, the right;
From paradoxes and koans entrepreneurs create and scholars postulate;
From complications and compromises ascend substance, convictions and consensus;
And lastly, from mechanical exactness movement to chaotic wholeness.

The Essence

For in the end, each master guides and enlightens the neophyte.
Each teacher and mentor must—
Pursue the truth,
Perfect the praxis, and thus,
Preserve the discipline.
As the work of change is not that of the elusive muse;
The discipline speaks to the world only through the "dance" of each practitioner, the
Individual nurse.

Expressions of Cultural Care: Faculty and Student Experience

by Rita Sperstad, Leah Luedke, and Heather Nelson

Rita Sperstad

Holy Family Services (HFS) at the heart of the Rio Grande Valley in Weslaco, Texas, is a very special place. From the roadside, Holy Family appears as a conglomerate of yellow buildings, bordered by gardens of vegetables and flowering plants, dogs and cats lazily soaking up the sun, clothes hanging on the line blowing in the wind, and the chatter and laughter of people sharing time while enjoying a snack in the community kitchen or attached screened patio. In the middle of the setting is a small, octagonal-shaped chapel that calls for the start of mass each morning by the ringing of a bell hanging outside the door.

Holy Family Services is a nurse-managed birth center that was started in 1984 by three Catholic sisters. The mission of Holy Family is to provide comprehensive health care from conception through four weeks after birth for underserved women and families in a God-centered atmosphere of compassion. Ninety-four percent of the clients at Holy Family are Hispanic, speak no English, and most were born in nearby Mexico. The poverty level of Holy Family clients is high, yet no one is ever turned away because of an inability to pay. Instead, women and family members may volunteer in a variety of ways at Holy Family in exchange for health services. Sister Angela Murdaugh, a certified nurse midwife, is highly esteemed and well known in the circle of midwives and is the director of Holy Family. She receives the help of several other Catholic sisters, a social worker, nurse volunteers (who receive room and board and a monthly stipend) and other volunteers. Communal living is the way of life at Holy Family. Each resident shares duties in maintaining the household. Each day at noon, a large community lunch is served for all to share. The philosophy of care given to women and their families exuberates holism—honoring the natural process of birth and helping women to connect with the inner wisdom that birth provides.

As a nursing educator from a baccalaureate nursing program in the Midwest, I have been blessed with discovering Holy Family Services and the honor of sharing this special place as a learning environment with nursing students. I initially took a group of three nursing students and my 12-year-old daughter for a weeklong immersion clinical experience during spring break in 1998. As a group, we lived as guests in the La Casa on the grounds of the birthing center and participated in the care of clients at Holy Family, as well as in the communal activities. I have since returned on three yearly visits with differing groups of nursing students. On each visit, I have asked the students to keep a journal, and we have processed the meaning of the experience for them (and me) in different ways. This last year (March 2001), I asked the students to use a creative journal activity (Capacchione & Bardsley, 1994) to analyze their written journal content. This creative journal activity was chosen because it utilizes both the right and left sides of the brain. The intent was to help students (and myself) become in touch with the artistic meaning of this nursing experience. And that it did! The outcome of our "assignment" was a poetic expression of the meaning of this cultural care experience. Each poem expresses individual life changing experience—to each of us, the heART of nursing. ♥

The following is a description of the creative journal technique, cluster writing: A quick look at feelings, adapted from Capacchione, L. & Bardsley, S. (1994) *Creating a joyful birth experience*. New York: Simon and Schuster (p. 72).

Purpose:
To explore your feelings about an emotionally charged work. To learn more about yourself and what is important to you.

Technique:

1. Begin by rereading your journal entries from the clinical experience at Holy Family Services.
2. Choose a single word that most fully describes the thoughts, feelings and descriptions from your journal.
3. Using your *dominant hand*, write that word in the center of your paper. Then draw a circle around the word.
4. Now think about five words that reflect your feelings about that center word. Using your *non-dominant hand*, write those words around the circle.
5. Think about the five words or phrases you have written and circle them one at a time. Connect them with a line to your central word.
6. Using your *non-dominant hand*, continue writing words around each of the five words that more fully describe your feelings. Continue writing until you have filled the page. Draw a circle around each of these words and then draw a line connecting the words to one of the five words it describes.
7. After your diagram is completed, read all the words you have written and reflect on them. Then using your *dominant hand*, write a poem with the words from your cluster exercise.

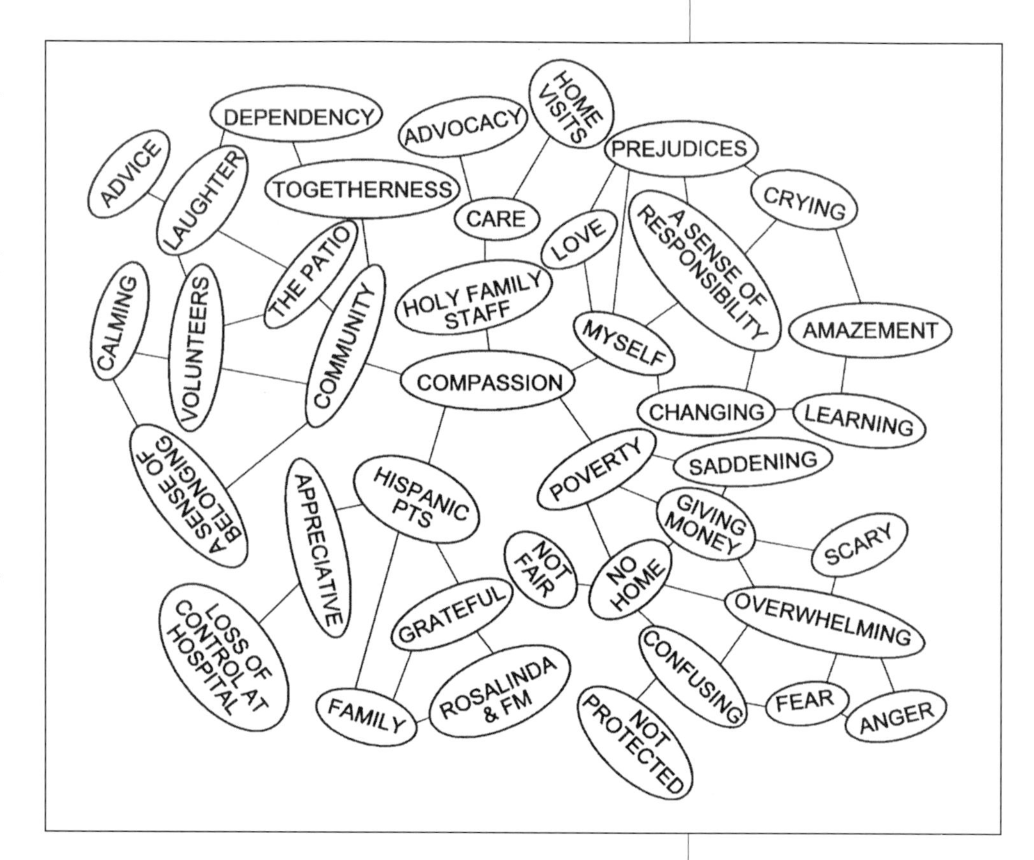

The poverty is overwhelming and fills my
heart with compassion for them.
It is confusing, scary, and simply
not fair.
The staff shows compassion for all.
I am changing, no more prejudices.
I am crying as I am learning in amazement.
I am dependent on the community as
they are depending on me.
The compassion is all around.

Leah Luedke

People have different
priorities in life.

People can survive and thrive
on only the bare necessities.

Sometimes the poor are the
rich and the rich are the poor.

Midwives provide for a
natural birth experience.

God is present everywhere
and will always provide.

Volunteering is a new door
that has been opened.

Heather Nelson

I live my LIFE inspired by wisdom;
Committed to service and love for others, challenged with sacrifice,
But joyful with caring, for these are moments on life's journey.

I see the wisdom in my CHOICES;
We do not have control, but must let go and be led by God, enjoy
A nap, and allow some downtime.

I feel the fullness in knowing DIFFERENCE;
Caring for those with a different color of skin, different foods, and different music,
less money, and simple living conditions.

I am enriched by RELATIONSHIPS;
The gifts of: my connection with Holy Family, touched
By each member at Holy Family, the unique person of each
Student, and growing with the maturity of my own daughter.

I know more about my SELF;
Strengthened in my spirituality with God,
On my search for identity, discovering my needs
For caring, my loving heart, feeling peaceful, on the
Path of doing God's will.

Wisdom comes from deep within
Beyond my human understanding— but
Inspired by the Spirit

WISDOM FROM WITHIN
Rita Sperstad

Thoughts from a Caregiver

by Nancy King

You and your children have been my teachers. From you I have learned that the really important aspects of nursing aren't taught in a classroom or found in a textbook. I learned to be technically skilled and I learned a lot about the human body and disease in school. I passed the examination and got the slip of paper in the mail that said I was a nurse. My second day on the job, I learned more about being a nurse than in four years of school. My first teacher was Dawn. She was three months old.

From you and your children I have learned that life is precious. Whether the length is minutes, hours, days, or years, a lifetime is a lifetime and we have the obligation to use that time to the fullest and to take nothing for granted. I have learned to savor moments of joy, to treasure peals of laughter, to take time to share with another, to make lemonade when it seems life is giving only lemons. I have learned that sometimes we say the most when we say nothing at all or when we simply sit with someone and hold their hand. I have learned that it is sometimes more important to sneak in a puppy or a kitten, or even once a piglet, than to follow the rules. I've learned that laughter is indeed powerful medicine and should be dispensed liberally. That syringes were really invented for water fights and trashcan liners for the protection of nurses whose patients have figured that out! I've had the honor to share in the joy of all sorts of life's milestones—baptisms, birthday parties, weddings, school plays, graduations, choosing prom dresses, meeting boyfriends and girlfriends, and funerals. It awes and humbles me to be included in these celebrations and I never take that gift lightly.

I have learned how parents value competency and skill and knowledge and how much they rely on nurses to help untangle the jargon. I have also learned that all the technical skill in the world is not enough if I do not deliver it with love, compassion, and always with creativity. I've learned that sometimes you throw out the instruction book and do it the way that works best for the child and the family. That sometimes medicines and tests and procedures can wait until after naptime, but if they can't, I'd better know the reason and be able to explain it. I've learned to be an advocate and ally to help the hospital experience work for the family rather than making the family work to accommodate the hospital.

I've learned how important it is to parents that I not just give care to their child, but that I care for their child. I have learned the hard lesson that I cannot fix everything, but if, in some small way, I can give a little comfort, bring a smile, share a tear, or empower a family to succeed then perhaps I have done the best I can do.

From you I have learned that one can face or do whatever must be faced or done with strength, courage, and grace. From you I have learned the value of self-sacrifice for another, of making heart-wrenching choices because you knew what was in the best interest of your child. I have learned that I need to listen to and respect your intuition because you sense things I cannot about your child. That my voice added to yours is a powerful way to help you be heard by others who do not hear you. I have learned that there is no greater force on earth than a parent's drive for their child's welfare and we caregivers better get on the same boat or get out of the water!

Through every child I have cared for to the end of earthly life, my faith in God and my belief that there is life after death has been cemented. As I have sat by their bedsides, held them in my arms, or made sure the light stayed on if they were frightened, many children—even the very young—have entrusted me with their thoughts, hopes, dreams, and visions of angels. I have been awed by their serenity, the wisdom beyond their years, and their concern for those they will leave behind. I have watched parents as they kept vigil and I am always reminded of Mary at the foot of the cross. I cannot comprehend the depth of that parental sadness. I am not a parent and I have never lost a child. I can only compare it to losses in my own life and empathize with the emptiness and pain grief brings. I, too, have grieved as I walked with children and families down that sad path when there is nothing more that can be done by medicine. I grieve the loss of each child, for the parents and family members, and for myself that someone I care very much about is no longer here. I know their souls fly free in a place where there is no pain or grief and that is a great comfort to me, but I still miss them.

For me, the children and families I have cared for are not simply faces from the past. There is a place in my heart where I remember each and every one and I have a unique legacy from each of them that spurs me onward. I am a better nurse because of them. I am a better person because of them. ♥

Springfall '98

*by Bernadette Dragich**

There is the gentle thud of an occasional acorn
  dropping on the ground
I have talked far too long to a distant son on the phone
After spending time in pleasant conversation
  with new acquaintances
While taking in the pleasures of a quiet small town night
A humid mountain breeze is in the air and the hour is late

I sit quietly grading your care plans
Because you will be there in the morning,
And my mind has captured your faces in pleasant memories
Faces that have been there often
As I reflect on the honor and pleasure it is
That you surround my day
With bubbly conversation and inquiring minds

In my mind I see lovely smiles in white uniforms
With blue and gold stripes
You are in conversation around the table
As I pass by the window at the hospital

Now I sit in my dark room capturing memories
While the big black cat lays on a folder and softly purrs
And the little brown "weenie" dog is asleep on the couch
Acorns fall from the oak trees outside
And I fear October will come far too quickly
Then I will begin again with new faces and folders...

* *To Jamie, Tara, Robin, Heather, Tracey, Kelley, Karen and Becky*

Nurturing Aesthetic Knowledge in Nursing

by Beryl Cable-Williams with Jennifer Bress

The volume of empiric knowledge and psychomotor skills thought necessary for the safe practice of nurse work is immense. As a result, nursing educators have focused on prescriptive knowledge, which can be directly applied in clinical settings, and critical-thinking skills. This can be done efficiently using verbal teaching/learning and evaluation techniques and observation of practice. However these strategies tend not to address the soulful attributes of nursing, the contribution of aesthetic knowledge, and the needs of visual learners.

In the stories told by nurses and those who have been nursed, the significance of soul-satisfying care is valued along with psychomotor competence. Indeed in some stories, soulful care is the only aspect that counts! While some would say that nurses are born, not made, others hope to nurture the capacity for soul-satisfying caring in the process of becoming a nurse.

The art of students in the second year of the Trent/Fleming BScN Program is the result of one such effort. Students are asked to explore illness-related concepts, such as hope and suffering, and present their understanding in a visual way to their peers. They were to consider the empiric, ethical, aesthetic, and personal ways of knowing (Chinn & Kramer, 1999). Results have been remarkable in terms of the insights developed, the creativity expressed, and the students' reports of personal impact.

In one example or student work, Jennifer Bress portrayed fear in her artwork with a stark white figure lost on a white background and isolated by an invisible barrier. The poem that accompanied this work appears below.

Photograph by Kirk Doughty

FEAR

by Jennifer Bress

Within the borders of this bubble there is a place
A place very different than most
It does not have an exact location, nor does it bear a name
It has no identifiable surroundings
and depends on only one thing for
Sustainability
This place recruits and allows only one guest at a time

There is a gate that governs this place,
As you enter, the very feelings that accompanied you on your travels to this
Place intensify
The apprehension, the anxiety ...
You take a look around and realize no one else is there
The gate is no longer in sight,
You realize that you have lost your sense of direction
You are now all alone in a place occupied by only you
You are scared because you are unaware of what really is happening
Panic sets in
You are alone
All alone in this place
A place very different than most.

REFERENCES:

Chinn, P.L. & Kramer, M.K. (1999). *Theory and nursing : integrated knowledge development*. (5th ed.). St. Louis : Mosby.

Poetry: Student Reflections of Psychiatric Clinical Experiences

by Patricia A. La Brosse and Sudha Patel

As two faculty members responsible for managing inpatient psychiatric clinical experiences for senior nursing students in the final semester of a baccalaureate program, we continually seek new and different methods to help bring additional meaning to the nursing care of a patient population that often fills students with fear, trepidation, and a myriad of other emotions.

Olson's (2002) description of the use of a poetry assignment with nursing students during psychiatric clinical rotations inspired us to implement this teaching strategy to expand the opportunity for students to reflect on encounters with psychiatric patients who are experiencing the acute phases of their mental illnesses. Most of our peers were intrigued by the incorporation of a poem into a psychosocial paper assignment for this rotation. When met by the comment, "But what do you two know about writing poetry?" we made it abundantly clear that this was not a poetry-writing class. Students would receive full credit for their poems with instructor feedback addressing only our personal responses to their individual work.

Poetry as an Expression of the Aesthetic

Multiple patterns of knowing, including empirics, ethics, aesthetics, and personal knowing, are identified in the profession of nursing (Carper, 1978). Aesthetic knowing is the art of nursing, and is the component that fosters the creative expression of nursing practice. This pattern "is the dimension of knowing that connects with depths of human experience that are common but expressed and experienced uniquely in each instance" (Chinn & Kramer, 2004, p. 193).

Poetry, as an aesthetic expression of nursing practice, affords the opportunity to deepen personal knowing through the examination of nurse-patient interactions. It provides a framework for self-reflection related to significant clinical perceptions and facilitates reconstruction of these perceptions into a nursing experience unique to the individual practitioner. This exemplar presents the use of poetry in a psychiatric clinical rotation for senior students in a baccalaureate nursing program. The art and science of nursing merged as students approached their clinical requirements using both right and left sides of their brains. The experience enhanced their understanding of holistic communication, provided them with an opportunity to grow as reflective practitioners, and facilitated expression of nurse-patient connectedness through an aesthetic modality.

Students' Experiences

Initial student reactions to the assignment ranged from groans to questions examining the relationship between the assignment and psychiatric/mental health nursing practice. During this, their final semester of nursing education, students frequently display ambivalence and anxiety related to what they know, how much they know, how much they need to know, and how they will know what to do in their chosen practice settings. Student focus at this point of their academic career is usually on the science of nursing, with limited concern for the art of nursing. A common question is, "How will writing a poem help me learn how to be a better nurse?" Usually by the end of the psychiatric nursing experience, this question has been sufficiently answered and the student has experienced some form of personal growth.

Conclusion

Significance to practice is the personal and professional growth experienced by the students. Each student incorporated the poetry created into their final course paper. One example, by student Hillary Jolivette titled "Friend or Foe?" demonstrates reflection in action, as the student considered the nature of the patient's feelings as clinical groups rotate through facilities.

A Nursing Grand Rounds Model was utilized as a mechanism for students to present a psychosocial paper on a patient-related experience during the rotation. The poems were read at the conclusion of each paper presentation, and verbal comments during discussion reflected clear evidence that students were appreciative of the efforts of their peers. Personal reflective comments from each student revealed personal growth and a sense of satisfaction. In addition, students described their "aha" experiences as they recognized the relationship between the reflective aspect of the assignment and their own personal and professional growth. One student took his work to another level by composing music to accompany his poem.

Educational significance is demonstrated by the use of poetry as an aesthetic modality in the educative process, assisting students to find another "voice" as a professional writing tool in which to express their aesthetic experiences in the clinical rotation. The clinical experience with chronically mentally ill patients provided opportunities to engage in diverse nursing relationships heretofore not experienced by the students.

Friend or Foe?

by Hillary Jolivette

Another day, another group.
Why are they interested in me?
"Who are you? What's wrong with you,
And how long have you been this way?"
I've started to memorize these questions
Hoping that they'll change one day.
They smile, they laugh, and sometimes play.
Do they really care, or is it just something they say?
I'd like to believe that I'm important to them.
Like I'm human too, and not just "Oh well, I'll take him."
We talk, they teach, they leave
Well, I know it's just a grade
Wait, they're back, they're smiling,
I think that it's a friend I just made!

REFERENCES:

Carper, B. A. (1978). *Fundamental patterns of knowing in nursing*. Advances in Nursing Science, 1, 13-23.

Chinn, P. L. & Kramer, M. K. (2004). *Theory and nursing: Integrated knowledge development* (6th ed.). St. Louis: Mosby.

Olson, T. (2002). Poems, patients, and psychosocial nursing. *Journal of Psychosocial Nursing*, 40(2), 46-51.

Transcendent Connections: Students' Experiences with Dance as Metaphor for Nursing

by Cynthia Bostick

Primal experiences are the beginning and earliest life experiences; when aroused, the primal touch is so powerful that the experience remains with the participant even after the birth of artistic expression.

One art form that embodies physical and emotional expression is dance. Dance is closely related to nursing praxis through its movement, rhythms, and touch. Dance is holistic in that all aspects of the human experience are connected—the physical, the social, the psychological, and the spiritual. Through these connections, learning dance fundamentals may help students identify with patients and family members and may enhance their abilities to comprehend and manage the complexities of illness. The purpose of this piece is to describe a qualitative study in which students, exposed to dance, describe their responses and experiences.

Background

Dance, Nursing, Rhythm, Touch, and the Primal Experiences

Dance is a creative art form that allows expression of unspoken and subconscious emotions through movement and rhythms. The combination of these is infinite and eloquent. Without one spoken word, dance can communicate emotions of love, awe, sorrow, tenderness, hope, desire, peace, and comfort. Dance and nursing praxis are intertwined because they each contain mathematical rhythms, geometrical movements, and are also performed solo, partnered, or in groups. Both begin with a living self that expresses through the art form and physically and transcendentally connects with others.

The transcendent connection for students occurs just as a dance evolves between partners and reaches into our primal emotions and experiences which began even before birth. Prior to learning speech and developing intellectually, from simple to abstract conceptual thoughts, humans learn from the environment through touch, sounds, and movement. This even happens pre-birth: As a fetus grows there are rhythmic sounds of the mother's heartbeat. For the fetus, life is experienced as oneness with surroundings because it does not have the ability to think concretely or abstractly. The fetus experiences movements in the womb with the stretching of limbs, floating in comfort and safety. The fetus also experiences sounds of his or her future surroundings.

Upon birth, an infant experiences movement through the womb and into bright lights and cold air. Baby is quickly wiped, aspirated, swaddled, and place in the comfort of a parent's arms. When laid upon its mother's breast, the infant hears the familiar rhythm of mother's heartbeat. Within a matter of minutes, the infant is cared for and comforted and quickly feels comfortable and safe once again. These early life experiences are primal and known only through rhythm, touch, and sound. Other primal experiences include being cradled, bathed, creamed, stroked, changed, swaddled, fed, and rocked.

The infant may hear singing, humming, musical instruments, and tender words. While infants do not understand the meaning of these sounds, they are associated with comfort and nurturing. Because rhythm, movement, and touch experiences began prior to language development, these memories are stored in the subconscious mind. When primal memories are evoked, the early feelings of nurture, care, comfort, safety, and general well-being come forth. The ability to evoke early memories of comfort is an important element of nursing art.

When a nurse begins providing care, the movement, touch, rhythms, and words elicit these primal memories, and healing is promoted. There is a connection that transcends time and space. In nursing, transcendent connection is achieved through mastery of movement that is human-focused and not skill-focused.

A comparison of dance and nursing, as shown in Table 1, helps one understand how the two professions are artistically linked. They are best seen through their movement, rhythm, and touch association:

Table 1. Comparison of Dance and Nursing

Dance	Nursing (Human Focused)
Teaches body placement centering and balance	Teaches body placement centering and balance
Reverence and beauty for body	Respect the aesthetic body
Coordinated and timed movements	Coordinated patient-rhythm and movement centered
Expression of movement with self	Caring for others begins with self
Vulnerability, authenticity enhance artform	Vulnerability, authenticity enhance nursing art
Evokes spiritual connection	Transcends and connects

"The art of nursing involves having the ability to sense the meaning of a situation and the authenticity to share self and metaphysical experiences."

The internal experience created by human-focused nursing praxis begins with self-knowledge but is other-centered. Nurse and patient are matched in rhythm, movement, and touch. When art is created, there is presence in the moment and participants evolve into a transcendent connection.

The Study

Assumptions

Understanding assumptions helps to define the context of the study and provides a frame. The assumptions underpinning this study include the understanding that:

1. Through an artistic process, students can learn the aesthetic nature of human-to-human interactions and connections.
2. Transcendent connection begins with inner self and transcends the nurse artist to connect with primal experiences.
3. Transcendent connections evoke primal feelings, experiences, and memories associated with the womb and infancy.
4. Through art, one can artistically explore the self as a spirit-mind-body living system with the capacity to consciously link with others and promote healing.
5. Tenets of art forms can function as experiential doors for knowledge development of transcendent connections and nursing art.

Participants

After institutional review board approval was obtained, 15 senior nursing students were recruited into an optional experience focused on dance. Students ranged in age from 20 to 38 years; two were men and 13 were women. All were volunteers.

The Research Experience

Dance movement exercises were developed for beginners based on dance and nursing tenets of body positioning, balancing, and ergonomic concepts. The dance movement exercises were purposely designed for simplicity and ease, allowing participation at any skill level. Three categories of dance movement exercises were developed:

1. exercises with self,
2. exercises with partner, and
3. exercises with group.

The dance movement exercises described here are only a partial list. They were presented in a six-week course that met once a week for two hours. The sessions also included discussions of the history and cultural background of dance movement, correct body placement, balance, and sensitivity to self and other in relation to environment.

Group members participated in the dance movement sessions. They were asked to maintain a weekly journal in which they specifically reflected on any noted influence the dance movement exercises had on patient-student interactions during student clinical experiences. After the first week, each class began with a focus group to share, if

they chose, their journal entries. The group discussions and the journal entries became the qualitative data that was analyzed for categories and themes.

Results

Three basic themes and 12 experiential categories emerged from this rich data. The themes are: rhythm, heart and soul vulnerability, and transcendent connection. These themes, with their related categories, are diagrammed in Table 1. The 12 categories are: feelings, experience, rhythm, sharing, tuning in, silent rewards, good mood, relaxation, energy, natural high, connectedness, and spirituality.

Rhythm is the foundational theme upon which the other two themes emerged. Rhythm was described by students with such comments as "tuning into the music," and "my timing with my partner," or "just coordinating my timing to the beat...". Also, "once I relaxed, I almost thought my heart had feelings of beating in time with the music..." and "the experience of concentrating on moving in sync with the rhythms is relaxing...".

Heart and soul vulnerability, which flowed from the notion of rhythm, was the second theme to emerge from the data. This unique vulnerability was described as "I was afraid; I didn't realize that to really move in mutual rhythm with another person I would have to share my intimate space. When one of us was offbeat, there was no connection, but when the connection occurred, we realized we had to make eye contact, relax, and tune in to the music and what our bodies were doing." Also, "hey, quick bonding."

The overarching theme that connected all the data was transcendent connections, which was expressed as "once I got over the nerves, I was relaxed, and there was something like a sigh; I felt connected and in a good mood to be with you guys." Participants describe the process of connection as emerging spontaneously when movements were deliberate and positioned comfortably with the patient. The journaling process helped participants identify and understand the experiential differences between moving deliberately with a focus on patient (human focus) and moving with task focus or skill focus. Through the journaling and focus-group discussions, participants described connections as an experiential moment that transcends and seems to slow down time. Descriptions are categorized below.

Table 2. Experiential Themes and Categories of Transcendent Connection

Experiential Theme	Categories of Transcendent Connection
Rhythm	Tuning in, rhythm, feelings, relaxation, experience, silent rewards
Heart and Soul Vulnerability	Connectedness, feelings, sharing, spirituality, relaxation, tuning-in, experience, silent rewards
Transcendent Connection	Feelings, connected, rhythm, energy, relaxation, natural high, good mood, tuning in, experience, silent rewards

A Return to the Nursing Literature

Transcendent connection may be likened to Watson's (1988) transpersonal caring. Watson (1985) asserts the promotion of health and healing occurs as humans reach for higher degrees of harmony of spirit, mind, and body. With harmony of self, there is an increase in self-knowledge, self-reverence, self-care, and self-healing, all of which evolve from connectedness to self to connectedness between self and unitary consciousness.

In order to achieve the unitary consciousness, historical traditions of education and practice require modifications. Education and nursing praxis require applications that reflect and support universal knowledge with transcendent and aesthetic dimensions. The practice of an art form is one way to help a student experience the artist within.

The quality of interaction among people is an integral part of all therapeutic relationships. Dance exercises and the study of the movements and their historical content are a method for learning the experience of transcendent connection and sharing. The art of nursing involves having the ability to sense the meaning of a situation and the authenticity to share self and metaphysical experience. Dance tenets provide the foundation to experience and share spiritual space in a safe and non-threatening atmosphere.

REFERENCES:

Watson, J. (1985). *Nursing: Human science and human care: A theory of nursing*. New York: NLN.

Watson, J. (1988). *Human science and human care*. New York: NLN.

Hope: Looking Forward

10

For We See Through a Glass, Darkly

by June Heider Bisson

I am a wanderer on a voyage
I did not choose,
lost in a sea of thought, adrift
in silent expression.

I live in fleeting fringes of feelings
in solitary fear,
alone,
as hidden tears of sorrow fill my clouded senses.
My imperiled form floats on uncharted edges of restless, murky
space.

The somber shadows loom and past visions, remnants
of my life compass,
perplex my order of myself.
I seek refuge, a new mooring, from the voices of my separateness;
a renewal,
a restoration,
for yet my heart stirs to nature's sounds and waking spring.

Hope, come softly to me.
Liberate me from listing shadows of this dark sea.
replace my despair with your presence,
for I seek your healing,
steps to the essence of myself.

Outdoor Healing Spaces: Holistic Treatment In Mental Illness

by Emily Diehl Schlenker

Milieu therapy is a long-established treatment modality for psychiatric illness. Most of the thinking concerning the topic, however, has dealt with supportive indoor environments, covering the gamut from inpatient unit structure and governance to the colors used in carpeting and on walls in the physical space.

Human beings, however, have been outdoor as well as indoor creatures since we began. We have been garden-oriented at intervals throughout historical times. From the Garden of Eden to Solomon's garden, from the gardens of the pharaohs to Nebuchadnezzar's garden in Babylon, gardens were places of refuge and restoration. And even before recorded history, Neanderthal man buried his dead with offerings of flowers. Cave dwellers at Folsom and Sandia in New Mexico, and at Olduvai Gorge in Africa chose their sites with sweeping views of the surrounding land. Beauty, it seems, has been important since our origins.

An even more important concept is that of the interconnectedness of humankind and nature. Buddha was said to have been born, to have attained enlightenment, and to have died under specific venerated trees, illustrating a core Buddhist belief in the connection of all matter. Native American belief systems also emphasize deep connections to the natural world, and to be ill is to be out of harmony with this world. Healing for Native Americans involves being brought back into harmony with the natural world, as opposed to curing a disease state. This older concept of healing has largely been lost in Western medicine, with its technological focus on curing, often at great physical, emotional and financial costs. Thus to concentrate only on the indoor milieu is to neglect an important factor that contributes to the individual's perceptions of self and world, and to hinder one's response to the world as a whole person.

In ancient times, healing nearly always took place out of doors, and even early hospitals included gardens where herbs and prayer became a focus of healing. The advance of technology has gradually widened the gap between nature and the healing process. Physicist David Bohm (1980) sees such fragmentation as pervading society in general and as a particular problem for the individual. Bohm notes that we have become so fragmented that neurosis is seen as normal and unavoidable.

In the mental health field, we have also become specialized, with our increasing emphasis on psychotropic

medications as the primary, often only, treatment. This is encouraged by insurance companies who focus on standardized diagnostic labels and quick inpatient turnover. We have to ask, therefore, if we can achieve wholeness for our clients in this way.

What, then, is an outdoor healing space and how can nurses use this concept in the care of clients? Such a space contains features that foster restoration from stress, as well as exerting other positive influences on people entering and using it (Marcus & Barnes, 1999). The size can range from quite small to an expanse as broad as an urban park. Its contents, simple or complex, will depend upon the needs and sensibilities of the users rather than on the aesthetic tastes of a designer. There should be an individual sense of control and access to privacy, the opportunity for physical movement and exercise, and access to nature. Overall, the space should contribute to the person's sense of wholeness.

For a more intimate view of an outdoor healing space, or healing garden, it is helpful to consider some other elements. In my experience, I have identified roles played by texture, movement, color, light, sound, scent and shelter. When I design a healing space, these are all brought into play. In addition, my spaces are done on a very individual basis, considering the past history, present needs, and personal perceptions and preferences of each client.

Texture can be visual and tactile, and comes from such sources as tree bark, stone, leaves, flowers and mulch. The barks of tulip poplar and Japanese maple are smooth, while Hinoki cypress bark is rough and birch bark is papery. Leaves of trees and plants have a wonderful variety of textures, from huge, smooth waxy hosta to small crinkled chrysanthemum and river birch leaves, to the scales and needles of juniper and pine. Rock forms add anchoring substance, either left in their natural state or sculpted by human hands or natural forces. The simple lines of stainless steel spirals draw the eye from the ground upward to the leafy canopy overhead. Plant roses for velvety petals, mums for a soft brushy quality, or yarrow for stiff flat flower heads.

As nurses, we learned early about the profound effects of immobility on all of our body systems. We tend to think less often of the effect of immobilized feelings on our mental health. Movement, real or implied, has an effect on both, and is necessary in a healing space. Consider the action of a breeze on narrow, pendulous flower clusters or on tall supple stalks of iris. It delights the eye and stimulates the imagination. A path through the space invites bodily movement in a gentle walk to see what lies around the bend.

Probably more has been written about color than about almost any other aspect of a garden. Red has a physically stimulating effect. Because it is a dominant color, it can be tiring physically and mentally. It's also a warning color in nature, and we recognize this on some level. But it can also provide a spark of interest. The sun shining through a red maple leaf is a joyous sight. A soft shade of pink is soothing and restful to the eye. Orange can be a challenging color, but it's warm and rich, and can produce a like mood. Bright yellow, the color of sunshine, is cheering. Because of its reflectivity it can be seen in low light and can penetrate a somber mood. Green is restful in all its variations. It is also the color of growth and life and hope. The parts of a garden that are all green are incredibly subtle and peaceful. Evergreen plants like Nandina, azaleas, Heuchera and pine offer visual interest in all seasons but, more importantly, provide hope that spring will finally appear. Blues and violets are usually thought of as restful colors. Perhaps because the blue tones remind us of sea and sky, they evoke a dreamy, sedating reverie and calm the mind. Blues can also be associated with sadness, however (we speak of "singing the blues"), so they work best in combination with white and complementary colors. White is subtle and wonderful in its variations of itself. It reflects and contains all colors of the spectrum. White is calming and stilling, and gives relief from the multiple stimuli of a chaotic day or a chaotic mood.

Light and shade contrast in the space to create clarity, complexity and mystery. Clarity happens when pathways are created, along with thresholds and edges in the space. Pathways encourage use and lead us through a space confidently. A threshold offers a welcome, and edges define the perimeter. Although a healing garden does not necessarily have traditional walls, it needs to have a defined shape. As children feel better when there are rules and limits, so do adults feel better when we know where one space stops and another begins. The ingredient of complexity entices us into a space, with a mixture of full and empty areas, colors and shapes. And finally, mystery is not a surprise but a promise of more. It is an enigma that invites a solution and a remedy for boredom and self-involvement. All of these elements can be provided with areas of light and shade.

Animate elements are the source of healing sound. Many moods and feelings are generated from the sounds of insects, water and wind. The buzzing of bees and cicadas can bring back memories of a childhood summer, sunlit grass and warm twilit evenings. The breeze in poplar and bamboo leaves, the rushing, splashing and gentle dripping of water in a fountain or stone basin, all have psychologically healing effects and are an antidote to the strain of daily pressures and uncertainties. Birdsong, too, is almost always present in the daytime, and sometimes at night. The sounds of nature show her work as a composer, always full of power, into whose music we can dip at will, when needed.

The psychological effect of scent has been long recognized by the perfume industry, and we have also come to know the power of pheromones to attract in the animal world. The human olfactory response is highly individual, and smell is one of the most powerful stimulators of memory. In a healing space, plant scents that

have particularly happy memory associations can be a strong antidote to depression. The smell of rain on grass and leaves, and the smell of the earth in spring offer a lightening of mood and hope for the new season.

Humans have always needed a sense of protection from the vagaries of the elements, thus the concept of shelter is important in an outdoor healing space. Ideally the place of shelter will afford a view of the rest of the space, as well as a sense of refuge. Refuge supplies a welcoming setting, gives us a sense of having our own space, and makes us want to stay. The place of shelter also serves as a beginning and a destination for the healing journey, a safe place from which to set out and to which to return.

If we accept the idea that our perception is our reality, then a perception of this space as healing assumes primary importance. Sitting in such a space reinforces feelings of wholeness, contentment and union with nature, and supports our belief that there is a way to rid ourselves of dysfunction.

In addition to healing the psyche, there are other reasons for structuring our milieu in a healing or supportive way. Mihalyi Csikszentmihalyi (1996, p.72), writing about the phenomenon of creativity, comments that "even the most abstract mind is affected by the surroundings of the body." None of us is impervious to the sensations we receive from our environment. Csikszentmihalyi insists that even though creative people can seem able to ignore discomfort and chaos as they concentrate on their work, "... in reality, the spatiotemporal context in which creative persons live has consequences that often go unnoticed. The right milieu is important in more ways than one."

Human beings are truly "whole people." To ignore this fact is to foster continuing fragmentation, and to come perilously close to disintegration and chaos. To concentrate on only one, or a limited number of treatment modalities, such as pharmacotherapy, behavior modification, etc., to the exclusion of others, puts therapists at a disadvantage and patients at risk. No single method works for all. Outdoor healing spaces, as extensions of a therapeutic milieu, offer advantages for patients and caregivers and should be routinely considered in treatment. ♥

REFERENCES:

Bohm, D. (1980). *Wholeness and the implicate order.* London: Routledge.

Csikszentmihalyi, M. (1996). *Creativity: Flow and the psychology of discovery and invention.* New York: Harper Collins.

Marcus, C. & Barnes, M. (Eds.). (1999). *Healing gardens: Therapeutic benefits and design recommendations.* New York: John Wiley.

Louisiana Frigid

by Valera Jo Clayton-Dodd

"Louisiana Frigid" is a machine-quilted wall hanging that is embellished with Mardi Gras trinkets. The strands of beads are from a physician who yearly goes through St. Francis Hospital at Mardi Gras time and "throws" beads to all staff, patients and visitors that ate in the halls on "bead day."

This piece was constructed while taking a quilting class; quilting is my de-stressor. This was the first "advance time off" day that was spent doing something just for me after a little over three years of employment at St. Francis Hospital and three positions, necessary from several restructuring models. Louisiana is an adopted state for me, due to a move for a health-care job.

The piece hangs in my office to remind me and all those who come to my office that life has a softer side than what is often portrayed when one is Associate Administrator and Corporate Compliance Officer.

Fixin' Anne Carroll's Quilt

by Sarah Hall Gueldner
with Dale Hall, Cheryl Asbury, and Krystin Jacobs

Lillian, a "salt of the earth" country woman, was good with her hands. In her younger days, she had won blue ribbons almost every year at the county fair for her needlework and canning. She made the best iced tea and cornbread in the hills of East Tennessee, and in the past had helped the women of her church make quilts out of sewing scraps to give to the needy or sell at the fall bazaar. Like most country women of her vintage, she had learned to quilt by her mother's side, around a quilting frame set up in someone's living room. Her sewing expertise was apparent, even in just the comfortable and natural way she handled a needle and used a thimble. Then one day, as she was cutting up a chicken to cook for supper (the country term for the evening meal), using the big butcher knife that Chart, her 83-year-old husband of 57 years, kept sharp with a now worn "whet rock," she had a gradual stroke. She didn't fall, so Chart didn't even notice anything was wrong until a neighbor came in and realized she couldn't talk.

By the time she got to the hospital, the stroke had completely taken out Lillian's language capacity (she couldn't even make a sound), and the doctors thought she might never be able to speak again. But she had plenty of what country people call grit, and within three weeks she was making sounds—the first being when she laughed out loud when her great grandson Wesley playfully snatched her glasses off her face. Unfortunately, the stroke also left her with right-sided weakness, and her vision was affected so that she really had to concentrate to read; some numbers looked different to her, and she couldn't always arrange letters to spell even the most familiar words. Valedictorian of her high school class of 1930, now she had to look at a copy of her name in order to sign her checks.

Just two to three weeks before Lillian had her stroke, she had cheerfully agreed to repair a tattered family quilt for Anne Carroll, her daughter's college friend from Memphis. Anne Carroll was short on family, and so sometimes joined our family for holidays. She kind of felt like Lillian was her substitute mother now. In fact, almost everyone felt like Lillian was their mother! Anyway, flying through Memphis en route to a professional meeting, I had rendezvoused with Anne Carroll and brought the quilt back to her home in Georgia, meaning to give it to Lillian to fix the next time she visited me in Tennessee. I couldn't have guessed there was a need to hurry.

But as it turned out, the stroke happened before I could get the quilt to Lillian, and with her weakened right side, Sarah knew she wouldn't be able to work on it. Since she could hardly sign her name, she certainly couldn't take on a quilt that needed major repair! But before I returned the quilt to Anne Carroll, I thought Lillian would enjoy just seeing it, so I took it to show her. When Lillian saw the quilt, she perked up with interest, taking hold of it as if she was trying to figure out how to repair it. Thinking she misunderstood, I said, "No, Mother–Anne Carroll knows you've had a stroke—she knows you can't repair it now—I just wanted you to see it before I sent it back to her." But Lillian continued to examine the quilt with interest and struggled to say, in broken, faltering language, "No... I want... to... do it............. Present." I finally realized that she was saying she wanted to repair it for Anne Carroll as a Christmas present. In disbelief, I got out the quilt scraps right away and cut out some replacement pieces. Sure enough, Lillian could still sew...and what a blessing that turned out to be. Known for her sunny disposition and chatty persona before the stroke, Lillian's uncharacteristic quietness made it difficult for even her best friends to spend time with her after the stroke. So the quilt project gave Lillian a way to visit with her friends without having to talk. Everyone who dropped by, including dozens of her lifetime friends and granddaughters, sat for a while and replaced a threadbare patch or two on the Dresden china quilt as they visited. Slowly, almost magically, the quilt began to look bright and new again.

Anne Carroll got her more-precious-than-ever quilt back. But the real magic was in the human healing factor. There, sitting quietly for hours among her friends, listening to them speak even when she couldn't yet, Lillian made a remarkable recovery from her stroke. In time she learned to speak again in sentences, to sign her name, to make tea and cornbread, and even to dial telephone numbers; and she never lost her long-time sewing ability. ♥

Life Patterns

by Sr. Mary Ellen Lewis

Vital Questions

by Sr. Mary Ellen Lewis

Dying, sprouting, maturing.
Dare I say one's more
true to life than another?

Surfeited with Summer,
I doze and dream.
Is Fall alert with anticipation?

Glorious colors glowing.
Does Fall's short life
deepen joy or sharpen pain?

Light at seven, dark at five,
Wind freezing the snow.
What fool believes in Spring's return?

Budding trees, bird calls
soft snow, warns of a freeze.
Winter can't let go.
Days lengthen, ducks nest,
Earth softens.
Did Winter die without my notice?

Andy and the Butterfly

by M. Cecilia Wendler

The deepest of nursing's lessons, I'm convinced, are often the simplest. When learned, yet again, in another context, their power emerges and the humanistic impact is clear. And although this story does not take place in a hospital or even in a patient context, it is no less profound. This is the story of a boy—Andy—a butterfly, unnamed, and me—Andy's mom, a professional nurse. It is a tale of lessons learned with patients that have made me a better mother and the healing potential of *presence*.

This story unfolds over several weeks, when Andy, a 7th grader, worked to find his rightful place in the cavernous experience called Middle School. Andy is an athletic, independent boy, a strong and centered person, very physically capable and well liked in school. His science teacher, Mr. Zupfer, challenges students by asking them to raise—from egg—monarch butterflies. This is an extensive project, remarkable in its complexity for these 12-year-olds. The children are responsible for feeding and caring for their caterpillars and butterflies every hour of every day. They begin the unit by gathering 100 milkweed leaves—the diet of monarch caterpillars—freezing them so that there is plenty to eat while the caterpillars mature. Students are assigned one of several eggs that hatch into tiny caterpillars, and they carefully chart the growth and development of each creature. A science journal helps the students keep track of such important information as how much each eats and grows every day.

This project is fraught with danger, for it is not unusual for students to lose an egg or caterpillar or two before they can take care of one well enough to keep it alive. Despite a couple of such "false starts," Andy finally had himself a winner. A female, she grew well and strong and with each passing day, Andy became more and more fascinated–and attached. The jar with the caterpillar and the bag with the milkweed leaves went with him everywhere, for the caterpillars could not be left unattended for a full school day. I remember coming to a soccer game to discover the jar of Andy's caterpillar peeking out of his gym bag. Did caterpillars enjoy watching soccer? I wonder, for Andy had perched the jar just so, atop a pair of dirty socks, in a way that hinted he wanted the caterpillar to observe his game.

I was home the weekend that the caterpillar, now about 3.5 inches in length, decided to hang, "j" style, from the screen at the top of the jar. "She's ready to go into chrysalis!" Andy exclaimed, triumphantly pointing out to me that only about a fourth of the students still had live caterpillars a month into the project. "When she hatches, we will band her, and release her with the other monarchs and in the spring we will see which butterflies return from the migration!" His engagement and excitement in this lively project was very obvious.

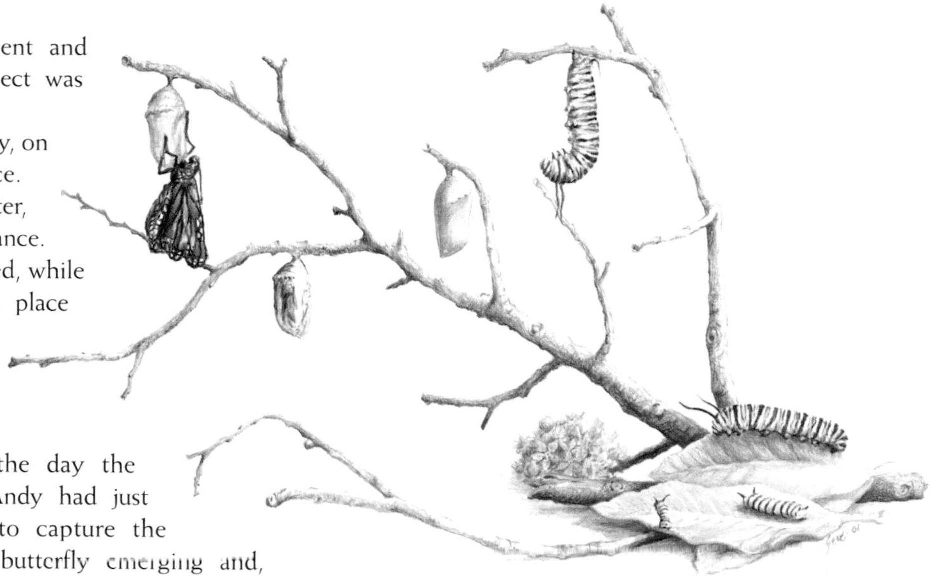

The jar was placed, reverently, on the mantle of our fireplace. Because it was not yet winter, there was no danger of disturbance. And there, the chrysalis matured, while the miraculous changes took place within. Every night, the family asked, "How is the butterfly? Any movement yet?" We all waited in anxious anticipation.

I was away on business the day the butterfly appeared. Indeed, Andy had just arrived home from school to capture the miraculous half-hour of the butterfly emerging and, delicately at first and, later, with vigor, pumped her beautiful wings dry. When I called home that night, Andy couldn't quit talking about this beautiful creature. "Mom! I did it! Only a few kids have butterflies and I am one!" I could hear his wide grin right through the telephone wires.

When I returned home two days later, I came into the house from the garage at the same time my son spilled out of his school bus. "Mom, Mom!" he cried happily. "Come, come, see my beautiful butterfly!" We raced, together, to the front door.

What we discovered when we opened the door and rushed to the mantle...Disaster. For the jar had been upturned, the screen top torn off, the rubber band that had secured the two together not found...and a butterfly thorax here, a wing fragment there...and, again, there... "Oh, Oh, Oh my God!" My son screamed, chasing our young cat under the couch. "Damn cat! Damn! Oh, Oh, Oh, Oh..."

The sobs began. I ran to his side, wrapped my arms around his head and shoulders and slowly guided him to our small couch. We fell as one onto its deep cushions. He cried the wretched cry of one who had lost a precious loved one, the cry of hate, angry, mean words spat out...he cried and cried until the entire front of my shirt was soaked with his sweat, his salty tears, the slime from his open mouth. His anguish was impenetrable.

And all I could do was to cling to him, hug him so tightly that he would know that I would not let go, ever, until he was ready. I whispered, "Oh, Andy, I am so sorry. I am so sorry this happened to you. Oh, darling, I know how much you cared. I am so, so sorry. I can hear your anger and your sadness. This is SO SAD! You worked so hard to raise that beautiful butterfly...I am so sorry this happened to you." My own tears rolled out of the corner of my eyes, down into his sandy hair, off into the netherworld of moisture that was his face.

Finally, finally, the sobbing slowed. I whispered to him how important it was not to blame the cat for the instinct of chasing something, enticingly moving, against the glass walls of a jar. I kept telling him how sorry I was, how important I knew the butterfly was, how much work it took to raise her. Andy said to me, "Mom, you never got to see her." I replied, "Oh, but I did. I got to see her through your eyes. I know how lively and beautiful she was, because of what you told me. I will always have her memory."

When he was, at last, spent, he pulled up and away from me. I was soaked with his fluids, and mine, intermingled. As he stumbled, puffy-eyed, away to make that final, agonizing entry into his science journal I realized the reason I knew what to say and what to do for my bereaved son. For I have held patients in much the same way, patients told that they need to have a new heart, patients told that there "was nothing more we could do," family members told their loved ones had died. And what I have discovered is a simple, but great truth for me:

People know that you cannot always "make it better."
All they want is for you to be "with them" when life is unspeakably awful.
Not to abandon, but to accompany. Not to always cure, but, ALWAYS, to care.

The next day, I was home when Andy arrived from school, this time with another 7th grader in tow. They were talking about the butterfly project when they came through the door. I positioned myself so I could listen to their chatter:

Andy: "So, how did your caterpillar do?"

Friend: "I got it all the way to chrysalis, but he died there. He never emerged."

Andy: "Well, mine emerged. I was home and got to see her come out and pump up her wings."

(I held my breath. Would Andy's sadness at the loss of the butterfly show when he talked about it? For, you know, boys in middle school must be tough. Strong. And never cry.)

Friend: "Wow. What was it like?"

Andy: "It was really lively. And beautiful. But our new black cat got into her, got up on the mantle and knocked over the jar and tore her apart."

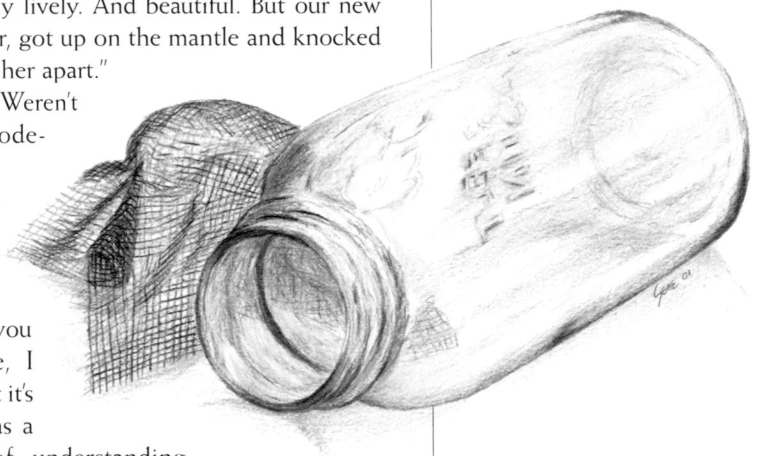

Friend: (Gasp!) "Weren't you mad?" (Boy codeword for sad.)

Andy: "Yeah, I was pretty mad. But that is the instinct of cats, and that's what happens when you live with cats. Sure, I was sad and mad. But it's OK now." There was a pregnant silence of understanding shared between these two good friends. Then, the tender moment passed. Off they ran to play soccer outside.

As nurses, as parents, it is so important to remember: *Stay with people,* even when whatever is happening is bad. Unspeakably bad. Awful. Terrible. Because your presence can provide important healing comfort and can express caring powerfully and deeply. So simple. So important. So imperative. ♥

Creating Healthy Work Cultures: The Role of Music, Verse and Stories

by Bonnie Wesorick

For 20 years the focus of my practice has been on creating healthy cultures for nurses and other health-care providers across the continent. The fundamental work to transform our busy, and often dehumanized, work cultures in order to support the essence of nursing is intense. A six-year pilot, based on organizational structures, processes and outcomes including theories of system thinking, complexity and chaos were vital to achieve the mission of creating "Best Places" to work and receive care. Yet, all of that was not enough. Although change was being called for and longed for by those who daily committed to be healers, I was surprised by the resistance to any type of change.

I learned the arts such as verse, stories and music touched the hearts of the practitioners. Only then would they engage in the change and lead the hard work to create healthy cultures that supported the practice of professional nursing. But what verse, what stories, what music, what words and in what way? I learned quickly that the arts needed to reflect the unique beauty, the essence of our practice. It was a verse such as the following that helped me connect:

Touching Souls

"I have marveled at the beauty of the mountain, the opportunity to be near the moose, the elk and the buffalo. I stood in awe of the glaciers reflecting the sun—while eagerly awaiting the next whale sighting. And then I noticed one person reaching out to help another. I wondered, how could I ever take for granted the beauty, the mystery, the potential of one uniquely splendid human being connecting with the soul of another? I have been in awe of mountains but failed to notice the beauty, the mystery, or the potential of the soul that invisible but tangible presence of my colleagues.—Bonnie Wesorick

However it was the combination of verse, made into songs that reflected the actual stories of the people the nurses cared for, and then placed on video, that had the most powerful impact. The combination of all three became a tool to bring alive the beauty and outcomes of nursing practice.

Here is one example. The verse *"In Your Eyes"* was written to reflect an incredible story of a nurse who under a short timeline changed the whole manner of care and outcomes for a 10-year-old who came into outpatient for an endoscopy. The knowledge of her scope of practice, not just around care during an endoscopy, but her nursing diagnosis expertise helped her put pieces together and make the nursing diagnosis of Rape Trauma Syndrome. The video is re-enacted through the eyes of the child while a song sung by Diane Penning is being played.

After watching the videos and hearing the music, there were hundreds of requests, resulting in the production of the following two CDs: *Celebration of Life: A Dedication to Nurses* and *A Place Within*. Over a half million of our colleagues have been moved by the music. Thousands have expressed the impact of the video, verse and music on their practice. I end with the words of one of our colleagues: "I play the music on the way to work everyday, it inspires and centers me on what matters. And I play it on the way home, especially on a hard day, to help me remember why I do this. It gives me courage to go back the next day." ♥

In Your Eyes

by Bonnie Wesorick

You come into my shattered world
I didn't think this nightmare would end
You see me thru my eyes, you speak thru my mouth
You touch me from within.
Now you see me as before, you feel me as I am
You know me beyond this moment
You've only known me a short time and yet

Verse
I see it in your eyes, I feel it in your touch
You care about my body, soul and mind.
I hear it in your voice, you make me realize
I trust you for I see it in your eyes.

You see beyond the rain, you're not
afraid to share my pain.
You know what to do to make me feel safe,
you know what to say.
And I understand, because you know me who I am
Because you see me beyond this moment
You've only known me a short time and yet

Verse
You see me whole again when right now
I feel so broken
You hear my heart cry out for help
when no words are spoken
I trust you for I see it in your eyes

Verse Repeated
Oh thank you, I needed you, you came you cared.
I trust you for I see it in your eyes.

I'll Still be a Nurse Tomorrow

by Rose Aguilar Welch

She looked at me with questioning gaze,
that asked ... why?
The mother's child is gone forever.
Why did her child have to die?

No answers to give, no cliches to utter,
I can only join in her tears and touch.
It's all so unfair, it's all so unjust,
And it hurts me far too much.

But I guess this is what it's all about,
one can't escape from the sorrows.
And despite the pain I see and feel,
I'll still be a nurse tomorrow.

Sometimes self-doubt enters my head,
can I face another hard day?
Weary body and mind...count down the hours,
I wonder if there's a better way?

What keeps me going? I ask time and again,
It's the satisfaction that I know.
From those in my care with thanks in their eyes,
And the warmth and caring that flows.

So I guess that is what it is all about,
The balance of joys and sorrows.
And despite the ups and downs I feel,
I'll still be a nurse tomorrow.

Unlimited Possibilities

by Terri Pauser Wolf

Unlimited Possibilities
Fiber art by Terri Pauser Wolf

I have been a fiber artist and quilter for almost a decade; a nurse for just a few years. I couldn't help but see the parallels between my art using fabrics and the healing arts of nursing. Fabric touches our lives from the first breath until death, and it is part of many special events. During a lifetime, quilts may provide warmth, comfort, and security. I see these same characteristics in nursing. I also realize these characteristics are just the beginning of the art of nursing.

Piles of fabrics in a myriad of colors and designs line the walls of my art studio. Within this space are countless possibilities for creating art. As I begin my practice as a nurse, I also see unlimited opportunities for creating art within the nurse-patient relationship. I've come to see that the materials to practice the healing art of nursing are always within us.

The quilt, "Unlimited Possibilities," conveys the sense of possibility that I see for the profession. Each square in the quilt is made from one of 25 unique striped fabrics. When the fabrics were cut into different shapes and reassembled, unexpected designs emerged. A new whole was created from these individual squares revealing just one of the possible quilted pieces. Through art-making, I've come to see that nursing also has an opportunity to take its art to new levels. Nursing can experience unlimited possibilities for healing by creating a new wholeness that comes from the heart.

Photography by Matthew Burke

Searching for Strengths
Fiber art by Terri Pauser Wolf

Afterword

The Healing Power of Art

M. Cecilia Wendler

The deeply personal works presented in this book reflect emerging notions of art and aesthetics in nursing. The artistic expressions offered reveal a diversity of ideas, approaches and products. However, there is an interesting thread that runs through all of the works. Specifically, nursing's artistic creations can be fleetingly embedded within the clinical moment, described clearly by Parse (1992) as a "performing art, [which is] the science creatively lived through the uniqueness of the artist" (p. 147) that is irreducible (Saylor, 1990), combining a professional repertoire with current clinical problems to invent unique responses to unique situations. Johnson (1996, p.169) asserts a hierarchical relation ship between nursing art and nursing science: "[Art] has primacy over science [and] nursing science must presuppose art... Nursing science must ultimately serve the art of nursing and not the reverse."

Nursing art is an expression of the "creative imagination [and] sensitive spirit" (Burke, 1992, p. iii) of the nurse. It is also an expression of unfolding relationship, expressed as authentic presence in the moment that transforms (Newman, 1994). Mallison (1993, p. 7) used a powerful metaphor when she spoke of the "butterfly beauty of nursing" that often expresses itself as the "quicksilver actions guided by intelligent hearts," often resulting in lifesaving actions for the patient.

This rich description of relationship, I believe, is critically important, for arts and aesthetics in nursing create a "sacred space" (Quinn, 1992, p. 27) for healing to occur (Wendler, 1996). There are two dimensions of relationship that are specifically addressed in this book that demonstrate healing has occurred or is unfolding. First, there is relationship between the nurse and the nurse's self. The artistic production that emerges as a result of this relationship is often a story, a thought, a sculpture, a teaching vignette or other, more tangible item. These productions often help the nurse to provide closure on an especially difficult chapter in the nurse's life: A witnessed painful death of a patient; a loss of one's own family member; a bout with illness or injury; a sense of social disruption from a health-care system that leaves many persons marginalized. These artistic products become items or objects in the world that help provide a subjective expression of emotions, story, feelings, thoughts, values, or beliefs that can then be engaged in by others and that can create space for others who may have encountered similar experiences. These become human cultural and artistic artifacts, amenable to reflection, study and response, therefore helping to more clearly identify and define the inner life, struggles, and little deaths that occur for nurses over the course of a lifetime of commitment to others.

Much more fleeting is the second relationship, the artistic, in-the-moment approach expressed as nursing art as it unfolds in everyday life (Chinn, 1994). This "art/act-in-the-moment" (Chinn, p. 27) is an expression of relationship between patient and nurse, patient and family (as witnessed by the nurse), or nurse and family. This form of nursing art is deeply embedded within practice, within the instant of unfolding as nurses and patients meet each other for the purpose of improving health... for example, the important self-comportment of the nurse as s/he pulls back the bedclothes for the first time to examine a mastectomy incisional site...or new ostomy... or a not-perfect infant. These moments of intense presencing, although they may be physiologically driven in our highly technological environment of health care today, are "moments of truth" for both the patient and the nurse. For here is the unique opportunity, with artful caring and expert practice, for nurses to use their hearts and their hands and their heads to create a moment in which healing, for example, of a ruptured body image, may begin. Tone of voice, warmth of touch, cadence of language, intentionality of respect, and a calm approach are only a few aspects of the dance of clinical practice, carefully choreographed to allow expressions of healing to emerge. When performed with precision and care, these actions provide a few heartbeats of time, allowing patients a sacred space for expression of grief, or surprise, or disdain, or sorrow, or joy; and the nurse, dancing now with the patient, responding by leading the dance, guiding the conversation with a heart full of caring and compassion, so that the patient can learn more about the surgery, the scar, the problem, the solution, the future. This intentional therapeutic use of the nurse's self is a powerful agent for healing and yet, the artistic moment, like a performance on stage, evaporates, existing only in the memory of the performers and those who witnessed the performance, and available to others only if the story of the moment is told. Perhaps this is why nursing appears to be, at times, invisible. The transient nature of much of our art can make it appear inaccessible to those outside of the world of hospitals and sick people and nursing.

However, I believe it is becoming increasingly important for nurses to illuminate these moments—for students, for fellow nurses, for health-care colleagues—so that there can be a growing appreciation for the powerful healing ability of nursing artistry.

In the end, then, nursing art lies within relationship and continues to emerge because of its intense power to contribute to healing. This healing can be of the nurse, or of the patient, or of family members; it can also be healing of the profession. The sacred space for healing created by countless nurses in art/acts embedded within nursing's moments is an expression of nursing's caring, compassion, and interest in the health and well-being of human persons and their families around the world. For many nurses, like myself, nursing art unfolding within the crushingly vulnerable moments of clinical care help to define the essence of nursing for us all. May these efforts inspire others to claim once again nursing's important artistic legacy, to illuminate and exclaim, "This is nursing art!" ♥

REFERENCES:

Burke, C. (1992). *Pentimento praxis: Weaving aesthetic experience to evolve the caring beings in nursing.* Unpublished doctoral dissertation, University of Colorado.

Chinn, P. (1994). *Art and aesthetics in nursing.* Publication No. 14-2611. New York: National League for Nursing.

Johnson, J. (1996). Dialectical analysis concerning the rational aspect of the art of nursing. *Image: Journal of Nursing Scholarship, 28*(2), 169-175.

Mallison, M. (1993). "Begat" of a nurse. *American Journal of Nursing, 93*(7), 7.

Newman, M. (1994). *Health as expanding consciousness* (2nd Ed.). Publication No. 14-2626. New York: National League for Nursing.

Parse, R. (1992). The performing art of nursing. *Nursing Science Quarterly, 5*(4), 147.

Quinn, J. (1992). Holding sacred space: The nurse as healing environment. *Holistic Nursing Practice, 6*(4), 26-36.

Saylor, C. (1990). Reflection and professional education: Art, science and competency. *Nurse Educator, 15*(2), 8-11.

Wendler, M.C. (1996). Understanding healing: A conceptual analysis. *Journal of Advanced Nursing, 24*, 836-842.

Contributors

Gabrielle Beasley
HeART Chapter: The Nature of Nursing
Page 41

Sr. Connie Beil, RN, MS, MSA
Manager, Helkath Services Advisory Group
Glendale, Arizona, USA
Lambda Omicron
HeART Chapter: The Nature of Nursing
Page 30

Mary R. Benkert, RNC, MS
Nurse Care Coordinator
Denver Health Children and Families Program
Denver, Colorado, USA
HeART Chapter: The Other is Me
Page 138

Rita C. Bergevin, RN, MA, BC
Clinical Lecturer
Decker School of Nursing
Binghamton University
State University of NY
Binghamton, New York, USA
HeART Chapter: The Nature of Nursing
Page 29

Janis Bible
HeART Chapter: The Nature of Nursing
Page 43

June A. Heider Bisson, RN, MS, CS
Retired
Liverpool, New York, USA
Omicron
HeART Chapter: The Other is Me
Page 137
Hope: Looking Forward
Page 179

Mary Bliesmer, RN, PhD
School of Nursing
Minnesota State University
Mankato, Minnesota, USA
HeART Chapter: Art in Research
Page 49

Deborah B. Borawski, RN, MSN, CNA, CPHQ
Director of Quality Services
Northern Hospital of Surry County
Mount Airy, North Carolina, USA
Gamma Zeta
HeART Chapter: Reflections: Nurses' Interiority Unfolding
Page 123

C. Anna Reyes Bostick, RN, CS, PhD
HeART Chapter: Preparing Others to Nurse: Teaching
Page 172

Jennifer Brees
HeART Chapter: Preparing Others to Nurse: Teaching
Page 168

Sharon Brown, RN, MSN
Oncology Services Director
Robert Wood Johnson University Hospital At Hamilton
Hamilton, New Jersey, USA
HeART Chapter: Preparing Others to Nurse: Teaching
Page 158

Jeanne Bryner, RN, BA, CEN
Staff Nurse, Emergency Room
Forum Health Trumball Memorial Hospital
Warren, Ohio, USA
Delta Xi
HeART Chapter: The Nature of Nursing
Page 25
HeART Chapter: Bookends: Birth and Death
Page 55
HeART Chapter: Reflections: Nurses' Interiority Unfolding
Page 119

Michele G. Burkstrand, RN, CCRN
Charge Nurse, Surgical Intensive Care Unit and Clinical Analyst II
Fairview University Medical Center
Minneapolis, Minnesota, USA
HeART Chapter: Reflections: Nurses Interiority Unfolding
Page 127

Beryl Cable-Williams, RN, BNSc, MN
Nursing Professor
Fleming Collaborative BScN Program
Peterborough, Ontario, Canada
HeART Chapter: Preparing Others to Nurse: Teaching
Page 168

Jackie Carlisi, MS, HT
Horticulturist, College of Applied Life Sciences
University of Louisiana at Lafayette
Lafayette, Louisiana, USA
Delta Eta
HeART Chapter: The Extraordinary Ordinary
Page 75

Mark H. Clarke, RN, BSN
Administrative Supervisor/Clinical Educator
Enloe Medical Center
Chico, California, USA
Kappa Omicron
HeART Chapter: The Nature of Nursing
Page 28
HeART Chapter: Delicate Artistry: Nursing of Children
Page 96
HeART Chapter: The Other is Me
Page 154

Valera Jo Clayton-Dodd, RN, MSA, CHE, OCN
Associate Administrator
St. Francis Specialty Hospital
West Monroe, Louisiana, USA
Lambda Mu
HeART Chapter: Hope: Looking Forward
Page 184

Palmer W. Cook
Salisbury, North Carolina, USA
HeART Chapter: Bookends: Birth and Death
Page 67

Helen Currier, RN, BSN, CNN
Assistant Director
Renal/Pheresis
Texas Children's Hospital
Houston, Texas, USA
Zeta Pi
HeART Chapter: Delicate Artistry: Nursing of Children
Page 88 & 96

Kimberly Daughtery, CCLS
Heartland for Children
Florida, USA
HeART Chapter: Delicate Artistry: Nursing of Children
Page 88

Mary Louise De Natale, RN, EdD
Associate Professor, School of Nursing
University of San Francisco
San Francisco, California, USA
Alpha Gamma and Beta Gamma
HeART Chapter: The Nature of Nursing
Page 35
HeART Chapter: The Extraordinary Ordinary
Page 73

Susan K. DeCrane, RN, MA, ARNP
Assistant Professor
Clark College
Dubuque, Iowa, USA
Gamma
HeART Chapter: The Extraordinary Ordinary
Page 74

Bernadette Dragich, RN, MSN
Associate Professor, Nursing
Bluefield State College
Princeton, New Jersey, USA
Alpha Rho
HeART Chapter: Preparing Others to Nurse: Teaching
Page 167

Patricia Earle, RN, PhD
School of Nursing
Minnesota State University
Mankato, Minnesota, USA
HeART Chapter: Art in Research
Page 49

Sandra Eggenberger, RN, PhD
Associate Professor
School of Nursing
Minnesota State University
Mankato, Minnesota, USA
HeART Chapter: Art in Research
Page 49

Rebecca J. S. Elsbernd, RN, BSN
Public Health Nurse/Nurse Educator
Fillmore County Public Health
Preston, Minnesota, USA
Nu Epsilon
HeART Chapter: The Nature of Nursing
Page 26

Valerie S. Eschiti, RN, MSN, CHTP, AHN-BC
Assistant Professor
Midwestern State University
Wilson School of Nursing
Wichita Falls, Texas, USA
Xi Iota
HeART Chapter: The Nature of Nursing
Page 42

Julie Fitch, RN, MSN, CCRN
Clinical Nurse Specialist
Medical College of Virginia Hospitals
Richmond, Virginia, USA
Gamma Omega
HeART Chapter: The Extraordinary Ordinary
Page 71

Peggy Flauta, RN, BSN
Staff Nurse, Surgical Services
Tahoe Forest Hospital
Truckee, California, USA
Epsilon Eta
HeART Chapter: Reflections: Nurses' Interiority Unfolding
Page 124
HeART Chapter: The Other is Me
Page 145

Catherine Fraser, RN, BScN
Artist-Nurse, Public Health Nurse, VIHA
Duncan, British Columbia, Canada
HeART Chapter: Introduction
Page i
HeART Chapter: Delicate Artistry: Nursing of Children
Page 94
HeART Chapter: Reflections: Nurses' Interiority Unfolding
Page 129

Brenda Rushing French, RN, MSN
Clinical Instructor
Columbus State University
Columbus, Georgia, USA
Pi Beta
HeART Chapter: The Nature of Nursing
Page 25

Rodrigo Galindo
Mexico
www.sxc.hu/
HeART Chapter: Bookends: Birth and Death
Page 60

H. Lea Barbato Gaydos, RN, PhD, CS, HNC
Faculty, Beth-El College of Nursing and Health Sciences
University of Colorado at Colorado Springs
Colorado Springs, Colorado, USA
HeART Chapter: The Other is Me
Page 147

Kathryn L. Gramling, RN, PhD
Assistant Professor of Adult and Child Nursing
University of Massachusetts at Dartmouth
Dartmouth, Massachusetts, USA
Theta Kappa
HeART Chapter: Introduction
Page 5
HeART Chapter: Delicate Artistry: Nursing of Children
Page 93

Sarah Hall Gueldner, RN, DSN, FAAN
Dean and Professor
Decker School of Nursing
Binghamton University
Binghamtom, New York, USA
Beta Gamma Sigma
HeART Chapter: The Nature of Nursing
Page 43
HeART Chapter: Hope: Looking Forward
Page 185

Megan Hoffmann, RN, BSN
Nurse Clinician
Johns Hopkins' Children's Center
Adolescent Medical-Surgical Unit
Baltimore, Maryland, USA
HeART Chapter: Delicate Artistry: Nursing of Children
Page 88

Sharon R. Hovey, RN, MN, RNC, CNAA
Associate Professor and Great Falls Campus Director
Montana State University-Bozeman College of Nursing
Great Falls, Montana, USA
Zeta Epsilon
HeART Chapter: Reflections: Nurses' Interiority Unfolding
Page 122

Roberta Hower, RN, MSN, CCRN
RN Coordinator for Endocrine Testing
Lehigh Valley Hospital
Allentown, Pennsylvania, USA
HeART Chapter: Bookends: Birth and Death
Page 66

Grace C. Jacobson, RNC, PhD
Associate Professor, Department of Nursing
Idaho State University
Pocatello, Idaho, USA
Theta Upsilon
HeART Chapter: The Other is Me
Page 144

Linda Jerzak, RN, NP
Master's Student, School of Nursing
University of Wisconsin—Eau Claire
Eau Claire, Wisconsin, USA
Delta Phi
HeART Chapter: Preparing Others to Nurse: Teaching
Page 160 & 161

Hillary Jolivette, RN, BSN
Cypress, Texas, USA
Preparing Others to Nurse: Teaching
Page 171

Tyler Kellen
Sauk Rapids, Minnesota, USA
www.sleekcode.net/
HeART Chapter: Bookends: Birth and Death
Page 59

Nancy King, RN, MSN, PNP
Oncology/Hematology/Transplant
The Children's Hospital
Denver, Colorado, USA
HeART Chapter: Preparing Others to Nurse: Teaching
Page 166

Priscilla M. Kline, RN, EdD
Professor Emerita
Clemson University
Wheaton, Illinois, USA
Alpha Lambda, Gamma Mu
HeART Chapter: Bookends: Birth and Death
Page 56
HeART Chapter: The Other is Me
Page 149

Norma Krumwiede, RN, PhD
School of Nursing
Minnesota State University
Mankato, Minnesota, USA
HeART Chapter: Art in Research
Page 49

Patricia La Brosse, MS, RN, CS, CNAA
Retired – former instructor
College of Nursing and Allied Health Professional
University of Louisiana at Lafayette
Lafayette, Louisiana, USA
Delta Eta
HeART Chapter: The Extraordinary Ordinary
Page 75
HeART Chapter: Preparing Others to Nurse: Teaching
Page 170

Scott Chisholm Lamont, RN, BSN, CCRN, CFRN
Pediatric Critical Care Nurse, Flight Nurse, Educator, Researcher, Poet, Writer, Activist, Tree-hugger, and Shameless Rabble-Rouser
Clinical Instructor
Dominican University of California
San Rafael, California, USA
HeART Chapter: Bookends: Birth and Death
Page 57

Carla A. Bouska Lee, PhD, ARNP, C, CNS, FIBA, FAAN
Professor of Nursing
Holy Names College
Oakland, California, USA
Delta, Epsilon Gamma, Nu Zeta, Nu Xi-at-Large
HeART Chapter: Preparing Others to Nurse: Teaching
Page 162

Gene Leisz
Senior Graphic Artist
University of Wisconsin – Eau Claire
Eau Claire, Wisconsin, USA
HeART Chapter: Hope: Looking Forward
Page 188

Sr. Mary Ellen Lewis, FSM, RN, MS, MA
Parish Nurse Advisor and Chaplain
St. Mary's Medical Center
Madison, Wisconsin, USA
Beta-Eta-At-Large
HeART Chapter: Hope: Looking Forward
Page 187

Leah Luedke, RN, BSN
Alumni
University of Wisconsin—Eau Claire
Eau Claire, Wisconsin, USA
HeART Chapter: Preparing Others to Nurse: Teaching
Page 163

Sandra J. Lynch, RN, BSN
Staff Nurse, Pediatric Intensive Care Unit
Fairview-University Medical Center
Minneapolis, Minnesota, USA
Zeta
HeART Chapter: Bookends: Birth and Death
Page 58
HeART Chapter: Delicate Artistry: Nursing of Children
Page 90
HeART Chapter: Delicate Artistry: Nursing of Children
Page 95

Norrie L. MacIlraith, RN, MS, CNS
Nursing Consultant
N. Mac Limited: Nursing Facets
Rochester, Minnesota, USA
Zeta
HeART Chapter: Art in Research
Page 52
HeART Chapter: Delicate Artistry: The Extraordinary Ordinary
Page 78

Mary E. McBride Majkut, RN, BS
Interim Director, Emergency Department
Nashoba Valley Medical Center
Ayer, Massachusetts, USA
Epsilon Beta
HeART Chapter: Delicate Artistry: Nursing of Children
Page 98

Tonia Marine, RN, MN, FNP
Adjunct Assistant Professor
Montana State University
Bozeman, Montana, USA
HeART Chapter: Reflections: Nurses' Interiority Unfolding
Page 132

Veneta Masson, RN, FNP
Nurse, Writer Essayist
Washington, DC, USA
Tau
HeART Chapter: Introductory Material
Page vi

Candace Matthews
Medical Assistant
Chico, California, USA
HeART Chapter: The Nature of Nursing
Page 28

Colin Maykish
New York, New York, USA
HeART Chapter: The Other is Me
Page 154

Josephine McCall, RN, BSN
Lead Nurse
Julien F. Keith Alcohol and Drug Abuse Center
Tuckasegee, North Carolina, USA
Eta Psi
HeART Chapter: The Other is Me
Page 140

A. Gretchen McNeely, RN, DNSc, RNC
Associate Dean, College of Nursing
Montana State University
Bozeman, Montana, USA
Zeta Upsilon
HeART Chapter: Preparing Others to Nurse: Teaching
Page 157

Sonja Meiers, RN, PhD
Associate Professor and Graduate Program Director
School of Nursing
Minnesota State University
Mankato, Minnesota, USA
HeART Chapter: Art in Research
Page 49

Jyn Meyer
Designer, Jyn Meyer Design
Spokane, Washington, USA
HeART Chapter: Delicate Artistry: Nursing of Children
Page 91 & 92

Cheryl Bible Miller
HeART Chapter: The Nature of Nursing
Page 43

Mitzi G. Mitchell, RN, GNC, BScN, BA, MHSc, MN, DNS
Professor
York University
Toronto, Ontario, Canada
Lambda Pi at Large
HeART Chapter: Reflections: Nurses' Interiority Unfolding
Page 133

Elizabeth Lada Morse, RN, MPA, MSN
Director for Cancer Nursing
Hartford Hospital
Glastonbury, Connecticut, USA
HeART Chapter: The Other is Me
Page 150

Heather Nelson, RN, BSN
Alumni
University of Wisconsin—Eau Claire
Eau Claire, Wisconsin, USA
HeART Chapter: Preparing Others to Nurse: Teaching
Page 163

Christina I. Nieves, RN, MSN, CS, FNP
Family Nurse Practitioner, Emergency Department
Hartford Hospital
Hartford, Massachusetts, USA
Beta Zeta
HeART Chapter: In the Process of Becoming a Nurse-Artist
Page 101 & 116

Linda Norlander, RN, MS
Project Director
Minnesota Partnership to Improve End of Life Care
North St. Paul, Minnesota, USA
Zeta
HeART Chapter: Bookends: Birth and Death
Page 59

Nicole O'Reilly
Melbourne, Australia
HeART Chapter: Bookends: Birth and Death
Page 55

Maria Theresa "Tess" P. Panizales, RN, MSN
Vice President, Quality Improvement
VMT Long Term Care Management, Inc.
Silver Springs, Maryland, USA
Kappa
HeART Chapter: The Extraordinary Ordinary
Page 74

Sudha C. Patel, RN, MN, MA, DNS
Assistant Professor
University of Louisiana at Lafayette
Lafayette, Louisiana, USA
Delta Eta, Epsilon Nu
HeART Chapter: Preparing Others to Nurse: Teaching
Page 170

Barbara Kay Pesut, RN, MscN
Assistant Professor of Nursing
Trinity Western University
British Columbia, Canada
Xi Eta
HeART Chapter: The Nature of Nursing
Page 27

Cathy Peters, RN, MS, NP
Assistant Clinical Professor, School of Nursing
Adjunct Assistant Professor, Division of Medical Humanities,
School of Medicine
University of Rochester
Rochester, New York, USA
HeART Chapter: The Other is Me
Page 152

Durae Pfeffer, RN, BSN
Staff Nurse, NSICU
St. Mary's Medical Center
Duluth, Minnesota, USA
Delta Phi
HeART Chapter: Introduction
Page xiv

Mercy Mammah Popoola, RN, CNS, PhD
Assistant Professor, School of Nursing
Georgia Southern University
Statesboro, Georgia, USA
Mu Kappa-at-Large
Heather Robertson, MD
Houston, Texas, USA
HeART Chapter: The Nature of Nursing
Page 28

Ethel C. Ragland, RN, MN, EdD
Professor, Department of Nursing and Health
Benedictine University
Lisle, Illinois, USA
Lambda Upsilon At-Large
HeART Chapter: The Nature of Nursing
Page 41

Bonnie Jean Raingruber, RN, PhD
Professor of Nursing
Director, Center for Health and Human Services Research
California State University
Sacramento, California, USA
Zeta Eta
HeART Chapter: The Nature of Nursing
Page 27 & 39
HeART Chapter: Bookends: Birth and Death
Page 55 & 57
HeART Chapter: Delicate Artistry: Nursing of Children
Page 95

Tracy Rasmussen
Professional Photographer
Insight Photography
Lawrence, Kansas, USA
HeART Chapter: The Extraordinary Ordinary
Page 71

Michelle Rau
Tucson, Arizona, USA
HeART Chapter: Bookends: Birth and Death
Page 63

Karen Roberts, RN, MSN, NP
Nurse Practitioner, Writer, and Artist
Internal Medicine Group
Lawrence, Kansas, USA
Eta Kappa
HeART Chapter: The Nature of Nursing
Page 36 & 42
HeART Chapter: The Extraordinary Ordinary
Page 71

Heather Robertson, MD
Houston, Texas, USA
HeART Chapter: Delicate Artistry: Nursing of Children
Page 88

Enid A. Rossi, RN, MS
Assistant Clinical Professor, Department of Nursing
Northern Arizona University
Flagstaff, Arizona, USA
Lambda Omicron
HeART Chapter: The Extraordinary Ordinary
Page 72

Carol Rossman, RN, MSN, CFNP
Clinical Instructor II
University of Michigan – Flint
Flint, Michigan, USA
Pi Delta
HeART Chapter: The Nature of Nursing
Page 34

Emily Schlenker, RN, PsyD
Assistant Professor of Nursing
Tennessee State University
Franklin, Tennessee, USA
Pi Upsilon, Beta Omega
HeART Chapter: Hope: Looking Forward
Page 180

P.O. Sedin
Örnsköldsvik, Sweden
HeART Chapter: Reflections: Nurses' Interiority Unfolding
Page 125

Laurie Shiparski, RN, BSN, MS
Healthy Workplace Specialist
CPM Resource Center
Grand Rapids, Michigan, USA
Kappa Epsilon-at-Large
HeART Chapter: Bookends: Birth and Death
Page 39 & 40

Cathleen M. Shultz, RN, PhD, FAAN
Professor and Dean, College of Nursing
Harding University
Searcy, Arkansas, USA
Epsilon Omicron
HeART Chapter: The Extraordinary Ordinary
Page 81

Leslie Beth Sossoman, RN, MSN, ACNP
Cardiology Nurse Practitioner
The Sanger Clinic
Concord, North Carolina, USA
Mu Psi-At-Large, Queens College
HeART Chapter: Bookends: Birth and Death
Page 57

Rita Sperstad, RN, MS
Assistant Professor, School of Nursing
University of Wisconsin—Eau Claire
Eau Claire, Wisconsin, USA
HeART Chapter: Preparing Others to Nurse: Teaching
Page 163

Marietta P. Stanton, RN, PhD, RN, Cm
Professor and Coordinator of Graduate Program
University of Alabama at Tuscaloosa
Tuscaloosa, Alabama, USA
Upisilon
HeART Chapter: The Nature of Nursing
Page 29

Diane L. Stuenkel, RN, MS
Lecturer/Clinical Instructor, School of Nursing
San Jose State University
San Jose, California, USA
Alpha Gamma
HeART Chapter: Preparing Others to Nurse: Teaching
Page 159

Charles Tapley, FAIA
Architect
The Bayou Improvement Group
Houston, Texas, USA
HeART Chapter: Delicate Artistry: Nursing of Children
Page 96

Julie R. Tower, RN, BSN
Registered Nurse, Intensive Care
Christus St. Patrick Hospital
Lake Charles, Louisiana, USA
Kappa Psi
HeART Chapter: The Other is Me
Page 137

Joanne Calore Turco, RN, MS
Professor of Nursing
Salem State College
Salem, Massachusetts, USA
Eta Tau
HeART Chapter: The Extraordinary Ordinary
Page 72
HeART Chapter: The Other is Me
Page 140

Frances R. Vlasses, RN, PhD
Assistant Professor
Niehoff School of Nursing
Loyola University Chicago
Alpha Beta
HeART Chapter: Reflections: Nurses' Interiority Unfolding
Page 125

A. Lynne Wagner, RN, C, EdD, FNP
Department of Nursing
Fitchburg State College
Fitchburg, Massachusetts, USA
Epsilon Beta
HeART Chapter: The Nature of Nursing
Page 37
HeART Chapter: The Other is Me
Page 142 & 143

Anthony Walker, RN
Clinical Nurse RN
Division of Pediatric Gastroenterology and
Johns Hopkins Hospital
Baltimore, MD
HeART Chapter: The Extraordinary Ordinary
Page 83

Sandra M. Walsh, RN, BSN, MaED, MSN, PhD
Professor, Barry University School of Nursing
Research Clinician, South Miami School of Nursing
Miami, Florida, USA
Beta Nu
HeART Chapter: The Nature of Nursing
Page 44

Madonna Walters
HeART Chapter: The Nature of Nursing
Page 40

Rose Aguilar Welch, RN, EdD
Associate Professor, California State University
Dominguez Hills, California, USA
Xi Theta
HeART Chapter: Hope: Looking Forward
Page 192

M. Cecilia Wendler, RN, PhD, CCRN
Associate Professor, Department of Nursing Systems
University of Wisconsin – Eau Claire
Eau Claire, Wisconsin, USA
Delta Phi, Kappa Phi
HeART Chapter: Introduction
Page 1, 3 & 19
HeART Chapter: Reflections: Nurses' Interiority Unfolding
Page 120 & 131
HeART Chapter: Hope: Looking Forward
Page 188
HeART Chapter: Afterword
Page 195

Joan Stehle Werner, RN, DNS
Professor, Adult Health Nursing
University of Wisconsin – Eau Claire
Eau Claire, Wisconsin, USA
Alpha, Delta Phi
HeART Chapter: Bookends: Birth and Death
Page 67

Bonnie Wesorick, RN, MSN
Founder and President
CPM Resource Center
Grand Rapids, Michigan, USA
Kappa Epsilon
HeART Chapter: Hope: Looking Forward
Page 191 & 192

Carol Williams, RN, MSN, CPNP, FNE
Instructor of Pediatrics
Mt. Carmel College of Nursing
Columbus, Ohio, USA
Rho Omicron
HeART Chapter: The Nature of Nursing
Page 38
HeART Chapter: Delicate Artistry: Nursing of Children
Page 87

Maria Witt
HeART Chapter: The Nature of Nursing
Page 37

Terri Pauser Wolf, RN, BSN
Nurse-Artist, Consultant
Carmichael, California, USA
Zeta Chi
HeART Chapter: Introduction
Page 20
HeART Chapter: The Nature of Nursing
Page 30
HeART Chapter: Bookends: Birth and Death
Page 101
HeART Chapter: Hope: Looking Forward
Page 193

Jeannie Zuk, RN, PhD
University of Colorado Health Sciences Center
Denver, Colorado, USA
Alpha Kappa-at-Large
HeART Chapter: The Other is Me
Page 141